ADVANCE PRAISE FOR SACRED ECONOMICS:

"Occasionally in human history a clear voice of good sense and compassion rises from the multitudes caught in the memetic mud of obsolete ideas about current reality. Thomas Jefferson was such a voice when he stated: "All men are created equal" at a time when there was no equality, at all. So now Eileen Workman sends a clear and intelligent message: We can live beyond the current monetary economy better, longer, kinder ands more joyfully, and here is how to begin. Even though it might seem impossible, as the system continues to breakdown and the inequalities grow, her voice increasingly serves us as a guide to the next stage of evolutionary economics. We should all read it and place our faith and actions in the good sense it offers us, guiding us toward the next era of economics in the coming age."

Barbara Marx Hubbard
Co-founder and chairperson of the board of
The Foundation for Conscious Evolution

SACRED ECONOMICS

THE CURRENCY OF LIFE

EILEEN WORKMAN

MUSE
HARBOR
PUBLISHING

LOS ANGELES   SANTA BARBARA

SACRED ECONOMICS

A Muse Harbor Publishing Book

Publishing History:
Muse Harbor Publishing
published May 2012

Published by Muse Harbor Publishing, LLC
Los Angeles, California
Santa Barbara, California

Cover design by Timm Sinclair
Interior design by Typeflow

ISBN 978-1-61264-120-1

Visit our website at

http://www.museharbor.com

v2.0

For Dave, for restoring my innocence, gifting me magic and walking with me through this mystery that is unconditional love…I'm forever grateful.

ACKNOWLEDGEMENTS

THIS BOOK COULD NEVER have been written without the support of every human being who has ever walked this Earth and has—wittingly or unwittingly—contributed to the compendium of collective human wisdom. I thank every atom, molecule, energy field and level of consciousness that has ever participated in the wondrous, riotous act of being alive. What a blessing it's been for us to create and self-express in this world for the sheer joy of discovering what we can do...especially when we do it harmoniously!

That said I would also like to expressly thank my parents, Edward and JoAnn Moran, for gifting me with life, and for empowering me to blossom into the woman I am today. I thank my wonderful godmother, Loretta Fallon, for her unwavering support and faith in me, especially during those days when I had difficulty believing in myself. I thank my sister Kathy and my brother Paul, their spouses and children for collectively forging an astonishingly beautiful extended family unit; I'm forever grateful for the field of love we share. I also thank my ex-husband Eric and his lovely wife Ellen for continuing to participate in that field, and for making it easier for our children to experience family gatherings where mutual respect and appreciation abide.

Unimaginable gratitude goes to my beloved husband Dave and my children, Kristin, Nicky and Bryan, for all their love, support and patience during the days I pulled away from them and took the time to heal the wounds of my long-neglected, suffering inner child. Special thanks also to my dear friend Ani Ahavah (aka Jackie Martin) for sweetly and patiently midwifing me while I painfully birthed my essential Self into being. Thanks also to our wonderful friend and roommate, Matt Russell, for putting up with my three A.M. bursts of dialogue.

To all my other mentors and teachers—those of you who know me and those who have no idea how deeply and profoundly you've touched my life—I thank you for being who you are and for the gifts you've brought to this world. While that list is long, I feel it's important to give special mention to Barbara Marx Hubbard, Nassim Haramein, Neale Donald Walsh, Deepak Chopra, Eckhart Tolle, Duane Elgin, Bruce Lipton, Bill Bryson, Matt Pallamary, Lena and Jose Stevens, Bill Plotkin, Paul Ray, Jim Garrison, Paul Hawkins, Arjuna Ardagh, Ken Wilbur, Matt Taibbi, David Korten, Jeremy Rifkin, Stephan Dinan, Devaa Haley Mitchell, Lynne Twist, Rianne Eisler, Hazel Henderson, Jean Houston, Marianne

Williamson, Leonard Shlain, David Talbott, Wallace Thornhill, Donald Scott, Brian Greene, Michio Kaku, Lee Smolin, Stephen Hawking, Leonard Shlain, Lou Marinoff, Lynne McTaggert, Thich Nhat Hahn, H.H. The Dalai Lama Tenzin Gyatso, Michael Beckwith, Dr. Pamela Taxe, Ian Wood…whew! I suspect I could carry on giving thanks forever. So many amazing human beings have touched my life with their grace. Apologies to anyone I've unintentionally missed.

Last but assuredly not least, to my beloveds from the intentional community of Hummingbird Ranch: Carolyn Anderson, John Zwerver, Rich and Marie Ruster, Makasha and Katharine Roske, Robert Griffin, Linda Fischer, David Fischer, Mark Courtman, Michael Elliott and Ami Spangler, Ralph Huber, Sarah Senet, Bill Henson, Mandy Creighton and Ryan Mlynarczyk—I thank you all from the bottom of my heart for holding the vision and finding the courage to build the human dream you've created at Hummingbird Ranch and through the Living School. I'm so grateful you've invited me into your resonant field of love. You taught me what community feels like when individuals consciously live and work in harmony for the good of all concerned. It's my sincere hope that who you are and what you've created together thus far grows ever more appreciated and continues to expand ever outward, into a weary world that is sorely in need of the modeling, love and wisdom you can provide.

CONTENTS

PREFACE

I USED TO BELIEVE THAT PEOPLE WHO CLAIMED GOD SPOKE TO them were crazy. Then one day God started speaking to me, which forced me to reevaluate my position.

Let me state up front I never fancied myself the kind of person prone to spiritual revelations. Though raised Catholic, I left the church as an adult because so many of its teachings made no sense. Talking serpents, winged angels, an ark that held two of every animal in the world—those stories seemed no more believable to me than did ancient Greek myths about Helios sailing across the sky in his golden chariot. I couldn't help wondering what Noah fed all those animals for forty days and nights. Wouldn't the lions have eaten all the zebras and antelopes?

As much as I wanted to believe the Bible's stories were literal truths, I couldn't turn off my questions any more than I could stop my own breathing. How flawed I felt for being unable to accept those stories the way others did, but I kept that shameful secret to myself through college, where I majored in Political Science and studied History, Economics and Biology on the side. Only after graduating did I devote my attention to the study of philosophy and the world's many diverse religions, including Wicca and Shamanism. Even then, so far as God was concerned, I leaned toward an agnosticism that occasionally bordered on militant atheism.

Before I reached my questioning phase, however, I put in my time as a good little capitalist worker, achieving fortune and status just the way I'd been taught. After college graduation I worked a brief stint at Xerox, selling copying equipment. I then spent sixteen years as a successful stockbroker with Smith Barney, a highly respected Wall Street investment firm. At the peak of my career my clients numbered over three hundred and I managed nearly one hundred million dollars in financial assets. Still, despite the external trappings of success I'd managed to accumulate—a lovely house, an expensive sports car, annual vacations and clothes that announced how successful I was—something still wasn't right. I wasn't *happy*. I'd already considered myself a flawed person for a long time; now I added "bad" to my self-description. After all I'd raised three terrific kids, was married to an amazing man and lived in relative comfort. What was *wrong* with me that I couldn't find some way to be happy?

Part of the problem, I finally realized, was that the questions I'd been asking myself since childhood hadn't gone away. If anything they'd grown louder and more insistent underneath the day-to-day distractions of life. Who was I, and why was I here at all? It didn't matter how firmly I pushed those questions away; they bubbled over into every aspect of my reality. Eventually I began to question everything, including the economic system in which I worked, and which had provided me with so many material comforts. The only way to stop the questions, I finally admitted, was to allow myself some time to search for answers. I decided to take a leave of absence from work to give myself that necessary time.

My first interaction with God occurred shortly after my leave began, one afternoon while I was meditating. As was typical when I first tried meditation, my thoughts chattered ceaselessly inside my head. On that particular day I was tackling the question of whether mankind was essentially good or evil. If there was a God and he truly made us in his image, I asked myself, why would he then have punished us for being as we are? Why would he not do what any loving parent would do: guide us and gently teach us how to be? Suddenly, seemingly out of nowhere, I heard a loud male voice boom up from inside me that echoed against my skull: "Shut up and listen!"

It wasn't much of a dialogue, really, more like an imperial order. For the first time though I realized how little attention I'd been paying to the rest of the world because I'd been so busy struggling with the questions inside my own mind. My interior questioner at last fell silent and for a change I found myself listening—*really* listening—to life. Sounds I'd never noticed before began to penetrate my awareness in ways I hadn't known possible. My boundaries melted and the energy normally contained by my body seemed to expand in all directions. I no longer knew where my own skin ended and the rest of the word began. Bliss shot through me until I thought the top of my head would blow open; tears of ecstasy streamed down my face. When eventually I opened my eyes the entire room looked brighter, almost translucent. I knew I could never view the world the same as before. It had come together, all of it, with no distinction left between animate and inanimate, no boundary remaining between the rest of the world and me. The entire universe was one, and it was all alive.

A few weeks later I heard God's voice a second time, again during meditation. Since that earlier day I'd been trying to recapture my blissful experience without much luck. Dutifully I'd emptied my mind and allowed the outside world to flow into the space I usually claimed as my own, but that blissful state I longed for hadn't returned. As I sat cross-legged and struggled mightily to coax it forward, the sweetest female voice sang out from within my brain, "Lighten up, my child."

Lighten up I did. I began to laugh. I realized all my anxious seeking had been blocking me from simply sitting back, relaxing and allowing whatever experiences wanted to happen, happen. It was time, I admitted, to release my obsessive desire to control the world around me. In that instant it felt like my blood drained away and was replaced by a warm liquid light. The light radiated from me and bathed the rest of the world in a hazy golden glow. I don't know how long I remained in that state of being, but I do recall that later the same day I felt an irresistible urge to Google the meaning of my first name. I did so, only to learn that the name Eileen is an Irish translation for "light." That's when I first realized God has a wonderful sense of humor.

4

We continued our conversations, God and me. When God first suggested I quit my job to write this book, I rebelled against the idea and, since I can be awfully stubborn, I did a good job. Write a book? What nonsense! I was already slated to return to work in a matter of days, and had no choice but to start to earn money again. So far my family, friends, coworkers and clients had been very patient with me, but enough was enough. Besides, I was still the breadwinner of my family and writing a book wouldn't pay our monthly bills. How would we keep a roof over our heads if I didn't hold down a job that provided a paycheck? I resisted the notion so much that God finally granted me an illness in the form of a metabolic psychosis to press the issue.

That illness, as anyone who has had a psychotic breakdown will assure you, is a wildly terrifying experience. Mine came about as the result of a dangerous chemical imbalance in my bloodstream and lasted several days. In the days before it struck I'd been in a state of spiritual ecstasy. I'd encountered the still, formless aspect of my deepest self and realized it was both infinite and eternal. Unfortunately I then made the mistake of assuming the physical body containing that formless aspect of me must also be infinite and eternal. I stopped eating, drinking and sleeping, believing I no longer needed to do those things to keep myself alive. I ran around the house naked, convinced that the world would be better off if we all lived more transparently. I squatted and peed openly on my front lawn (which thankfully sits on a hill far removed from the staring eyes of neighbors). I scooped up spiders inside the house and tenderly placed them outdoors, singing them love songs along the way. My golden retriever began speaking to me in a language

I understood. The world was beautiful and I felt blessed to be so deeply connected to it.

Then, as day four of my experience dawned, a horrible darkness descended over me. The lack of food, sleep and water had taken its toll on my all too-mortal body, and the acidity in my bloodstream spiked to dangerously toxic levels. I passed a television set tuned to CNN and noticed nuclear bombs being dropped on the U.S. by China. Armageddon, it seemed, had suddenly arrived. In the valley below our home I heard chainsaws at work, and believed them to be wielded by roving gangs of murderers who were massacring my neighbors. Frantic, I began to call my family members and friends on my cell phone, desperate to hear their reassuring voices, only to "hear" their words cut off midsentence. Desolation overwhelmed me as I watched their phone numbers scramble and then vanish from my telephone's memory bank.

My terrified husband phoned 911 several times and begged them to hospitalize me, but since I managed to maintain my composure in the presence of paramedics, they couldn't force me to go with them. They came and left several times, until finally I attempted to steal their ambulance because I believed them to be aliens, there to inject me with nanobots that would later explode through my skin as they hatched into baby alien beings. The paramedics wrestled me out of the ambulance, handcuffed me and took me to the hospital, convinced at last that I'd become dangerous. I spent the next three days in intensive care, near death.

When the experience mercifully ended, I knew my shattered body and badly bruised mind were going to need time to recover. I made the decision to quit my job to tend my inner spirit and regain my health. Still, the overwhelming panic I'd experienced during my illness lingered, and I feared I'd severed my earlier connection with God. For a time I went back to my old pattern of blaming myself: perhaps if I'd listened better, if I'd fully honored the truths I'd experienced I wouldn't have gotten sick. Then again, I realized, maybe I *needed* to experience that full emotional gamut from bliss to terror in order to develop a deeper sense of connectedness to and compassion for all living beings—including myself.

The moment I stopped complaining about my situation and began to embrace my breakdown as a valuable experience, life improved. I stopped viewing it as something that happened to *me*, and instead chose to see it as a powerful turning point from which I could steer my life in a new direction. God and I became friendly once more, though admittedly I'd been humbled. I didn't have all the answers, nor did I care to know them anymore. My previously endless and repetitive questions about the past and the future lost their allure; my attention shifted to the only moment in which I had the power to engage and influence life—the here and now. I also realized I still had work left to do.

The work that had been calling me but that I'd been so strenuously avoiding revolved around the challenges facing our modern economy. Signs of an imminent economic collapse had long been appearing in the form of ballooning trade deficits, skyrocketing commodities prices, the rapid expansion of consumer credit and housing prices that had spiraled out of control. I'd rejected the thought of addressing those challenges directly, because I didn't believe myself capable of tackling such fundamental social problems and suggesting solutions. Besides, who'd take my ideas seriously? I wasn't a trained economist, just a person who'd been in the trench- es and noticed the absurdity of it all. Still, it seemed high time *someone* began a dialogue around how to shift us from unfettered growth to something more sustainable before the entire financial system self-imploded. Having already experienced a personal emo- tional breakdown, I didn't relish the idea of having a second one alongside our entire human society. Therefore prudence, if nothing else, dictated I follow my heart. I thus agreed to allow my spirit to direct my mind while my body composed this book.

Before I began to write in earnest, I gave myself some healing time, during which I enjoyed just being. I dabbled with learning to play the guitar and made feather wands and jewelry—not to any expert degree, but well enough to appreciate the abilities of my hands. Making money for money's sake had never taught me the value of true creation. What an eye-opening experience it was to make something I could see, hear, touch and feel joy around! I also attended a couple of educational conferences and did some volun- teer work for a non-profit organization. Through those activities I met amazing people who aided me with my recovery, and who also taught me the value of focusing on something greater than myself.

Once I felt healthy enough to tackle our economic issues, I began to examine the nature of capitalism – not through the tradi- tional economic metrics by which we currently measure our success and social advancement, but from the broader perspective of myself as a living creature operating within a complex, living plane- tary system that supports me. As such, I realized that the needs I had—for food, shelter, air, clean water, love, beauty, harmony, com- panionship and opportunities for creative self-expression—existed regardless of the monetary system we've designed to jealously guard and direct the distribution of life's necessities. What I truly needed to be happy, then, was access to *resources*, not money. What I further realized was that while we can print as much money as we want, whenever we want it, the resources we need to advance the cause of life on planet Earth are finite. Wasting them, exploiting them or commoditizing them in pursuit of the acquisition of limitless printed money (and using the amount of money we hoarded instead of the resources themselves to measure our true wealth) suddenly revealed itself for what it was: a collective form of species suicide.

Through this intentional broadening of the context of my own life, I found that capitalism contained many dogmatic beliefs, myths really, that most of us have never thought to question, ideas that can't survive scrutiny when viewed from a wider human perspective than the one from which they were birthed. I therefore began to explore new ways of thinking and to imagine how we might improve our system.

The first realization that came to me was that much of modern civilization revolves around the idea we're supposed to "get" something out of this life. Our religions tell us we need to "get" saved, and teach us to focus on what we'll *get* from the afterlife— be it heaven or hell or seventy-two young virgins. Our schools, families and teachers exhort us to *get* an education. Our economic system mandates we *get* a job so we can *get* money in order to *get* the things we need to survive. Our social structures teach us how to *get* love and approval from others, especially our parents, children, friends and intimate partners. The bulk of Western medicine is designed to *get* us back to healthy from a place of disease. The press encourages us to *get* rich and/or *get* famous—if necessary through acts of infamy. Our judicial systems, both criminal and civil, support us in the quest to *get* even with others. Our political systems are all about *getting* and holding power. Even new age spiritualism, which many have been turning to in search of a new way of being, urges us to *get* ourselves enlightened.

This focus on getting, which appears to be an offshoot of our survival instinct (must get food, must get water, must get sex, etc.), has been running our subconscious human programming for many thousands of years. It's fostered within us a deep-seated feeling of lack. That nagging fear we won't have enough, that we need just a little bit more to be happy, is very real for most. The irony, though, is that every human being has already won the mega-lotto of life.

Have you ever stopped to wonder what the odds were you'd be born? For you to exist, each of your ancestors throughout history had to survive long enough to give birth to the offspring who then begat you. Your mother and father, on a planet populated by over six billion people, needed to meet and come together in the exact month your egg was released, at the perfect moment for your creative inception. Additionally, the solitary sperm that was your father's contribution to who you are—out of the five hundred million or so that are released in a single ejaculation—had to connect with that egg. Those are incalculable odds, really. And yet here you are, blessed to exist yet conditioned by instinct and by society to worry about what else you need to "get" for yourself from this miracle we call life. Something seemed terribly backwards about that viewpoint.

The second realization that came to me was this: I'm a much happier person when I'm focused on what I'm giving to others instead of on what I'm acquiring for myself. I also noted I wasn't alone in that. I've seen the powerful need others have to be heard, to be appreciated for what they have to offer. We humans are so hardwired to *give* that when no one seems willing to accept our gifts we sometimes blow a circuit. In the main, people who've committed terrible acts of violence against others were loners who desperately longed to feel accepted for who they were, but couldn't find that. The biblical story of Cain and Abel describes just such a misplaced pained reaction to rejection by those we love.

Why do we react so negatively to perceived rejection by others? I suspect it's because we are at heart a generative and creative species, longing for loving connections. That's obvious when we look around at all we've managed to accomplish in such a short time on an evolutionary scale. If we can't give others what we have to offer, we may break down so completely that we resort to giving them what we believe they deserve for refusing to accept our gifts.

Having already won life's lotto then, it occurs to me that perhaps our true purpose for being here is to discover how much beauty and love we can give to this world with these forms we call our bodies, not merely for our own benefit, but on behalf of *all* life. Once we get that priority straight we'll have plenty of time to figure out how to share the wealth and creativity that are likely to explode in abundance, because we too are life and entitled to share in whatever it is we create. At present we humans are creating a great deal of suffering, which is unfortunately what we're sharing with the rest of the planet. When, however, a majority of us bring forth the best in ourselves out of gratitude for this precious gift we call life, how could joyful abundance for all *not* be the result? The good news is, an unselfish approach doesn't negate or diminish our innate desire for individual achievement and success. Individual achievement flowers even more beautifully when it's placed in loving service to the whole, instead of focused solely on what it gains for the individual.

Intuitively we all know this. Athletes who play for the love of the game are typically the best at what they do. Scientists, teachers and philosophers who work tirelessly and bravely to nurture others and bring forth new ideas, despite the risk of being mocked or attacked for their nonconformist thinking, are the people who change the world. Our most beloved icons—Buddha, Jesus, Krishna, Mohammed, Joan of Arc, Gandhi, Mandela, Mother Teresa, JFK and Martin Luther King, to name but a few—weren't focused on receiving financial rewards for what they were delivering to humankind. They gave of themselves out of love and the joy of giving, and taught that we could be "as them" *or better* if we embraced their messages.

A third realization came to me by way of Mahatma Gandhi: I needed to *be* the change I wanted to see in the world around me. That meant I had to adjust my internal attitudes by letting go of my need for external approval in order to feel more complete as a human being. I'm now practicing this every day, letting go of my fears whenever they arise. I'm learning to greet each moment as I would a trusted friend, and discovering where that attitude can take me. That I fail sometimes is teaching me the value of patience, which itself is a useful life lesson.

Stepping away from everything I'd been taught to believe in was terrifying, even though my life had become intolerable. Yet doing so gifted me a new perspective that enabled me to see where I'd been from both a higher and a broader vantage point. Through stepping away, my judgment became less clouded and I later found myself able to reconnect with others from a place of deeper wisdom. Perhaps all of us should be granted regular sabbaticals from our work so we might consider the strengths and weaknesses of the structures in which we're imbedded. We can't fully understand life's issues unless we make time to contemplate our own experiences. As Socrates once said, "The unexamined life is not worth living." I would expand on his thought by suggesting, "The unexamined society is not worth living in."

To trust in humanity's ability to ask and answer some hard, self-reflective questions seems a better application of human faith than to dedicate our faith to the notion that men who walked this Earth centuries ago knew more than we modern humans do about how to construct a social order that meets our present needs. Our understanding of the world changes constantly, which makes sense since the world itself is constantly changing. The ongoing expansion of human consciousness resulting from those changes is being accompanied by an equally powerful expansion of personal ethics. It's therefore time we learn to trust ourselves to successfully navigate the external changes we're experiencing as well as to embrace the internal ethical realizations we're having as we evolve.

At present we face many perils since our social systems seem on the brink of collapse, but if the universe has taught us anything it's that chaos and crisis are triggers for transformation. I remain hopeful we'll weather these storms, because we're a hearty species, and together we've already accomplished amazing things. I also believe, as the Hopi Indian prophesy says, that the time of the lone wolf is over; that no self-serving individual has the ability to destroy us if we band together and empower each other to thrive. There may always be people in the world functioning out of ignorance of our greater connectivity, just as there will always be loving, generous individuals to guide us through the uncharted waters of change. Our choice now is either to continue to build fear-based societies designed primarily to keep out or control the ignorant and the suffering while we toil to get what we need, or to promote more loving, generous societies in which the darkest regions of the human psyche are gently brought into the healing presence of light. My hope for us as we forge ahead is that we each choose to light our inner candles rather than continue to curse the darkness inside us all.

The ideas in this book may have flowed through me, but I don't claim them as mine. Feel free to accept whichever of them you like. If none appeal to you, surely there will be other books, other ideas that emerge to touch your soul, many with the power to change our world. Light, as I have come to understand it, cuts through the darkness from every conceivable direction, but all of it emanates from a single Source. That seems to be the way God speaks in our world.

As for me, I've held discussions with God many times since the first illuminating experience I had. Sometimes they occur in the form of images—multi-dimensional, multi-colored visions that seem to swirl from my brain and fill the air around me, displaying ideas mere words could never describe. Other times they occur in the form of feelings, powerful intuitive sensations I've learned to obey without question or hesitation. Sometimes I'll be taking a walk and God will command my attention through the form of a passing butterfly, the overhead screech of a red tail hawk or the sweet scent of orange blossoms wafting by on the breeze. By grace I've discovered I no longer feel an urge to question God's existence, or to challenge the direction in which he's guiding humanity, for God is always hanging around these days. God shines in the eyes of a child, reaches out through the neediness of a homeless person, smiles through the people I pass in the grocery store. In short, these days I notice God everywhere. If anything I suffer from an embarrassing abundance of God, because in my experience God and life are inseparable—they are always and ever One. As long as I remain conscious of that, I will never again feel alone.

HUMANITY AND
THE MONEY GAME

Before I built a wall I'd ask to know
What I was walling in or walling out,
And to whom I was like to give offense.
Something there is that doesn't love a wall,
That wants it down.

Robert Frost

WHEN I WAS A CHILD, THERE ONCE STOOD A WALL SO HIGH, thick and militarily defended that most of us couldn't imagine it would ever come down. It wound through the center of Berlin like a concrete snake, constricting the hearts and minds of those who were caught within its coils. Life for those who resided near the wall was a study in contrasts. Outside the wall spelled freedom— the freedom to be, do and experience life the way one wished to live it. Being trapped behind the wall meant enslavement: enslavement to a system that imposed its beliefs on people at the point of a gun. Which side people found themselves on was mainly an accident of birth—which made the wall seem that much more capricious. As unfair and absurd as it was, however, our knowing that which side of the wall you lived on was a function of fate and not free choice didn't make it less solid.

During the wall's lifetime, as many as eleven hundred people were killed while trying to escape from East Berlin, yet the people who lived behind the wall never stopped trying to make their way to freedom. Then on November 9, 1989, after the West Berlin television station ARD[1] inaccurately broadcast that East Germany would no longer defend the gates against unauthorized crossings, an immense crowd of East Berliners surged to the base of the wall and demanded their freedom. The wall's guards had in fact not been instructed to let them pass unmolested, but once they witnessed that sea of humanity clamoring for freedom, they put down their guns without firing a shot. Strangely enough, the wall we'd all thought was so solid, so impenetrable, gave way that day with an ease that would have been unimaginable only the day before. The amazing thing was it didn't fall victim to a violent civil uprising, but to a peaceful collective embrace of a new belief: the belief that the wall could no longer imprison its people. If history teaches us anything then, it's that when people hold to their truth and come together around an idea they know to be right, together they become so mighty a force that nothing can suppress their indomitable will.

---

1   Mary Elise Sarotte, "How It Went Down: The Little Accident That Toppled History," *The Washington Post*, November 1, 2009.

Humanity's present driving need for money isn't much different from the drive of the East Berliners to get past that wall. Money is nothing more than a psychological wall we've constructed to separate ourselves (and each other) from the global abundance that already exists on this planet. Everything we need to thrive as a species—food, land, shelter, water, educational opportunities, energy, clothing, furnishings, travel, health care, beauty, artistic experiences—exists in quantity outside the money wall. What we've been trained to do to access those things is work continuously for money, which we give away in exchange for what we need to survive inside the money wall. The ultimate goal of the game, however, is to escape, to make our way outside the wall by accumulating so much money that we'll never need to work for it again.

The money game was already in full swing for centuries before any of us were born. We certainly didn't invent it and, at this point, like all the Berliners born after their concrete wall was completed in 1961, we can hardly imagine what life would be like without it. The problem is, we can't afford to stop playing the game long enough to figure out whether it's still the game we humans want to play. We're all so busy surviving we don't have much time to wonder what the world might look like tomorrow if we deconstructed the wall and decided to share everything that already exists outside it. Much like those early intrepid East Berliners, we've instead turned our focus on finding new and creative ways to get ourselves over the wall and away from the forced labor camp that is our modern economy. Some of us steal from others to achieve success. Most of us, though, play the game by the rules: sacrificing our free time and the time we spend with our families, or surrendering our dreams, talents and passions in exchange for a shot at long-term financial security.

At this stage of the money game we're operating under an "every man for himself" style of play. We're exhorted from childhood to pull ourselves up by our bootstraps, to compete ferociously against our peers and to win at any cost, to be strong and proud and to strive against all odds. Those characteristics, we're told, are the mark of a noble character. We're taught that the end justifies the means, that it's a dog-eat-dog reality, that might makes right and it's a winner-take-all kind of world. We're taught that winners never quit and quitters never win, and that only the strongest and fittest among us survive. We operate under the theory of buyer beware, *not* seller behave. Anyone who fails at the game—who whines or complains or tries to attack the wall—is labeled a loser, deserving of punishment, blame and public humiliation. The animal rights movement, the civil rights movement, the feminist movement and the environmental movement, to name but a few, all have had their martyrs: leaders who were murdered, imprisoned or marginalized for speaking out and standing up for higher ideals they believed to be right. These people were punished for putting a chink in the wall—a window from which we could all view what life could be like on the other side. By daring to speak of providing real opportunities for all people, by insisting that everyone alive holds a birthright to whatever this planet has to offer, and by condemning the inherent inequities, abuses and exploitive practices of the economic system they opened people's minds and hearts to alternative possibilities.

This wall we're all trying to scale—this economic game we're all playing—is a win/lose game. It's one where we each try our best to hoard as much money as we possibly can while paying for our survival needs as we go, so we can eventually heave ourselves over the money wall and into abundance. Meanwhile, other people try their best to separate us from our money, so they too can hoard more and eventually get themselves over the wall.

Once in a while an intrepid individual—Bill Gates for example, or Oprah Winfrey—does manage to accumulate so much money that he or she successfully makes it safely over the wall. Suddenly that person finds they have access to unlimited worldly delights, as measured by all the best things money can buy. It's rather like becoming the biggest hotel-holding landowner in the game of Monopoly®. The moment a single player controls the bulk of Monopoly® properties he finds that money starts coming his way so fast there's nothing left to buy, so it just stacks up. Money magnetizes money, since money is the primary tool we use to separate others from their money. We call it capitalism, which is a nice way of saying that once we've accumulated enough seed money to start with (capital), we can invest it to invent new ways of making even more money—which we "earn" by extracting that money from other people.

The key to the money game is this: the more *dependent* we can make others on the products and services we offer in exchange for their money—particularly with regards to everyday survival needs like food, water, shelter, energy, etc.—the more likely we are to create a continual stream of ongoing wealth to enjoy…at *their* expense. We justify that behavior by rationalizing that we're providing a necessary service to those trapped behind the wall, while conveniently ignoring the fact that simply by *playing* the game we're embracing the premise that it's fine to deny life necessities to people who can't afford to pay for them.

The money game, then, doesn't eliminate poverty and human suffering, as is sometimes proposed. It can't, because it *created* poverty when it commandeered all the land, natural resources and human labor it could corral and moved them like chess pieces over to the abundant side of the wall, in exchange for the limited paper cash it placed in circulation *behind* the wall. The game's originators then began to guard all the stuff they'd moved beyond the wall through the establishment of civil property laws. They created governments to enforce those property laws, tax systems to preserve the governments, and religious and moral belief systems to control the minds and hearts of the people who remained trapped behind the wall. All those who were unable to escape were then either forced to go to work for the winners or suffer from deprivation until they died.

The game's winners—particularly those in our modern era who didn't invent the game but have played it well—often feel compassion for their friends and neighbors who are stuck behind the wall. They charitably reach out and try to help others climb over the money wall, but none of them are wealthy enough to make much of a difference for the rest of humanity. That's exactly the way the game was designed to unfold. The money game requires that there be many, many losers whose energy, tears, life-blood and sweat support the beautiful lifestyles of the winners. It then holds up those winners as social role models, to entice the losers to keep on playing in the improbable hope that they'll someday become a winner too.

Even if *all* the wealthy people gave away most of their savings to the multitudes still stuck behind the wall, all they'd manage to do is assist them in penetrating the wall for a day or two, before the powers that guard the wall got wise and forced the players back behind the gates. The prices of all our existing goods would immediately go up to capture that extra money in circulation, and brand new products would swiftly be invented to inspire more consumption to bleed off those funds. What, we must therefore ask ourselves, *is* this force that protects the wall and holds us all captive to the endless quest for money so we can't escape?

Hard as it may be to admit, *we're* imposing the money game on ourselves. Our shared belief that we need to buy anything this planet has produced (or is presently producing) from another human being who claims to own it is what keeps us all from living in shared abundance. We stubbornly cling to that belief, even though it goes against our own best interests to do so, because we've been trained from birth to *believe* two things are absolutely true:

1. There will never be enough to go around for us all to be happy.
2. Most of us wouldn't work if we didn't need money to survive.

We've long since forgotten that we humans enhanced our living standards and advanced our social behavior for tens of thousands of years before money ever became a part of our exchange process. (It's called evolution.) The thing is, though, because we've been playing this money game for so long, most of us have trouble conceiving of a world without the need for a paycheck to bind us to our jobs. We've lost touch with how hard we're willing to work when we apply ourselves to a vision for our future—which we do when we raise our children, when we care for our homes or explore our creative genius. We know that when we work for joy it doesn't feel like work, and that the rewards we reap from a job well done—when it's one we chose to do—are far more meaningful than dollars and cents. The problem with the money game, then, is that the work most of us are paid to do isn't work we love, nor does it enrich or advance society or our planet; it's work that games the losers and damages the planet so the winners can earn more profit.

We've also lost sight of the fact that one of the cornerstones of the money game is the way it fosters in people a continual sense of need, as well as creating a dependency that keeps the losers diligently working to try to "keep up" with the winners. The winners in turn push relentlessly forward in their quest to earn even more money, by producing more things the losers can't afford—but are told they need. We're all trained from birth (and by our religions) to fear being "left behind," as if that's the worst thing that could ever happen to us. Meanwhile, we're so busy keeping up that we fail to notice how running in place is slowly killing us all.

Even if Bill Gates *did* give away forty billion dollars to create four thousand new millionaires, those millionaires would soon be competing with each other to buy new houses, sports cars and quality educations for their children, so they too could live the "good life" in relationship to the losers. The problem is, the moment the people who manufacture and market the luxury homes and cars began to notice the increased demand for their products, they'd raise their prices to siphon more cash away from those new millionaires. We label that "making a profit," and it's a highly acceptable way to play the money game. The more cash that gets placed into circulation, then, the higher prices will generally climb to bleed it back out of circulation and into savings accounts. And, since money tends to beget more money, the savings accounts of the winners grow fatter while the losers' accounts keep shrinking.

We can't *blame* each other for jockeying to improve our individual financial positions so we too might someday scale the wall and gain access to all the stuff the millionaires have; after all, that's how the game is *supposed* to be played. The result, though, is that every time our government or our banking system prints or invents some new form of money and infuses it into the game to give it a charge, that money very quickly gets sucked right back out of circulation. Meanwhile, the amount it takes to be considered rich keeps rising as the bank accounts of the wealthy continue to grow. That's called inflation. Inflation reveals why stuff that today costs a thousand dollars to buy cost less than thirty-eight dollars in 1900.[2] Money can't buy what it used to because there's so much more of it lying around than there was back then. It's just not in the bank accounts of the people who really need things.

It seems that the more money we invent, lend, grow and trade among ourselves *behind* the money wall, the more each of us will need to hoard if we hope to scale the wall. That's because the value of money is relative, not fixed. To make our way to abundance, then, isn't a matter of whether we manage to accumulate a hundred thousand, five hundred thousand or even a million dollars for ourselves. It's dependent upon each one of us hoarding vastly *more* than most everyone else can hoard—no matter *what* that number

---

2   *http://www.measuringworth.com/calculators/ppowerus/*

of actual dollars may be. Since more and more people are born into the money game every day (or are seduced into playing through our continued global exportation of capitalism), increasing amounts of money need to be invented to entice the newcomers firmly in the game. Like a giant Ponzi scheme, the earliest players will always have a giant leg up on the newcomers who come into the game (or are born into it), with nothing, but it's really only the few at the top who manage to hoard enough money to scale the wall.

Logically, we must admit it's impossible for each one of us to accumulate relatively more money than everybody else. That means we must also admit that the money game has created a society where, for there to be *any* winners, there must always be a far greater number of losers. In order for the game to survive, the losers must remain compliant and continue to work very hard at playing the game. They may be eager or very unhappy players, but they must not be allowed to *quit* the game or else the entire pyramid structure would have to give way. Drugs, booze, entertainment, sports, advertising, politics and social punditry—all these are means by which the losers are kept preoccupied so they don't have time to think about the problems the game creates. Those are the game's carrots. The sticks are the endless streams of bills, the stress, the sleepless nights, the rising prices, the crashing markets, the criminal activities and the constant need to scramble to find a job that provides a paycheck. Between grabbing the carrots and dodging the sticks, most players have little time remaining to focus on why they're even playing the game.

No pyramid top can survive without a massive base to support it. The best players in the game understand that truth on some level, which explains why so many are willing to use the sticks. The sticks create the illusion that the bottom players will be crushed and destroyed by the top if the game collapses. In reality, though, when we dismantle a pyramid we find that the bottom stones are stable and remain intact; it's the *top* blocks that risk suffering the greatest damage as they tumble down.

Some very clever financial sticks are used by the game's top players, inventions like loan interest, mortgages, insurance policies, licensing fees, property taxes, utility fees and the like. Because they're ongoing fees or are annually imposed, they guarantee that money is constantly being bled away from most players before they can accumulate enough to get over the wall. Once the game-players become ensnared by these "trap fees," they can't quit playing the game without losing the items those fees permit them to have. People who rebel and try to get around the money wall (or tunnel underneath it), either taking what they need or otherwise refusing to play by the rules, are labeled criminals or insane, and are punished or isolated for their refusal to play the game. Brothers, fathers, uncles, sisters—even our very own children—it doesn't matter who these rebels are. We put them in jail to punish them for trying to cheat the game.

The winners can always afford to invest some of their money in inventing new ways to quit paying the losers who are stuck behind the wall. They create tax shelters, move their production facilities to countries where labor costs are cheaper, install automated assembly lines to eliminate human jobs. They make their remaining workers compete with each other for increasingly scarce positions, which gives them the clout to pay out lower wages. They reduce paid benefits, eliminate company-sponsored retirement plans and force their workers to cover ever more of their daily costs of living.

Our governments try to prevent the losers from violently rebelling by providing a minimal safety net for the people unable to meet their daily needs. However, because winners control the government, that net gets constructed by taxing the daily wages of the losers instead of taxing the hoarded wealth of the winners themselves. That bleeds more money away from the losers who are stuck behind the wall, and makes it the losers' problem to provide enough cash to care for their fellow losers. Many losers begin to resent their neighbors, who are receiving meager handouts from the net, and humiliate them by making them feel ashamed. In this way, the winners have entrained the losers to turn the sticks upon themselves, to try to force their fellow losers back into the game.

The winners don't want to take responsibility for the poverty and suffering they're continuing to create, because to do so reduces their monetary leverage and diminishes their power. In the game, money IS power. Money gives the winners the power to constantly write new rules that keep them safe beyond the wall. It enables them to make the wall higher, wider and longer so it can hold more losers in. It buys the winners political favors, allowing them to control the military might of their governments, which they then use against each other in mega-battles for natural resources and political control over vast farms of losers. The sons and daughters of generations of losers have become the expendable fodder the winners use to fight their bloody wars. Those wars are mainly fought inside the wall so that the men, women and children who become "collateral damage" don't come from the powerful moneyed families of the winners. "We'll take the war to them before they bring it to us!" is just another way of saying, "Let's fight for all the stuff we want in a place where we won't get hurt."

The danger for us in continuing to play this money game end-lessly can be grasped by noticing what's at stake—for us as people, and for life itself. Unlike the board game of Monopoly®, the money game allows its players to *die* if they can't buy what they need. While we all started playing it innocently enough, we quickly be-came enslaved to the game through the very real fear of dying if we don't win. Meanwhile, even those who *appear* to be winning must continually hoard ever more money to claim access to the abun-dance and privilege that exists outside the wall. They gobble our planet's natural resources and destroy its delicate ecosystems in their relentless quest to make more and more goods they can foist upon the losers behind the wall.

Long term, the money game can't continue without ultimately destroying the field of abundance that creates and sustains us all. No possible balance can ever be achieved in a game where the play-ers keep constantly changing, the finish line keeps moving and the need to consume more stuff continues to grow. There can be no *ab-solute* winners in the money game, only a few who beat the system in the short run (their own lifetimes) but who help bring down our entire civilization in the end.

The entire point of the money game—which places maximum emphasis on unfettered consumption—is to siphon money away from the losers so they can't ever quit working, so the winners who made it over the wall can be lavishly taken care of. That means the losers must remain slaves to the game for their entire productive lifetimes, after which they become society's elderly discards and are labeled financial drains on the safety net.

Our children too, aren't revered as the precious life gifts they truly are. They come into the money game naked, with nothing, which means they're a constant drain on their cash-strapped parents. The losers, who are required to pay for their children's needs from their meager and highly taxed wages, can't afford to encourage their children to explore their talents, deepest passions and dreams to their heart's desire. Instead, they raise them to be practical and become monetized future commodities: loyal, energetic workers who will step willingly into the money game and support its continuation so they each can eventually afford to take care of themselves. We therefore educate our children only so far as their knowledge can be standardized to enable them to move seamlessly into the game and play it well once they mature. What we've missed is that our focus on standardized testing, which requires each child to memorize specific information and regurgitate it with as few alterations as possible, inhibits creative thinking. Instead of teaching children *how* to think, we're teaching them *what* to think. How can we possibly expect future generations to help solve humanity's challenges if every young adult is mentally encoded with the same information and the same narrow range of ideas as everyone else?

The money game offers no wondrous vision for a brighter human future. It degrades the sustainability of our planet and abuses its natural abundance for short-term gain. It commoditizes life and disrespects that which is unique and precious in each of us, and in doing so reduces us all to its lowest common denominator:

price. All the money game really promises to do for us is slowly bleed the life energy out of most of us in exchange for an endless effort to survive.

The questions we must ask ourselves, then, are these: Do we really want to continue to play this game? If not, how do we *stop*? Can we quit playing it without descending into societal chaos, without triggering violence and rebellion and surrendering to fear? Can we do so without creating massive needs shortages that will cause even more suffering before we figure out how to fairly distribute what we have? What kind of mindset (and heartfelt approach) is required of us to inspire us to love the work we need to do to thrive? How do we tear down this mental wall we've erected inside our own heads?

It's possible we can—if we take the time to examine what we're doing rationally and look at its long-term effects—collectively admit the money game is a failed experiment in social design. Any good scientist will tell us it often takes numerous failed experiments before the best way to proceed is finally found. If we can learn to appreciate the money game from an experiential perspective, *and* if we agree to work together to decide what we liked about it and what aspects of it we don't wish to see repeated, we could then begin to formulate a brand new social design that weaves the best ideas from the money game with the best of our newer ideas. One starting point might be to design a loving, cooperative win/win game instead of a fear-based, win/lose competition. We could then begin again from a place of deeper wisdom and greater social compassion, with the understanding that while we still might not get it exactly right, we'll be that much closer to what we hope to become as we evolve.

This book examines both what went right in the money game and what we might learn from the many ways it went astray. It poses tough questions that challenge our shared beliefs. It isn't intended to *change* minds, so much as invite them to question for themselves and decide what they know to be right. It is, at rock bottom, a love story: an ode to our wild, wonderful, wacky human experience.

I honor us all for our willingness to be feeling, thinking rats running through this experimental laboratory maze we call "life." We are indeed the trailblazers, the unsung heroes, the warriors and the courageous world explorers. We are the ones who are being called upon now to trust each other—and trust in a higher evolutionary process—as we give ourselves over to adventures in the unknown. We are the surprisingly patient, kindhearted and occasionally very frightened ones, yet we nevertheless keep bravely soldiering on. We are the ones who have, over eons, learned to feel sorrow, to worry, to dream, to imagine, to share, to create, to express, to give freely of ourselves to those we love. We are the ones who have only just lately realized we are capable of it all, from mass destruction to unconditional love. And *we* are the ones who must live with that terrible wisdom. We are, in fact, the ones we've been waiting for: our own messiah. Not *a* One, but a multitude of amazing ones. Because we *can* create it all, it's up to us to decide—right now—what we wish to create for ourselves, and then create it.

I invite you now to try an experiment. See if you can set aside your personal beliefs about money and its meaning and role in your life as we investigate how and why we relate as we do with each other. I promise you, your beliefs won't disappear simply by opening up some space around them and shining a light on some alternative points of view. Your beliefs will be right where you left them should you need to hold them again.

The crucial question to ask yourself as we explore new ideas is this: Do I want to live in a world filled with love or destruction, joy or fear, enslavement or peaceful freedom? I believe that every human heart already holds the answer. It's therefore up to each one of us to align our thoughts and actions with our highest spiritual truths, so we can consciously envision and collectively design the best road for humanity to take. Godspeed and safe journeys to all of us as we continue down this wild road that is life.

AN EXAMINATION OF HUMAN BELIEFS

IN THE BELOVED MOVIE *THE WIZARD OF OZ* THERE IS A POW-
erful, dramatic scene where a hungry Dorothy starts to pick apples,
when suddenly the apple tree slaps her hand and scolds her for
stealing. The scene surprises us by shifting our perspective away
from ordinary reality, because in real life apple trees don't care who
eats their fruit. Even so, we don't dare pick an apple from a neighbor's tree just because we'd like to eat one. What stops us isn't the
tree; it's our fear we'll get into trouble because we've been taught to
believe that taking fruit we don't own is wrong.

We observed similar self-limiting behavior in New Orleans
after Hurricane Katrina. While some people swiftly released their
beliefs about stealing and scavenged items they thought they needed from local shops, most struggled to survive with whatever goods
they had on hand. What is it about our beliefs, we therefore need

to ask, that makes them so powerful some of us are willing to suffer or die before we'll ignore what we've been taught to believe is right? At what point do we allow society's fabric to flex enough to honor the need of people to survive? As we observe in *Les Mis
ables*, the tale of Jean Valjean who stole a loaf of bread to save his family, when we place group beliefs about right and wrong above an individual's need to survive, we've elevated our love of abstract ideals above the very essence of life itself. Yet without life to enable them to flower, our abstract moral concepts can't survive. The trick, then, is for us to learn to balance our ideals with the needs of reality: actual people who need apples.

Beliefs are behavioral motivators. Each of us has been raised to embrace a distinct set of beliefs that pertain to our cultures, nationalities, faiths and genders. The worldview of a Muslim boy raised in a village in Indonesia will likely be very different from the beliefs held by a Christian woman in Madison, Wisconsin. Can we determine that one of their belief systems is absolutely more "right" or "wrong" than the other, or does the "rightness" of a belief system depend on the location and culture that produces it? This isn't an easy question to answer. Some beliefs feel absolute, like "thou shalt not kill." Others, like "don't work on Sunday" may have pertinence to one culture but not another. Deciding which beliefs are absolute and which are dogmas born of local customs is crucial to our ability to connect with each other across the divides of our various social cultures.

Many historical documents, including the Bible, the Magna Carta and the U.S. Constitution, are byproducts of thousands of years of shifting beliefs that eventually coalesced into a new way of thinking about the world. These great documents were drawn up to promote the continuation of their radically new beliefs. As any culture advances, then, one of its greatest challenges is to periodically examine and update its teaching materials so beliefs shift in alignment with the leaps the culture has made in its world understanding.

To redesign our belief systems without collapsing our society may seem like an insurmountable task, but it isn't impossible. A number of modern societies have survived for centuries despite having experienced hugely disruptive economic, political, social and religious upheavals due to changing beliefs. When a society does collapse, as evidenced by ancient Egypt, Rome and the Mayan civilization of Central America, the culprit is often the society's *inability* to change its beliefs—hence adapt its behavior—to meet its rapidly changing reality.

Beliefs have power over us because of the way they're structured. They tend to come in an "if/then" format, such as: "If I pick this apple, I then could be arrested and sent to jail." Our fear of the negative consequences thus lends many beliefs an emotional charge that makes it harder for us to test them. Sometimes the warnings are valid, as in, "If you eat cyanide you'll die." To discover whether it's true all we have to do is research the history of cyanide poisonings. We don't need to try the cyanide ourselves. Other times we have no way of knowing whether the consequences we've attached to a belief are valid until we challenge it, as in, "We can't afford to make products without polluting the environment, because the added costs will put us out of business." To test that belief we'll need to act as guinea pigs and perhaps use our own company as an experimental laboratory, which is scary due to the consequences associated with failure. That's the way civilizations have always advanced, but when people grow comfortable with the way things are—even when things aren't going terribly well—they become fearful of testing changes that might make life worse instead of better. We think, "Bad as reality is, it can always get worse."

Most of us tend to avoid scary choices by refusing to admit our beliefs might not be true. In the above example, the belief that not polluting is more expensive than continuing to pollute isn't usually true, especially if we attach the cost of environmental destruction to the cost of doing business, but discovering the truth means we need to be willing to explore our options without fear overpowering our ability to reason. To reduce our fear of the consequences we must therefore first determine how accurately they've been linked to our beliefs. That requires good information, critical thinking, and—when necessary—real world testing.

OPINIONS, NOT FACTS

All beliefs are opinions, not facts. That cyanide can kill us is a *fact*—tested, proven and known beyond any reasonable doubt. That people won't work unless we force them to do so, through the application of an external reward and punishment system, is *opinion*. It hasn't been scientifically tested or proved, and is only grounded in social bias and current mental conditioning. Facts represent data we can perceive with our senses and can test and experience; therefore, we can know them to be true. Beliefs, on the other hand, are ideas we're trained to accept. Indeed, beliefs *must* be entrained, because no real data exists to prove them factual. That's because beliefs don't always reflect reality. We don't need to "believe in" giraffes or cotton candy for them to exist, but we do need to "believe in" Santa Claus and the Tooth Fairy as aspects of our cultural customs. Beliefs, unlike facts, can and should be periodically reexamined for validity over time, but too many—particularly religious beliefs—have been crafted in ways designed to discourage real world examination.

For ages now, humanity has crafted beliefs in ways that punish and frighten those who would reject them. Fear is a powerful way to enforce the unquestioned embrace of beliefs, which is necessary when we're addicted to our beliefs and don't want them challenged. Absent facts, cultures have historically chosen to adopt a shared set of beliefs to give our world structure so we can comfortably carry on living by pretending we know what we don't. For instance, before humanity understood the energy behind volcanoes, entire civilizations adopted the belief that the gods must be angry with them whenever the volcanoes rumbled, so they sacrificed their virgin daughters to the fires to appease those gods. It would have been unthinkable to most families living within those cultures to defy the dominant belief system, particularly since the sacrifice was framed as a high honor, while to shirk that duty was viewed as a grave threat to society and was punishable by death.

We take comfort in the stability beliefs provide, and worry that if others abandon or reject our belief system our shared reality might be destroyed. Centuries ago we went so far as to torture, crucify or burn people at the stake for daring to challenge society's cherished beliefs. Nowadays we fancy ourselves more civilized, so instead we label those who think outside our personal belief boxes unpatriotic, naïve, ignorant, terrorists, crazies, infidels, racists, etc. It doesn't matter so much what we call them, so long as whatever word we use enables us to view the imagined heretics as "other." That enables us to dismiss people who challenge our beliefs without having to pay attention to their ideas.

For eons we've inflicted an incalculable amount of suffering on one another doing battle over our conflicting beliefs. If we look at the hostilities the world is engaged in today, at the root of each we'll inevitably find opposing beliefs about how the world "should be" and how "the others" ought to behave. Were one side's position based on fact, every conflict would end of its own accord. Falsehoods can't survive long in the light of truth. Since beliefs, however, are based on personal (or group) opinions of how things should be, facts don't exist in abundance to settle these quarrels. The preponderance of whatever evidence we have to support our beliefs rests almost solely on our subjective life experiences and personal biases, not facts.

For example, Americans live in an open and democratic society, with an economy based on free trade and entrepreneurial profits. Most Americans believe the system is a good one and therefore assume it should be the foundational social platform for everyone else. What we miss, though, is the way outside observers can spot the flaws and inequities in our system that we've either ignored or have rationalized away for the sake of its preservation—and there are many. Were we to look more deeply at ourselves, we might create a better system all others would *want* to emulate, and democracy would spread through the world by its shining example. That's hard work though. Instead, looking outside ourselves and judging what's wrong with everyone else allows us to avoid the tough but necessary introspection to improve our own experience.

In a fashion comparable to Western thinking, fundamentalist Muslims believe firmly that living under Sharia law promotes an orderly and righteous society, and that the entire world would be better off if it followed Sharia law and eschewed capitalism's immorality. As outsiders looking in we can swiftly spot flaws and injustices of Sharia law that Muslims ignore or rationalize away for the sake of preserving *their* system. Since it's always easier to label something wrong when it isn't our own accepted way of life, we love to impose our beliefs on others whenever we engage in discussions of how the world "should be." Conflict ensues because others hold different opinions.

WHAT WE PAY ATTENTION TO
IS WHAT WE MAKE REAL

Our minds have the power to collectively change reality. For instance, if we believe earning a profit is the most compelling reason to declare a business successful, we'll reward companies that make a profit and punish those that don't. When a company's stock rises because investors are pleased by its profits, that company finds itself able to borrow more money, expand its operations and increase its future profits. Conversely, if a company's stock declines because it failed to make a profit, it must then shrink its operations, lay off employees and perhaps even close some locations to try to restore its profitability.

That overriding need for companies to turn a profit explains why so many businesses commit moral atrocities for the sake of improving their earnings. Most of us were outraged when we learned that the CEOs of big tobacco companies had known for decades that their products were harmful, and yet hid the scientific data from the public. That they'd willingly forfeit human lives for the sake of higher profits seemed unbelievable. But why wouldn't we expect businesses to get away with as much as possible in search of higher profits? We've chartered them to believe that money means everything, and that people and nature are expendable in that quest.

Though we're constantly writing laws to curb the worst excesses of corporate behavior, we haven't yet drawn up a social code to inspire moral behavior in businesses. We have religious codes that instruct individuals how to behave, but as yet we've no secular moral code on which we all can agree. The problem with writing laws that tell companies how *not* to behave is that it's much harder to continue correcting them as we go forward than it would be to teach them how to behave in the first place. In this day and age of rapid human advancements, we can't write laws fast enough to keep up with the creative ways employees can invent to get around them. How much simpler life would be if, rather than constantly hunting down and trying to correct bad behavior, we reached a consensus on how we might all behave more honorably toward each other and this planet, and then each of us worked toward embodying that. Genuine self-governance—which is the ultimate goal of every democracy—blossoms from the inside out, not the outside in.

COMPANIES ARE COMPRISED OF LIVING PEOPLE

Most of us work in private enterprise. Our ability to survive is dependent upon the survival of the institution that issues our paycheck. Unfortunately, our entire economic belief system has unwittingly given our companies (and its employees, by proxy) permission to turn a profit at the world's expense. In fact, our current global financial crisis can be directly traced to the deeply entrained human belief that a person can only succeed if he or she hoards more money than anybody else, and that what we do to achieve that objective is less important than the achievement itself. If you haven't read Matt Taibbi's wonderful book, *Griftopia: Bubble Machines, Vampire Squids and the Long Con that is Breaking America*, which breaks down how and why this is such a destructive belief system for our society, you should.

So blinded have we become by our own ambitions to accumulate ever more money, what we've failed to notice is the awful cost of all our paper profits. We prefer to ignore the gobbling up of our limited planetary resources, the increases in environmental pollution, the destruction of crucial natural habitats and the extinction of other life forms, the outsourcing of middle-class jobs to cheaper labor forces, the exploitation of poorer nations, the ongoing disintegration of the family unit, the continuous engagement in war to support the military-industrial complex and the growing loss of consumer and employee trust in the overall system. Perhaps the time has come to reexamine our cultural beliefs around the importance of monetary profits—or at the very least redefine what we mean when we use the term, "for profit."

Corporate management's present motivation to succeed by turning a profit (accompanied by the fear of what will happen to themselves and their employees if they fail) is clearly out of step with the longer-term objectives of society, at least if we hope to survive without collapsing or going extinct. What happens when business's objectives are out of alignment with humanity's objectives is predictable. People feel betrayed when they suffer the consequences of immoral corporate behavior and react defensively. Some even begin to view corporations as our enemies, when the root problem lies in the pathology of our economic system itself.

What needs to change, then, is our definition of what constitutes a successful corporation. We must shift our attention away from believing that economic profits are of utmost value, particularly since all recent evidence points to the contrary. If we fail to take into account the importance of nurturing people and protecting and preserving nature when we measure our business profits, someday there won't be any place left for people or nature in this world. And what good are businesses without customers or natural materials upon which they can rely? The plain fact is, we're on a steady suicide course if we continue along the path of ignoring life in favor of money, so it's time for us to thoughtfully change directions.

Rather than wasting energy trying to fix blame on somebody else for the mess we're in, it would instead be most helpful for us to turn our attention toward consciously and methodically experimenting with other forms of economic design that embrace the values of nature and encourage the evolution of the human spirit. That's where our true profits lie as we advance as a civilization. It's not through more money or toys or competition that we find happiness, once our basic material needs have been satisfied, it's from loving and giving and creating and reveling in the wonder that is our world.

We humans gravitate toward beauty, toward light. We want to create and live in a world that's as joyful, humane and peaceful as we can make it. The difficulty lies in reaching consensus around our varied cultural ideas of what peace and happiness look like. As our species evolves, however, our understanding of how to reach peaceful accord and live in harmony with nature has been evolving along with us. Yet our instructions to our corporations haven't nearly kept pace with our advancements in social morality and our rising understanding of our civic duty to this planet. That *must* change if we hope to evolve a way of life suitably worthy of the respect and cooperation of future generations.

MODERN BELIEFS ABOUT ECONOMICS

People today are espousing some very strange beliefs about the state of our modern economy. We frequently hear things like: We can no longer afford to educate our children, provide universal health care, clean up our polluted environment, innovate around renewable energy resources, provide food, water and basic shelter for all, share our wisdom and planetary resources with other nations, protect our ecosystems or explore the farthest reaches of our universe. The reality-check question we must therefore ask ourselves is this: Will humanity survive as a species if we fail to do any or all of the above?

Once we shift perspective we may be shocked to realize the only thing preventing us from doing everything we hope to achieve is our mental attachment to the idea of money as both the driver and the reward for what we do. Money, a tool invented by people to aid in the exchange of our creative and productive output, has, over time, become our main barrier to the free expression and exchange of creativity. We're granting a collective belief—a group delusion about the power of money and its ability to determine our destiny— precedence over the immediacy of life's needs in the here and now.

We have the option to collapse as a civilization or go extinct as a species because we believe we can't afford to create a more loving, more sustainable way of life for all. We can cross our fingers and hope somebody somewhere figures out how we can all "muddle through" these current crises so we don't have to rock our belief boats to the point of personal discomfort. Or we could just leave it to our children to clean up our ever-expanding world mess in the hope the next generation will figure it out before the problems we're creating grow too vast to fix.

Those choices don't assume much responsibility for where we are right now. If we want to take responsibility for ourselves we must first look at the world as it is—not through the lens of the childlike beliefs we've accepted as true without question, but through the open and discerning eyes of mature adults. The collective way back from the insanity of any group delusion begins the moment we admit we are, in fact, insane; that we've left reality far behind in favor of what we've imagined to be true.

Once we acknowledge that our beliefs are self-imposed, that we've been taught to "believe in" the significance and power of money instead of the true creative capacity of humanity, we can see a need to reexamine economics in a whole new light. We need take none of our system's principles and practices for granted, nor assume any of its so-called values are absolute truths. What makes that process hard is this: we've all been born into the monetary system and were entrained to accept it without question, so challenging our beliefs may cause us some discomfort. Take heart in that. Personal growth and discomfort go hand in hand—just ask anyone who's been through adolescence. Besides, the anxiety we're already feeling due to our current economic problems should be all the encouragement we need to push through that angst and discover new solutions.

We can't view our world for what it is if we're afraid to acknowledge we may have outgrown our beliefs about how it works. The good news is that if we find the courage to examine and burst the collective myths under which we've all been operating, we become free to recreate our world in the way we want it to be: as a living reflection of who we truly are.

Einstein said, "You can't solve the problems of humanity with the consciousness that created them." At the moment, the level of consciousness under which we've all been operating for a long time is a worldview of separation: "I must protect and preserve what's mine, even if I do so at your expense." We've come to view most "others" as lazy, untrustworthy and in need of constant supervision and control, which is why we live in a world choked by greed, suspicion, fear and insurrection. Why we attribute to others all the worst qualities we have in ourselves and fail to acknowledge the collective best in all of us might have something to do with the fact we've become deeply disconnected from each other and from our own spirits. The belief that we're each independent, that what I do doesn't affect you and vice versa, is one that has failed us for many centuries now. History is replete with examples where isolationism hasn't worked, which is why wars have become increasingly dangerous. Our modern world actually reflects the truth of our interconnectivity through its relentless march toward human globalization. We can continue to cling to a belief in our absolute separateness and encourage our social structures to reflect that belief until they crumble beneath the weight of its inherent falsehood, or we can embrace our connectivity and learn to work together so we all can thrive.

FOLLOWING THE LAWS OF NATURE

To view humanity from a higher perspective, to recognize that we each want to put an end to suffering and that at heart we are all connected by our shared desire for love and happiness can inspire us to evolve our social structures until they reflect this new and higher faith in humankind. That's the new level of consciousness necessary to resolve the problems created by the old way of thinking.

We can begin making these changes by letting go of the beliefs that no longer serve us. But then what should we use for our new social model if our entire system was modeled on a false belief in separation? I suggest we try applying the successful models for interconnected living systems that are functioning all around us, and for which nature has so generously offered us blueprints. Nowhere in nature does a system—any system—survive independently of everything else. Nothing in the realm of nature works or succeeds alone.

Before the very first atoms in our universe coalesced, many billions of years before the emergence of human consciousness, creation apparently wondered whether this world would work better if things came together with order and intent, or went flying off on their own without regard for anything else. For eons our cosmos has explored and experienced the joy of binding different atoms together to form an amazing variety of molecules, each capable of being more and bringing more into the world than any atom could be or bring by itself. Those molecules eventually collaborated to become the building blocks for more and more complex structures, including us. It seems, therefore, that creation has already asked and answered the question about isolation and its limitations for us. It seems to delight in making multiple novel connections as much as it loves the interdependence such connections foster.

In nature, any whole system is always greater than the simple sum of its parts. A tree, for instance, isn't just a simple combination of root cells, trunk cells, capillaries, leaves and branches. It is a living, highly adaptable *enterprise*, capable of reproducing itself, sheltering other creatures, contributing oxygen to the atmosphere, depositing nitrogen into the soil, adulterating the climate and adding amazing beauty and stability to the landscape. Not only that, but its very existence enables all the cells that comprise it to activate themselves to their highest potential, and to be part of something greater than themselves.

So, too, is a human being more than just a mere collection of cells. The cells in our toes may not know they're part of a thinking, feeling person whose capacity to love and experience life is so much more than the product of its many cells, but they nevertheless go on, doing the essential work of being toes—and, because we *are* thinking and feeling, we have the power to protect our toes and appreciate them, even if they don't realize they're being protected.

We humans can stubbornly continue to insist we're better off not relying on each other. We can refuse to believe what we've learned about our own universe, but the truth won't change no matter how firmly we deny it. In our universe, any living system whose diverse parts don't learn to collaborate in order to form something greater than a random collection of units eventually fails. What's called for in any whole-systems design is an overarching benefit that every single part can enjoy in exchange for its willingness to work for the well being of the whole. Clearly then, humanity can't long sustain an economic system that benefits just a few of us by exploiting the capacities of the many.

BECOMING CONSCIOUS OF OUR PART IN THE WHOLENESS

Unlike cells, we do have the power of reasoned thought. With thought we've been granted the ability to consciously change our ways of being, thinking and interacting through learning how to successfully balance our personal needs with the overarching needs of the whole. If we truly want to heal humanity—as well as the larger living planetary body that has been suffering under our ignorance for so long—we must collectively change the false beliefs that are causing our dis-ease…one individual human cell at a time.

We've long been honing our ability to apply the gift of reasoned, creative thinking to the world around us. One thing we know about the human mind is it grants us the power to learn. The evolution of thinking enables us to craft our understanding of the world consciously, patiently and carefully, based on new information and insights. That we now understand volcano activity isn't caused by angry gods is one such an advancement. That doesn't mean anything was "wrong" with our old beliefs or ways of interacting. We've always done the best we could with the information we had at our disposal at that time, so judging those who were working with less information than we now have is a pointless exercise. It's foolish to declare that the people who proposed those now-debunked ideas were bad or evil. What matters is that we're learning to behave in more coordinated and supportive ways as we evolve in consciousness. That's exactly as our world was designed to unfold.

Rather than warring over our beliefs with whomever we don't agree—which has been our historic approach—we're gradually gaining the maturity to take an emotional step back to examine the reasons why we don't agree. In political debate, for example, we're beginning to hear more rational arguments around whether it's better for us to practice fiscal austerity and reduce taxation, or whether it's more important for us to stimulate the economy through government spending in the form of higher taxes. What's really interesting is that—as we continue to run the experiments pro and con—what we're really learning is that neither seems to provide the answer, and that what's needed may be something entirely different. Experimental failure, frustrating though it may be, sets us up for an expansion in human consciousness. As we continually try and fail to achieve our desired objectives through the same tired means, ultimately we're forced to rise above our limiting beliefs and embrace something new—an idea that propels us closer to the truth.

Because each person brings a unique set of life experiences to our shared world reality, there will always be multiple points of view on any given situation. Still, it seems the fine art of agreement can be learned, as evidenced by the existence of coordinated living systems all around us. If nearly a hundred trillion brainless cells[3] can learn to cooperate in a system as complex as the human body, why can't we?

---

3   Isaac Asimov, The Human Body, New rev. ed., Plume, 1996, p. 79; C. Van Amerogen, The Way Things Work Book of the Body, Simon and Schuster, 1979, p. 13.

MONEY AND
OUR FOR-PROFIT
WIN/LOSE GAME

WHAT IS WEALTH?

Imagine I'm holding a pack of matches and a twenty-dollar bill. If I asked you to select one and offered to give you whichever one you wanted, which would you pick?

If you're like most people, you'll choose the money. You know you can easily go to a supermarket and purchase dozens of packs of matches for twenty dollars. And when you consider that most days you have very little use for matches, while cash can get you anything you need, the decision becomes a no-brainer.

Let's next pretend, however, that you've already got both the matches and a twenty-dollar bill in your jacket pocket. Let's further imagine you've set out for a long hike on your own, perhaps in the hills or a thickly wooded forest not far from your home. You've been walking a while and have been so enjoying the scenery you forgot to pay attention to where you were going. Suddenly you realize it's getting dark. Alone in the woods and with your cell phone out of range of satellite service, it occurs to you that you're lost. Soon it'll be getting cold. As you contemplate what to do next, a gentle rain begins to fall. Shivering, you reach into your pocket and discover the twenty-dollar bill and the pack of matches.

In that moment, which item do you think you'd feel most grateful to hold in your hand? What do you think is the likelihood you might burn that twenty-dollar bill to start a fire?

When we place ourselves in such an extraordinary situation, we make an important discovery. Money, it seems, is only as good as our ability to exchange it for something we can actually use. As such it isn't wealth at all; it merely acts as a proxy, or substitute, for wealth. True wealth can be found in the things we need to improve our life experience. The question then becomes: how can we know the difference between true wealth and proxy wealth?

When we have true wealth we don't need others to agree with us on its value. If I happen to find a potato and I'm starving, that potato becomes real wealth to me. Whether or not you like or want a potato becomes irrelevant. Likewise, if loving someone makes my life feel richer and more complete, I don't need you to approve of the person I love for me to be happy.

Money, since it acts as a proxy for wealth, is only as valuable as we collectively believe it to be. I can't acquire true wealth with my twenty-dollar bill unless I can convince another person to accept it in exchange for what I actually need. I can't eat my paper money, wear it, shelter beneath it or heal myself with it. I can only hope to trade it away so I'm able to get what I need to improve my life. How *much* money it will take for me to get the things I need depends upon the nature and desires of the other person (or business) who is selling whatever it is I happen to want.

THE DANGER OF TRUSTING IN PROXIES

The trouble with elevating the proxy wealth that is money to our most desired form of wealth, the way most of us do today, is that it provides us with no guarantees. Read a dollar bill and you'll discover it's classified as "legal tender for all debts, public and private." Right there we find that the cash we invest so much of our time and energy acquiring offers us nothing tangible to secure a better future for ourselves. So then, what does that slippery phrase "legal tender" actually mean?

When we investigate the meaning of legal tender (which we can easily do by visiting *http://www.treasury.gov/resource-center/faqs/ Currency/Pages/legal-tender.aspx*), we learn it gives us the right to offer our cash to any *creditor*, which is a person (or business) to whom we owe a debt. Nothing in that arrangement, however, mandates a vendor must accept our money in exchange for goods or services we haven't yet purchased. Just as each vendor has the right to demand as much of our legal tender as she deems reasonable in exchange for her products, she also has every right to refuse our money.

What, it's fair to ask, would cause a vendor to turn down perfectly good legal tender? What would she prefer to accept instead? Peer into the shadows of history for answers and we find countless examples of nations whose citizens lost faith in the integrity of their currency and suddenly refused to accept it, as occurred in Germany in the early 1920s, Chile in the 1970s and Yugoslavia in the mid-1990s. Varied as their citizens' reasons might be for doing so, at the heart of every national currency collapse is the fact that money has never been actual wealth, but rather a proxy we've chosen to help us *acquire* real wealth. Even when most nations were on the gold standard and their cash could be exchanged for actual gold, gold was simply a more solid proxy for wealth than paper is now.

The average person has little use for gold other than to trade the rare metal away for something they need. For the most part gold has been prized for its relative scarcity, not its functionality. That it's also beautiful, easily melted, shaped and considered useful for making jewelry is a bonus, not a necessity. What *is* necessary is that whatever item we choose to define as a proxy for wealth remains scarce; otherwise we fear too many people will collect proxy money and grow rich without contributing something of value to society. If you doubt for a moment that the whole point of making money is to gather enough of it so you have more of it relative to everybody else, consider this: if pebbles or tree leaves were money, we could all be rich. What then would be the point of using money to purchase what we need? As Don Henley says in his wonderful song, "If dirt were dollars, we'd all be in the black."[4]

Scarcity, it's important to note, is purposefully built into every proxy wealth system to press people into working in exchange for the things they need. And for whom, we must ask ourselves, do the pressed poor (and more recently the declining middle class) work? The answer, of course, is that poor and middle class men and women are required to work for the very small number of individuals who have accumulated enough money to be able to pay them a wage in exchange for their labor. In the United States that number refers mainly to the one percent of people who own nearly half of the nation's wealth.[5] That figure includes corporate stock that designates ownership of America's private corporations, as well as bonds (outstanding debt) issued by those private enterprises, along with the debt of all federal, state and local governments.

While many middle-class Americans may own shares of corporate stock in their investment and retirement portfolios, they are no more the actual owners of those businesses than they are possessors of tangible wealth because they have money. The de facto owners of our so-called "publicly held" corporations are the individuals who have amassed large enough blocks of company stock to dictate how the business is run. That includes how its profits are distributed, how its employees are paid, what it produces and how, where and with whom it does its business. Typically such decisions

---

4   Don Henley, "If Dirt Were Dollars," from the album *The End of Innocence*, Geffen Records, 1989.

5   G. William Domhoff, Wealth, Income, and Power, September 2005 (updated September 2010). http://sociology.ucsc.edu/whorulesamerica/power/wealth.html

are made by ultra-wealthy individuals who sit on the board of directors, in concert with a company's chief executives.

It thus seems that a scarcity system, by its very design, promotes a separation between those few who manage to accumulate vast amounts of proxy wealth (which equates to social power) and the many more who do not. A scarcity system naturally concentrates power in the hands of the wealthy because it wrests power from those who must work to acquire enough money to survive. Whenever wealth begins to seep too rapidly into the broader population, as happened in the 1950s during the rise of the middle class, the wealthy change the rules or behave in ways to ensure that wealth re-concentrates. The poor, it therefore appears, will always be with us because we function in a scarcity system—not because we have no choice in the matter, but because we've embraced a way of life that institutionalizes a large underclass to service the needs of the rich.

PROXY WEALTH AND INFLATION

Whenever people begin to lose faith in their nation's currency, inflation results. Inflation reflects the risk that comes from accepting proxy money for goods and services. The problem with trading proxy money for actual wealth is that there's no guarantee some other vendor will later accept that proxy money at the rate of exchange the first vendor used when he calculated the prices at which to sell his own merchandise.

Imagine for a moment you're a storeowner during a high inflation period. If the goods you need to buy to provide for your
family will cost you ten dollars today, but those same goods might
cost you as much as twenty dollars tomorrow, you might decide to
charge twenty dollars today for all the items you sold in your store
for ten dollars yesterday. Inflation, then, is a matter of every merchant trying to squeeze more money out of his inventory than the
next guy so that he will have a bigger pile of money to spend in relationship to everybody else.

It helps to remember that proxy wealth is *relative* wealth, not
real wealth. That means it's only a net positive for me if I have more
of it in my pocket than you happen to have in yours. If I have more
money than you and we both want the same thing, I can afford to
outbid you for that item. In short, I win and you lose. How wealthy
or happy do you think you'll feel in that moment when I beat you,
regardless of how much cash you happen to have?

It's easy to see how money's relative value creates bidding wars
and perpetuates the cycle of inflation that, to some extent or another, bedevils every currency. We also begin to see how price and
wage increases, considered by so many to be a sign of economic strength, are in reality a sign of monetary weakness. Wage and
price increases occur whenever we inject more cash into our economy, which fuels a bidding war as people compete to buy finite
goods and services. Certainly that happens during times of economic expansion, but it also happens during recessions when the
Federal Reserve floods the banking system with money to stimulate spending. In recent years, for example, the Federal Reserve has
poured literally trillions of dollars into the economy to encourage

both spending and borrowing. Where it's showing up as inflation, since we're still suffering from high unemployment, are in costs that aren't particularly discretionary—in food prices, oil prices, health care costs, education costs and the price of goods imported from foreign countries. In reality, inflation is a byproduct of money's inability to retain its value over time.

Realize that whatever labor we've outlaid to earn our money is energy that's gone forever; we can't summon it back and offer it over again to a higher bidder. That means whenever the buying power of our annual salary declines because prices have increased (inflation), we've essentially worked for less than we bargained for. That outcome is great for businesses and corporate profitability, but not so great for living human beings with physical needs. Realize too that the longer we're expected to wait to collect our wages, the greater the chances our money will buy less than it would have on the day we earned it. Somewhere along the way, "give us this day our daily bread" mutated into "I'll pay you the money you've earned at the end of the month."

How, we must also ask ourselves, does this steady erosion of money's buying power due to inflation affect the value of all our other assets? To understand that, think back to the house your parents or grandparents may have owned in the 1940s. Perhaps they bought it for as little as fifteen thousand dollars. That very same house might sell today for as much as two hundred and fifty thousand dollars—nearly seventeen times its original purchase price.

On the surface it seems like an amazing profit, right? Except essentially it's the same house it always was. It didn't magically become more special than the other houses on its block, or suddenly sprout more acres and ten new rooms. If you checked you'd discover all the houses listed around it would probably be selling for about the same price, so if your grandparents chose to sell their house their standard of living wouldn't markedly improve. Whatever money they earned off the sale of their house would have to be fully reinvested in order for them to acquire a new house of comparable size and value. What we're witnessing, then, is the way the buying power of money has decayed over time. That we've been trained to label most monetary decay as "price appreciation" or "capital gains" helps to confuse the issue, so people don't grasp the truth of what's really going on.

When a monetary system becomes *too* weak, it may cause the collapse of a nation's entire economy. Tales abound that after World War I, Germans pushed around wheelbarrows full of cash to try to buy a single loaf of bread. A similar collapse occurred in the United States just after the Civil War. Confederate currency, that proxy monetary darling of the South, lost one hundred percent of its value when the victorious Northerners refused to accept it. All those formerly wealthy Southerners who'd invested their life's savings in Confederate dollars and war bonds suddenly found themselves destitute and unable to pay the property taxes on their homes and plantations. A deep-seated hatred of the so-called carpetbaggers—those Northerners who moved south with their Union-backed money to buy up homes and farms in foreclosure sales—reflected the unfairness of it all.

It's not only distant history that offers us examples of economic collapses. Currencies collapse around the world all the time. In Mexico in 1993, for example, the government was forced to strip three zeros away from the peso because the prices of goods had gotten so high that calculating prices and change had become unmanageable. The new peso was priced at one for every thousand old pesos being exchanged, and the old pesos were eventually phased out. Imagine witnessing your half-million dollar retirement account reduced overnight to a piddling five hundred dollars and you'll understand the pain of that experience. Meanwhile halfway around the world in Zimbabwe, inflation in 2008 exceeded one million percent per year.[6] Imagine for a moment that items you could purchase in January for a dollar each would cost a million dollars to purchase in December and you'll grasp the extent of that fiscal tragedy.

People who live in relatively stable nations prefer to believe such awful things could never happen to them. Then again, Germany was fairly stable before it begat World War I, as was the United States before the Civil War. It's also important to note that wars aren't the only cause of financial destabilization. Natural disasters provoke a tremendous amount of personal reckoning around what's valuable and what isn't. Additionally, corporate criminality and bad conduct, particularly in the financial services industry, which collects and controls the public's money and can easily abuse that trust, trigger monetary collapses. This is a scenario we are all too familiar with in modern times.

The United States has experienced two episodes of financial panic generated by banking shenanigans within a short span of only twenty years. The Savings and Loan scandal of the late 1980s was triggered by imprudent real estate lending and compounded by political corruption (the Keating Five) of the federal investigatory

---

6   Steve Henke, "R.I.P. Zimbabwe Dollar," The Cato Institute, last updated May 3, 2010.

process. It led directly to the failure of nearly eight hundred bank-ing institutions and cost the people of the United States nearly one hundred thirty billion dollars.[7]

The next panic, the financial crisis of September 2008, was also caused by imprudent real estate lending and political corruption of the federal investigatory and regulatory processes. It triggered the failure of at least one hundred sixty-five banks, along with millions of home foreclosures. As for the net costs to the American people, they're still impossible to quantify as of this writing since the mess continues to unravel day by day, but they're estimated to run into the many *trillions* of dollars.

Both banking collapses were driven by greed and fueled by all the political corruption that corporate money could buy. Although they caused massive suffering to ordinary citizens, they succeeded in their primary objectives, which were to re-concentrate wealth in the hands of a few and to reinforce the power of the wealthy. If you think for a moment we've learned our lessons from these re-cent financial debacles, consider the fact that about a year after the financial collapse of 2008, the United States Supreme Court ruled that corporations were entitled to spend as much money as they chose to influence the outcomes of political campaigns, labeling it a matter of free speech.[8] The decision to equate campaign spending and free speech granted people with access to large pools of money (i.e. corporate owners and directors) the power to influence polit-ical outcomes to a far higher degree than people who don't have

---

7   Resolution Trust Corporation's 1995 and 1994 Financial Statements (PDF), U.S. General Accounting Office, July 1996, pp. 8, 13.

8   Citizens United vs. Federal Elections Commission, January 2010.

access to large pools of cash. For example, a multinational oil company now has the power to influence the outcome of a community election by flooding the local airwaves with ads and radio spots attacking the character of a politician who holds an environmental position on oil and gas that the company dislikes or feels might threaten their profitability.

To equate spending money to influence political outcomes with an individual's freedom to speak his mind is a perversion of the Founding Fathers' belief in the right of *every* individual to be heard. The *de facto* result is to hand the political process over to those who can best afford to buy a desired outcome.

That proxy money is unreliable *matters*. That we tend to be complacent about the corrosive effects of inflation, and that we blithely surrender power to those who control money's distribution only increases the chances we'll some day wind up on the losing side of another financial collapse.

Had you visited Haiti shortly before the January 2010 earthquake and offered a random sampling of people a choice between food and proxy money, most would have happily taken whatever amount of money you had to offer. Immediately after the earthquake, however, odds are good those same people would have preferred whatever food, water or medical items you offered over cash. How many starving Haitians do you think would have traded their precious food for a fistful of proxy dollars?

THE POWER OF OUR BELIEF IN PROXY MONEY

A "dogma" is defined as a settled or established opinion, belief, or principle. Clearly, we live in a world that long ago embraced the dogma that says money is the principal method we humans will use to go about the business of exchanging our labor, creativity, goods and services. We need to acknowledge that this dogma was set into motion long before any of us were born. Over the centuries it's become so widely accepted as "the best way" for doing business that most of us have never bothered to ask ourselves the simple question, "Why?"

To question a dogma is always to risk discomfort. Any time we look deeply into a dogmatic belief we may discover that beliefs we once assumed were true no longer make sense. While certain beliefs may have seemed perfectly reasonable in the past, even the most ingrained dogmas eventually give way to new realizations as human understanding and awareness advance over time. For example, slavery used to be a perfectly acceptable social dogma, as did burning people at the stake for crimes of heresy or witchcraft. In ancient Mayan cultures, cutting out the beating hearts of one's still-living enemies and offering them up to the gods was acceptable dogma. In Biblical times, stoning women for adultery was perfectly fine, a dogma that continues to apply in some Islamic nations today. That many of us now view these traditions as barbaric is a reflection of our intellectual and spiritual evolution. As we humans grow ever more aware of our profound interconnectedness—to each other, to our planet and to all living things—our collective attitudes and values slowly shift to reflect that awareness.

Therefore, for us to regularly and unflinchingly examine our inherited dogmas to determine if they remain appropriate in light of our modern day values is an important part of helping society change to meet the challenges of new times. Unfortunately, many of us become so enmeshed in our dogmas that we suffer a failure of imagination when it comes to visualizing a different way to be. That's the power dogmas have over us; they become so institutionalized that for us to imagine behaving in any other way is almost unthinkable. The key word, of course, is *almost.* For once we examine a dogma and see the problems that have resulted from our clinging to a particular belief, we find the strength to free ourselves from its grip. We can begin to imagine a world without the suffering caused by those problems, which helps us envision a way beyond the dogma.

This doesn't mean we reject our past. The lessons we've learned will forever be part of our story. All the pain, joy, fears, suffering and happiness of our personal life experience is already inextricably woven into the colorful and complex tapestry of human history. We must appreciate and honor those lessons as integral to our shared wisdom, even as we leave behind our outmoded dogmas.

THE ORIGINS OF HUMAN CREATIVITY

There can be no doubt that money once served a vital purpose. To grasp that purpose and to explore whether or not it remains relevant today, we must first take a journey down the dark and tangled path of human history. Peer deeply into the shadows behind us and they'll whisper stories of how we got from there to where we now live.

Human history can best be described as imagination in motion. If necessity is indeed the mother of invention, then surplus—particularly of time—must be its father. For early man, the thing he had the least surplus of was time, yet time is what's required for us to advance our understanding of how to navigate our way through reality. Once the first hominids shimmied out of the trees and figured out how to pick up rocks to use for weapons, it then took many hundreds of thousands of years for them to next figure out how to attach a stone to a stick and make a useful bludgeon. They then spent another hundred thousand years learning to throw a spear. What strange circumstances, we must therefore ask ourselves, prodded these apparently slow-witted creatures to develop the massive creative edge we have over other life forms today? What changes in our environment enhanced our ability to build tools and imagine new ways of doing things that would eventually help us evolve into modern man? And how many eons of learning were required for us to get from there to here?

While opposable thumbs and a reasonably good-sized brain were helpful assets, the best guess of most historians is that the taming of fire prodded humanity down its long and winding journey toward creative advancement. Fire gave early hunters the ability to cook and cure their meat, which kept it from spoiling as fast as did raw meat. That skill would have enabled them to lay down a decent surplus of food, and our ancestors would have suddenly found themselves with a bit of free time on their hands. Free time granted them a newfound opening to pursue whatever creative ideas might have occurred to them previously, but which they'd not been able to explore because they'd been too busy surviving. Their evening fires would have additionally provided them light in which to work long past the setting sun. Just think about it for a moment: without the twin surpluses of food and productive time, how would humankind ever have managed to test its more complex theories?

Imagine yourself as an ancient man, forced to stand in the shallows of a river for ten hours a day trying to bash a fish on the head with a rock so you could have something eat. You might well spend those tedious hours envisioning how to craft a net that would make your task easier. You'd also recognize such a net would take you many days to craft, and you could hardly afford to stop eating in order to try it. Suppose you decided to try anyhow, but your net came apart in the water on your very first cast? Having already gone many days without eating, you'd likely be too weak to fish the way you knew how, and so would perish. Net construction, therefore, came about due to surplus *and* necessity, not just necessity.

Think too where humanity might be today if Thomas Edison had been forced to meet all his needs through bone-crushing labor. How would he have found the time to invent anything? Clearly, then, no matter how creative early man's *thoughts* may have been, until he harnessed fire, his need to work through the daylight hours would have barred him from exploring his own creativity.

Luckily for us, fire *was* discovered and tamed by ancient man, and humanity eventually evolved beyond its original hunter-gatherer behavior to establish primitive agricultural communities. With the advent of agriculture, humanity for the second time in history found itself in a state of wealth surplus, only this time the excess being produced met the needs of many more people. Before agriculture, humans had the capacity to lay down food provisions for a week or maybe two. The cultivation of grains, however, enabled people to store adequate food supplies to last an entire community a whole winter. The power in that cannot be overstated.

Stonehenge, the great pyramids of Egypt and the giant stone cities of Central America were all constructed during the great agrarian period—because for the first time such feats could actually be achieved! No evidence exists to prove that the laborers of these great city-states were slaves or in any way coerced into building their monuments; on the contrary, excavations of cities where the pyramid builders lived prove the workers lived well and were properly nourished and cared for. We've also recently learned that in Egypt, pyramid construction ceased each year when the Nile receded, which signaled it was time for the farmers to plant their crops for the following season. Pyramid construction was again taken up just as soon as the harvest was in, which indicates most laborers were ordinary farmers and citizens.

We marvel today at the energy and devotion it must have taken for these ancient cultures to create such immense and precisely engineered public works. We also attempt to ascribe great religious or astronomical importance to these monuments, because we have difficulty imagining any society would put in so much effort for all but the most important of reasons. We do this, though, through the prism of our own times and modern life experiences.

These days we tend to take our great cities and civilizations for granted. Having been born into them we know no other way of life. Back then, however, imagine how exhilarating it must have been for hardworking citizens to watch their creative efforts bear such amazing fruit. Perhaps the joy that came from working for a cause that was greater than their individual capacities was enough to spur them to see their projects through. In this fashion, the whole of each of these societies became greater than the simple sum of their parts, just as nature tells us it must be. Any other motive we attempt to ascribe to our ancestors may in actuality spring from our present-day biases and beliefs.

Along those same lines, imagine how some sentient being many hundreds of thousands of years in the distant future who happens to stumble upon the undersea ruins of Manhattan might marvel at the skyscrapers we once built in the twentieth century. Such beings might wonder why we puny humans would have struggled to invent and use such difficult technologies. Why build up when we could more simply spread out? Perhaps they'd speculate we were trying to connect with (or worship) our own gods through our physical achievements, not realizing we'd constructed certain buildings because the task seemed so hard, and we wanted to find out if we could actually do it.

When we gaze into history, we tend to forget the immense embedded power behind our impulse to imagine and create when spurred by will.

THE NEXT GREAT SHIFT: MONEY
AS THE MEDIUM OF EXCHANGE
FOR HUMAN CREATIVITY

Deep in the shadows along the trail of our human history, as free time became more readily available and each person was required to devote less energy to support the basic survival needs of the whole community, something wonderful happened. Human beings discovered the bliss of art, music and dance, the excitement of creative storytelling and the beauty of craftsmanship. We began to design fine furnishings and make better tools, jewelry, artwork, clothing and pottery. Originally such items were traded through barter; there is evidence of such transactions from as far back as a hundred thousand years. Eventually, however, the idea of creating a proxy wealth system to make it easier for people to exchange their creative products was birthed into being. The first proxy wealth arrived on the scene around 3000 BCE. Many of these early societies used shells or stone beads for their trading, mainly because they were pretty and had some utilitarian purposes for scraping hides or creating jewelry. Gold and silver coins were minted much later, around 650 BCE (the first coins were introduced by the ancient Lydians, in what is now the modern Republic of Turkey). Coins offered the advantage of being easily melted down, and they could also be broken into smaller pieces if a seller needed to make "change."

In its original incarnation, money functioned as a convenient way for people to exchange their labor, goods and services. It made complex trading easier, hence the term "currency." Much like a river, money formed an energetic flow whereby the fruits of one person's creativity could travel to another person and then on to another and another, without any of them actually having to meet. Just as importantly, the invention of money triggered a third wave of surplus accumulation (one still underway today) by granting people the ability to set aside reserves *not* just for a few weeks or a few winters, but for an entire lifetime.

Before money arrived on the scene, material wealth couldn't be hoarded for very long. Grain crops eventually rotted and livestock inevitably died. These facts required people to trade away their surplus before it deteriorated in value, which meant that most of the time, the collective wealth of humanity was either actively circulating or being consumed.

Money changed all that. Suddenly hoarding became a noble goal. Excess gold and silver could be set aside for years and only brought back into circulation when the need to buy goods arose. Eventually people realized money could be stored beyond a single lifetime, so inheritance and property rights were invented. Such laws were likely written for the benefit of those who'd already amassed enough wealth to pass it along to their children, since the wealthy tended to be the very people who made the rules. Hammurabi's Code, written around 1780 BCE, contains the earliest recorded laws we've so far uncovered. The code makes multiple references to property rights and suggests punishments for various forms of theft. This indicates most people by that time had already shifted their thinking away from a communal belief in "ours" to the dogma of "mine" that persists into modern times.

With the invention of money people gradually developed an urge to accumulate enough for the future so they wouldn't have to worry about not having enough anymore. While early man would have thought it foolish to worry about the future beyond doing what he needed to do each day to survive, once money appeared people began to pursue personal success with relentless enthusiasm. Additionally, money gave individuals the power to hire out tasks they didn't wish to perform for themselves anymore, which in turn began to divide humanity into classes of "haves" and "have nots." Those with wealth were afforded the privilege of purchasing the time and labor of others, while those without were forced to sell their time and labor to the highest bidders.

We must remind ourselves here that money's value is strictly relative, not absolute, so the fact that you possess a lot of it won't help my cause at all. Since I'm required to compete with you to buy the things we both need, the more money you have, the more of it I'll need to accumulate so I can outbid you. This means that the more financially successful you are, the greater the problem you'll pose for me in the long run. Subconsciously then, we're all being programmed (by what is fundamentally a win/lose system) to resent the successes of others and to resist those policies that require us to support or assist other human beings in need. On some level, whether we realize it or not, we recognize that such assistance must come at our own expense. Therefore, while our personal morality may be telling us to behave one way, our economic system is encouraging us to behave the opposite way. Is it any wonder so many of us feel conflicted? What we often label hypocrisy is actually a manifestation of this internal conflict between our quest for monetary survival and our desire to do the right thing by other people.

While its earliest users may not have understood the negative effects of money's relativity, the consequences of it have been profound. Over time any desire we may have once had to try to create a world that worked for everyone (a win/win scenario) dissipated as the individual's need to hoard relatively more than all others (win/lose) became our new societal dogma.

Along the way, our creativity and our desire to direct it for social benefit became subverted to our increasing need for money. Nowadays we see massive amounts of creative energy unable to find an outlet, either because people can't afford to test their ideas or businesses won't pay them for their efforts. Nor can the average person afford to purchase the many creative outpourings of humanity. The sad result is that we've got far more gifts to offer each other than we've granted ourselves the ability to receive.

THE INHERENT STRESSES IN A WIN/LOSE GAME

When we understand the negative influences our attachment to proxy wealth has had on our own behavior, we begin to understand why we're expected to pay as we go for our needs, and why many of us don't see fit to help other people. We can better comprehend how hard it must have been for our parents to provide for us while we were still too young to provide for ourselves, and why life wears down so many of us and leaves us bitter, discouraged and fearful. We grasp why, as soon as our children reach their teen years, they're encouraged to take on some menial job to help pay for their own needs while they're still in school. We see why children get pushed into academic programs as babies and are forced to surrender their childhood so they can learn how to fit into the system in the future.

We all know that getting an education unfairly requires many young people from impoverished families to take on debt before their earnings power comes into play, but it all makes sense once we realize that—beyond our own loving family members—the rest of society has no real incentive to help young people succeed. Given the relative nature of the money game, if your child does better than mine, my child's lifestyle will suffer. What possible benefit can I therefore gain by helping your child succeed at my child's expense?

When our young adults do at last begin their careers at entry-level wages, our society then expects them to meet all their own needs while paying back the debts they were forced to incur while still in school. At the same time they're expected to set aside money in case anything goes wrong. We also expect them to purchase insurance and pay annual premiums to protect themselves from accidental disasters or catastrophic illnesses, which might hinder their ability to provide for themselves in the future. On top of that, they're expected to build up large retirement nest eggs to ensure they've got enough money to live on when they're too old to work.

Given that modern human life expectancy now exceeds eighty years and is rising, is it any wonder so many of us walk around feeling frazzled, anxious and fearful? So much of our daily ener-gy gets spent on meeting our future personal needs (or worrying about how we're going meet them) that we've lost track of the one gift our shared explosion of human creativity was supposed to pro-vide for us—more free time to create in the here and now! Without that free time and without the mental alertness we need to use our free time wisely, human creativity becomes even more bottlenecked and a vast amount of our collective potential gets wasted.

How many wonderful ideas, we have to wonder, have never been explored or experimented with because a would-be inventor got too busy taking care of his many future needs to extend him-self any further? How often have *you* dragged yourself home from work, exhausted from traffic or the pressures of the day, craving only a cocktail and a mindless TV show to relax your brain? What happened to all that amazing human exuberance we once had? We see its remnants everywhere we look. Why don't we feel the same thrill our ancestors must have felt when they pulled together to cre-ate something really BIG? Could it be we've gotten so busy taking care of ourselves, so wrapped up in meeting our individual future needs, that we've forgotten how amazing it is to do something re-ally terrific as a species?

Unlike our ancient fisherman, who each day needed to pro-vide enough food for only a single day, modern man is expected to provide—right now—for *all* his needs; past, present and future, as well as for those of his offspring. Creativity can hardly flourish in a mental and social prison so confining. Surely the inventors of money never imagined such an outcome when they began using wealth proxies to trade the fruits of their own creative endeavors.

THE BIRTH OF BANKING

We've already seen how the introduction of wealth proxies led to hoarding, an obsessive focus on the future and all the attendant stresses that come from it. Less obvious is the way the two most powerful negative drivers of human behavior—greed and fear—spring directly from those experiences. The problem we all confront is this: we fear the future and what it might do to us if we're not financially prepared to meet it, so we greedily hoard whatever we can to try to protect ourselves from the awful unknown.

The fact, though, is that no amount of money we can hoard has the power to protect us from an unknown future, because proxy wealth holds no absolute power to address the very real events that may occur in life. Only life itself holds the power to adapt to whatever challenges it may be asked to face. No amount of money in our pockets can buy us out of harm's way should a meteor strike our planet, a super volcano erupt, a massive earthquake hit our city, or climate change flood our coastlines. The cosmos isn't interested in our cash. It seeks only our most intelligent and creative response to its actions.

As impossible as is our ability to hoard enough money so we won't ever have to worry about life's challenges, inflation renders it impossible for us to know that money's future value will be what we need it to be when we're older, even assuming we confront no huge disasters. Because of inflation, stuffing our cash into our mattresses doesn't guarantee we'll be able to provide for ourselves in the future. Inflation, therefore, forces us to invest our hard-earned proxy wealth in items that represent real wealth—things like real estate, stocks and bonds and investment loans—in ways we hope will cause our net worth to rise over time. That involves running the risk of losing some (or even all) of the money we've so far managed to save.

The need to assume risk creates a whole new set of problems that colors our behavior when it comes to money. We desperately want our net worth to grow so we'll never run out of cash or be in need (the greed factor), yet we're terrified we might make a poor decision and lose more than we can possibly recover (the fear factor). These two emotions drive our stock markets, the real estate market, the markets for collectibles and even our consumption and savings habits.

The financial services industry initially arose to help people manage their money more efficiently and with less emotional decision-making distortion. Banks, in their earliest incarnation, were little more than glorified safety deposit boxes, secure places where people could store their money and presume it would be safe. Early banks were neighborhood businesses, owned and operated by people who lived in the town their bank served. If a local merchant or farmer needed a loan because he needed to expand his inventory or had suffered a major crop failure, the banker's job was to make the loan from money he held on deposit for other families. The banker negotiated personal terms for each loan's repayment, depending on the reason behind the loan. Bankers in those early days went out of their way *not* to call in loans or foreclose on friends and neighbors, because to do so might upset their other customers. The person who'd suffered the setback was a neighbor too, and everyone in the community understood any one of them might someday fall on hard times. Everyone wanted to be able to rely on their neighbors to help them get through a rough patch.

Keep in mind that the mature insurance industry we know today didn't exist a hundred years ago. If someone got sick, his community stepped up to help the afflicted family. If someone's barn burnt down, the entire town would gather to raise a new one. If someone's crop failed, other farmers pitched in to provide new seed stock and food to help the family through that first winter. People still recognized the value of sharing whatever they could afford without demanding something in return, because most had experienced both good times *and* personal hardships. The idea of spending hard-earned money to buffer themselves from as many of life's risks as possible, the standard practice of buying insurance today, would have seemed very strange to our ancestors.

THE EVOLUTION OF MONEY

Not only were our early banks different, our money was different as well. Although still only a proxy for wealth, the earliest paper money was backed by federal gold deposits and could be exchanged for gold. Because gold couldn't be mass-produced to dilute our proxy wealth, its scarcity helped to keep inflation in check. Over time, although more and more gold was extracted and hoarded to back more and more cash dollars, the amount of cash in circulation remained restricted by gold's natural scarcity.

Although it helped control inflation, the fact that gold remained scarce created other problems for money—problems that had festered in Europe for several hundred years before the United States was founded. By the early 1900s, those problems led to at least one financial crisis (and often many more) in every single monetized nation, including the fairly young United States.

The greatest problem money faced at that time was that a post-Middle Ages population boom had been accompanied by the onset of the Industrial Revolution. That combination led to a massive explosion of human creative output as more people began to produce more and more goods more quickly. That creative explosion guaranteed gold's scarcity would clash with humanity's growing need for enough money to move around all the goods that were being produced. The battle between scarcity and abundance set the two wealth proxies—gold and paper money—on a supply and demand collision course with destiny.

The growing number of people, multiplied by their exploding creativity as human ingenuity expanded upon itself, was multiplied yet again by the introduction of new technologies to mass-produce those goods. All that productivity needed to be distributed, which meant every industrializing society had to flood its system with enough cash to ensure its people could actually acquire all the things that were being manufactured. This, however, was not a new problem. As early as the late 1400s, most European nations found themselves in the awkward position of not being able to mine gold fast enough to produce the immense amount of cash and coinage necessary to support their own economic expansion.

We often think of the historic period of European global expansion that began in the late 1400s as a romantic time of exploration and planetary discovery. The truth, however, is the reason for the furious exploration was that most European empires were desperately seeking new sources of gold, precious minerals and other natural resources to refill their depleted royal coffers. All the great arboreal forests of Europe had long been cut down for construction, firewood and to make room for grazing and farmland. The mineral resources the Europeans had uncovered had mainly been tapped and all available land had been settled, deeded or sold.

By contrast, the vast untouched forests and expansive unsettled plains of North, Central and South America must have indeed seemed like a "new world" ripe for pillaging when viewed by those early explorers. Settlements sprang up as an afterthought; the early explorers' original intent was to plunder those virgin lands and relieve of their gold any savages they encountered, as well as to enslave the indigenous people. That the Maya, Inca and Aztecs used gold in their jewelry making and building adornments explains why Cortez and others focused on exploring and conquering the wilderness to the South rather than on the North American plains. It seems the North American Indians had found little use for gold, so the conquistadors were unaware it existed in those parts.

How important was the search for gold? At home in Europe, legends spread like wildfire about a famous jungle city named El Dorado, said to have been built entirely of gold. European explorers dreamed of discovering El Dorado for their own country, and of being rewarded with titles and wealth for enriching their monarchy's coffers.

Other explorers eventually ventured southeast from Europe to Africa. Africa appeared to be disappointingly void of great forests or rich mineral deposits—at least on the surface, since the natives did not wear gold—but what Africa *did* possess in abundance was a human population so unlike the people of Europe they were thought to be of another species entirely. The physical and cultural distinctions of native Africans were strange enough for Europeans to justify capturing them by the millions and selling them into slavery for the benefit of a growing business economy.

Slavery eventually thrived in the Americas because it behooved plantation owners to capitalize on the vast amount of "free" labor needed to work their fields, especially since money for wages was relatively scarce in the South. Feeding and housing slaves in the South didn't much burden a landowner, not when the land was vast and food grew in abundance. In the North, on the other hand, great manufacturing cities populated by a constant flood of European immigrants sprang up near virtually every river mouth, lake and natural port. There cheap human labor abounded; but property costs were high and food was scarce. That made it less expensive for a factory owner to pay his workers a miserly weekly wage than it would have cost to feed, clothe and house them in perpetuity.

Due to these local differences, most northerners didn't grasp the advantage awarded a plantation owner for utilizing slave labor. Nor did he notice his own barbarous attitude toward the immigrant underclass he himself exploited. A steady influx of immigrants meant job competition stayed high, ensuring that factory owners needn't pay much to keep their businesses running. Wages were held so low that immigrant children were forced to work in the factories, often for twelve or fourteen hours a day, to help provide for their families' basic needs. Things got so hard for city dwellers that every new wave of immigration sparked an adverse reaction from those who'd already arrived, because every hungry new immigrant posed a brand new threat to the existent population's ability to survive on their meager factory wages.

Even with wages kept artificially low and the use of slave labor for farming, there still wasn't enough available gold being mined globally to enable the various governments to produce the necessary paper money to support their swelling economies. Over the centuries, countless wars had been fought in Europe to determine control over land, resources and wealth, and that pattern began to repeat itself in the newborn United States. The war of 1812 represented a thwarted attempt by the United States to wrest control of Canada from England. During the Mexican-American War of 1846-1848, the United States successfully grabbed what is now Texas and most of California from Mexico. That war was followed closely by the Civil War of 1861-1865, a conflict that forced the South to remain part of the United States and that ensured the abundant Southern-produced food supplies would continue to flow to the great Northern factory cities. Close on the heels of the Civil War came the Spanish American War of 1898, in which the United States successfully dislodged Spain from its territories in Cuba, Puerto Rico, Guam and the Philippines.

Wars weren't the only result of these national obsessions to acquire or hold new lands or grab natural resources. The United

States economy suffered through five major recessions in a brief fifteen-year period between 1890 and 1905.[9] By December of 1913 the United States government finally seemed to have had enough of financial ups and downs. Embracing the "helpful" advice of J.P. Morgan and John D. Rockefeller, the major bankers of that era, the government under Teddy Roosevelt established the Federal Reserve Bank to assist it in managing monetary policy. Roosevelt's hope was that by creating an independent central bank to regulate the creation and flow of money into society, the booms and busts so often triggered by the easy availability—or sudden shortage—of money would disappear.

It's interesting to note that before 1913 the United States government carried no debt, even though it had already fought a multitude of wars. The establishment of the Federal Reserve enabled the government to begin to borrow cash from the Fed that could be collateralized against any future gold discoveries. The government's ability to borrow what it needed instantly inflated the amount of cash placed into circulation.

The creation of the Fed worked well enough for a few years, but by the late 1920s it once again became clear that all was not well with the American financial system. The stock market crash of 1929 left people reeling as their personal balance sheets shed more than forty billion dollars in savings (an amount that equates to over half a trillion dollars today) and was followed by massive bank failures. Deposits then were not insured, so if a bank failed, its depositors

---

9 Remarks by Governor Edward M. Gramlich, The Samuelson Lecture, before the 24th Annual Conference of the Eastern Economic Association, New York, New York, February 27, 1998.

lost their life savings. Those savings losses, combined with stock market losses, triggered a reduction in personal spending that depressed business's ability to hire workers and manufacture goods.

Heavy tariffs had also been recently placed on imports, which reduced the amount of goods coming in from overseas. The sudden scarcity of goods made things even more expensive, just as people found themselves with less and less money to spend. Last but not least, a multi-year drought hit the great agricultural plains of the American Midwest and turned them into a dust bowl that only increased the people's collective misery. Food prices skyrocketed, forcing desperate city dwellers to flee to the country to seek a way to survive.

World War II at last pulled the United States out of its Great Depression. A "good" war—which we'll cheekily define here as one being fought on someone else's turf, but that requires a dramatic buildup in military might and enhances a local economy—can always be counted on to raise industrial production and lead to an increase in wages, a fact history has illustrated time and time again. For Europe and most of Asia, World War II must have seemed like a very "bad" war—in that it was fought at home, caused the deaths of millions of innocent civilians, wiped out the bulk of the healthy male labor force and reduced their social infrastructure to rubble. America, however, profited greatly in the war's aftermath. Perhaps this explains our fascination with and nostalgia for this war and for that generation, while Europeans hold a very different perspective on its "value." We must remember that the charter to rebuild Europe fell on the one nation that still had an intact infrastructure, plenty of available natural resources and a healthy enough labor force to create and export the goods Europe so desperately needed for its reconstruction. That direct financial windfall led to the rollicking decade we call the 1950s.

Unarguably the most romanticized era of modern American history, the 1950s were marked by an expansion in productivity accompanied by an explosion of new technology. Higher real wages swelled the ranks of the middle class, as money from the reconstruction of Europe and Japan flooded American business coffers. The great consumer society, one in which businesses began to design products primarily targeted at the people most able to buy them—America's rising middle class—was born.

We must pause here a moment to ask ourselves: from where did the shattered European nations find the cash they needed to rebuild their decimated nations? The answer, of course, is that much of it was lent to them by the United States, which in turn was borrowing whatever cash it needed to operate (over and above its income tax collections) from the ever-helpful Federal Reserve. By 1950, then, the United States federal deficit had ballooned to over two hundred fifty-seven billion dollars. That number, we must remember, expanded from a deficit of precisely zero dollars when the Federal Reserve first formed in 1913.[10] Now, while on occasions prior to 1913 the government had indeed fallen into deficit spending, it typically righted itself as soon as the event (often a war) that had triggered the need for deficit spending was over; it was only after the creation of the Federal Reserve that deficit spending came to be more acceptable as a standard operating procedure.

10   Historical Tables, Budget of the United States Government, Fiscal Year 2009.

YET ANOTHER FINE MESS

One might be forgiven, even after reading all the above, for believing that a proxy wealth system works quite well and is only periodically punctuated by minor difficulties that require a bit of readjustment before the happy parade of economic prosperity continues. One would, however, be wrong.

Unfortunately for us, the disturbing truth about the evolution of human economics is rarely discussed in our schools or history textbooks. They tend instead to focus on the high dramas of human conflict: the wars, the political upheavals, the great social and religious clashes that checkerboard our violent and passionate past. We've therefore been taught to believe that those dramatic events alone reveal our human story in full. We're missing, however, a major piece of our own historic puzzle—the driver behind most political, social and spiritual upheavals, which is the ongoing quest for monetary power.

From the first introduction of proxy wealth around 3000 BCE to the introduction of gold and silver coins around 650 BCE, from the development of monetary gold standards around 700 AD to the introduction of borrowing from the Federal Reserve in 1913—throughout *all* those periods and without exception—economic collapses, destructive wars and the disappearance of entire civilizations have occurred with frightening regularity. Far from protecting us from life's many risks, proxy wealth seems to have led to greater suffering and larger social imbalances than we experienced before we invented money.

Even the wonder years of the 1950s were frustratingly short-lived. During the 1960s inflation spiked from just over one percent annually to greater than six percent per year. Given an annual inflation rate of just six percent, a dollar's value declines by over sixty percent in a decade. Although people were earning more, the steady erosion of their purchasing power meant they needed to save more money instead of spend it if they hoped to provide for themselves in retirement.

Meanwhile, by the early 1970s, the shortage of gold had again reached a crisis point. "Fiat" money is money that is not backed dollar-for-dollar by actual gold, but backed by the total gold reserves of a nation. The massive infusion of fiat money triggered by the need to rebuild Europe led not only to inflation but to a growing international distrust of American currency. That problem finally came to a head in 1971. For some time France had been making aggressive demands on the United States' gold bullion reserves by cashing in over one hundred ninety-one million dollars in paper treasury notes at the long established federal rate of thirty-five dollars an ounce. Fearing that the run on America's gold reserves would gather steam and would undermine the nation's gold supply, President Richard Nixon, with the stroke of a pen, eliminated the gold standard. That decision, known as the "Nixon Shock," allowed the dollar value of gold to float based on market demands. It immediately thrust the cost of gold through its previous price ceiling. That decision also eliminated any last wisp of tangible value paper money possessed. From that day forward money became nothing more than "legal tender." Any relationship it once had with gold had been irrevocably severed.

Other nations quickly recognized the value of releasing their currency's attachment to gold and followed suit. It wasn't long before *global* inflation—the erosion of worldwide monetary purchasing power—accelerated beyond anything that had been seen before. By 1974 inflation in the United States had climbed to just over eleven percent per year, and it remained close to or in double digits each year for the next nine years. Meanwhile the federal deficit spiraled to nine hundred nine billion dollars by 1980, the year Ronald Reagan took office. Servicing the national debt became an important part of the United States budget, as interest costs on the federal deficit skyrocketed. By the time of Reagan's first inaugural address, the top tax rate on wage earners in the United States had risen to a walloping seventy percent of adjusted gross income, which meant seventy cents out of every dollar earned over a certain amount went straight to the government till in the form of taxes.

While many Americans praise Reagan's handling of the financial crisis, including the way he reduced federal tax rates on the nation's top wage earners, they may be missing the point. The *real* point of the mess we found ourselves in by the late 1970s—the root illness that no amount of policy tweaking, tax relief or increase in the deficit was ever going to cure—was that proxy wealth was unable to do the job it was meant to do.

As we've already seen, human population growth, combined with a centuries-long explosion of human creativity and the continual introduction of new and more productive technology, ensured that any system designed to value scarcity in exchange for human output would surely fail. We can't attempt to match something that needs to be deliberately kept scarce to preserve its value (money or gold) with something that can't help but grow increasingly more abundant (human creativity and productivity) and end up with a system that offers us any reasonable hope of maintaining balance or promoting social fairness. The abundance in such a system will inevitably flow to the possessors of that which is scarce—but in high demand—the way water gravitates toward a narrow crack in the rocks and creates a waterfall. Individuals who, through luck of birth or by virtue of talent and skill, are able to accumulate more money than most others will wield a disproportionate amount of power when it comes to both the distribution of and the consumption of humanity's scarce resources.

What we wound up with is a two-tiered social system in which an increasingly few wealthy "haves" exercise near absolute control over the lives and welfare of a massive (and growing) number of "have nots," mainly for personal benefit. We then fail to notice the way our politicians, who receive the majority of their campaign contributions from the financial "haves," conceal their economic policies within ideological political concepts like personal freedom, excessive governmental intrusion into private affairs, private property rights, etc. in order to mask their underlying economic agendas. Such inflamed rhetoric, particularly when it's encased in patriotic terms that make us feel guilty for not embracing it, creates confusion and encourages people to vote against their own economic interests based on what seems like higher morality, but is actually immorality in disguise. Many people—as witnessed in the rancorous health care debate of 2010—erroneously believe they're taking a moral position on the proper role of government in private affairs, when in actuality they're voting to preserve the immoral status quo of the win/lose game. The irony is that they're the very losers the game is rigged to exploit, but they can't see the truth beyond the propaganda.

What makes matters worse is that human creativity confronts a near constant shortage of money that hinders our efforts to produce the things we most need. We no longer have enough teachers to educate and support our children because we "can't afford" to pay teachers for their efforts. We don't have widespread renewable energy platforms because we "can't afford" to do the research and development necessary to produce them in mass quantity. We don't have enough clean water, healthy food and living quarters for the vast majority of people on this planet—not because we don't know how to create those things, but because we "can't afford" to create them for each other.

Creativity is crucial for our survival because it brings the best of our talent and wisdom to bear on the challenges that confront us. Unless we learn to treasure our ability to respond creatively to life's challenges *more* than we value our attachment to financial security, humanity will likely go extinct. Pretending that real obstacles don't confront us because we're unwilling to make that difficult shift is not a reasonable option.

In the past, the most grievous creative bottlenecks and social imbalances frequently led to uprisings, revolutions and the wholesale massacre of the ruling classes. Consider the American Revolution of 1776, the French Revolution of 1789, the Bolshevik Revolution of 1917 and the Civil Rights movement of the 1960s and we see that the downtrodden have time and again made it clear to the upper classes they will not be suppressed or dominated for long. How many more bloody revolutions are necessary before the privileged few finally get it? How much longer need the masses suffer before the wealthiest people realize that their wealth won't buy them much once all the servants who support them disappear?

The answer is still unclear, but in 2011 we witnessed massive populist uprisings in totalitarian states like Tunisia, Egypt, Iran, Bahrain, Jordan, Yemen and Libya. We also see increasing dissatisfaction in failed nation states like Haiti, Zimbabwe, Sudan and the Democratic Republic of Congo. We find it too in nations that have been struggling to meet the basic needs of their people: places like Venezuela, Cuba, Bolivia, Afghanistan and Pakistan. Surprisingly enough, we're also beginning to hear stirrings of civic unrest due to financial instability and government cutbacks in some of the so-called first world nations: places like France, Italy, Greece, Mexico and even the seemingly impervious United States.

In the United States in 2011 we witnessed an entirely man-made fiscal crisis when politicians voted to cut taxes on corporations and the wealthy after first spending trillions of taxpayer dollars shoring up companies they'd proclaimed "too big to fail." Those same politicians then decreed that to solve the budget crisis they'd just created, they now needed to slash government spending to the bone. Their budget "solution" was to cut spending on programs that support the most vulnerable Americans, to disembowel the agencies that protect the environment and to financially hamstring agencies that oversee and regulate the behaviors of private industry. All are policies designed to increase corporate profitability on the backs of the middle class and working poor, without regard for human life or the environment. None of it demanded that the wealthiest Americans suffer the slightest inconvenience to help resolve the politically created budget crisis.

Democracy, the most compellingly moral system we've imagined so far for a people to effectively self-govern, cannot survive the overwhelming lust for money that eventually undermines social morality. Morality time and again falls victim to the ongoing imperial lust for corporate profits, to feed the selfish self-interest of a wealthy few.

WHERE WE ARE NOW

No discussion of the history of money would be complete without a brief evaluation of our *modern* Federal Reserve System and an explanation of what it is, how it works, and why it continues to fail. To understand the present-day state of banking and what's been happening within the system, we have to fast-forward from President Reagan's election in 1980 to the economic nightmare inherited by President Obama in January of 2009. When we do, we find that the giant inflationary mess we once were in has morphed into a full-fledged monetary crisis of epic proportions.

By late 2009 the United States' federal deficit had ballooned to well over twelve *trillion* dollars.[11] That number is so enormous the human mind is unable to grasp it as other than an abstract concept. To bring it into a form that we can truly appreciate, reflect for a moment on the fact that one trillion dollars laid end to end would

---

11 U.S. Treasury Department national statistics.

stretch from the Earth to the Sun. That's a distance of about nine-ty-three million miles. Now make the round trip six times over and you're starting to get the picture.

Clearly we don't have enough forests on our entire planet to even *begin* to print the amount of money necessary to satisfy that debt. And that's just the U.S. federal debt; it doesn't speak to private debt, which topped forty trillion dollars by January 2008. That's twenty trips to the sun *and back* on a road of paper dollars! If we tack onto those figures all the debts that have been incurred by other nations, their private citizens and their businesses, the mind truly begins to reel. And the question that begs to be asked as we visualize a dollar bill road that carries us beyond our own solar system and out towards Proxima Centauri, our nearest star, is *to whom* are all those trillions of dollars owed?

The answer, crazy as it may seem, is this: *to ourselves.*

How did we reach the sorry state of affairs where we owe more money to each other than is possible for us to manufacture? For starters it helps to realize that since the gold standard was elimi-nated all the money in circulation can at best be described as pure debt, and most of that is in digital recordkeeping.

Here's how it works: Whenever the government needs to spend more money than it's able to collect in taxes, it contacts the Feder-al Reserve Bank and asks to borrow additional funds. The Federal Reserve Bank then orders the United States Treasury to print more cash so the money can be placed into circulation. In exchange for that cash, the Fed accepts treasury bonds as payment from the U.S. government. Treasury bonds are essentially I.O.U's of a nation, promissory notes to pay back the amount of cash being borrowed from the Fed, plus interest, over time. In 2009 alone, the citizens of the United States paid three hundred eighty-three billion dollars in interest to service the outstanding national debt. That's one giant credit card being proffered on our behalf by the government!

If borrowing our own cash and then paying ourselves back with interest represented the extent of our monetary system it would be foolish enough. But there's more—much more—to it still. The Federal Reserve Banking system isn't a federal agency but a conglomeration of privately owned member banks, each of which are permitted to borrow cash as needed at a privileged rate of interest from the Federal Reserve. Member banks then make loans to private citizens and businesses, a process that theoretically is supposed to help "capitalize" new enterprises and improve the living conditions of the people. In practice, however, something else inevitably seems to happen.

Because private banks adhere to the same capitalist principles as do all private businesses—their main objective is to earn a profit—the bank's focus is on continually finding new ways to increase the amount of interest and fees they can collect from borrowers to enhance their profitability. It is therefore in the bank's best interest to keep us all deeply indebted and continually working to pay off our bank loans, because that generates a constant flow of cash to the banks and delivers steady profits to their bottom lines.

It's crucial to note that member banks are required to hold on deposit a mere ten percent of all their depositors' cash. That means if a bank borrows a billion dollars from the Fed, it can lend out nine billion *additional* dollars (against that borrowed billion) to its customers. The nine billion dollars of so-called new "money" gets distributed as *digital* cash by way of mortgage loans, credit card borrowing, small business loans and the like. It doesn't exist in paper form; it exists only as customer I.O.U.'s on the ledgers in the bank's computers. That explains how we've wound up with so many trillions of dollars in outstanding debt.

All that digitized (imaginary) money then gets lent out to the public with genuine interest charges attached for the privilege of borrowing it. Much (if not most) of the cash we borrowers earn through the sweat of our hourly labor thus goes straight to the banks to compensate them for lending us their imaginary money. The interest we pay on our home mortgages, for example, is owed against digital money that's been created by banks as a result of the Federal Reserve's ten percent depository rule. It's not money the bank has taken on deposit from your neighbors and owes back to them in the future. It's smoke-and-mirror money, borrowed from no one. Yet the banks seem to have no trouble charging the public exorbitant rates of interest for money they've created out of air.

Imagine me lending you a thousand dollars for virtually no interest, then telling you that as long as you keep that money stored safely in my home cookie jar, you're free to print up your own certificates representing nine thousand additional dollars you can then lend out to all your friends and neighbors. Other businesses must accept those certificates as payments for customer debts (because I said so) while you get to charge your borrowers interest on the nine thousand dollars you've just manufactured. Even if a few of your buddies fail to pay you back, so long as you collect lots and lots of interest (along with some principal payments) on the imaginary money, you'll get pretty rich very fast. Your only obligation is to "return" the original thousand dollars to me at some point in the future—though I don't care when. And don't forget, the money I lent you is already stored safely away in my cookie jar. You can't lose it, so where's the risk to you for making this deal?

Now imagine you do that over and over again, lending and collecting interest against the certificates you've created without having to answer to anyone for it. Multiply that by many, many trillions and you'll begin to understand how banking works.

Any member bank can borrow a billion dollars from the Federal Reserve at an interest rate of, say, one-half percent per year. It can then deposit all that cash into the Federal Reserve vaults (the cookie jar) and lend out nine billion dollars of newly digitized money. It may charge as much as thirty percent interest on credit card debt, fifteen percent on personal loans, ten or twelve percent on business loans and perhaps eight or nine percent for high-risk home mortgages. Even if some loans don't get repaid, all the bank really stands to lose from that is the ability to re-lend those digital dollars to somebody else for more interest! The bank loses *nothing* by way of actual money. It only loses the future potential to make even more obscene profits. Meanwhile it gets to collect huge amounts of principal, interest, fines and service fees from the people obligated to repay its imaginary money. Remember too that the bank is collecting interest on a full *nine billion dollars* of imaginary money, while paying the Fed at a much lower rate of interest on only *one billion* real dollars. Last but not least, let's not lose sight of the fact that the one billion dollars in the federal vault that backs the imaginary money being lent to the public is money the public is already borrowing from itself with interest. It got into the bank in the first place by way of the Fed, who issued that cash in exchange for a Federal Treasury I.O.U.—an obligation created by the government "on behalf of the people"—with interest owed (and the principal due back as well) out of public taxation. How's that for a profitable business model that sticks it to the people on both ends?

If you're not *yet* sick to your stomach, think about this: most bank loans are *collateralized*, which means the bank has the power to repossess your house, your car, your furniture or force you to sell your business and liquidate your assets to pay off your loan if you happen to default. All that represents *profit* for the bank, since the money it *lent* you was imaginary and the money it *borrowed* is still safely tucked in the vault. A bank may "book" a loss on its accounting ledger if a repossessed home is sold at foreclosure for less than the bank originally lent the buyer, but the *real* pain gets felt by the family that has forfeited a hard-saved down payment, has made monthly payments that were heavily frontloaded with interest and—after all that—is left broke and homeless.

Consider the recent sub-prime mortgage debacle. What made sub-prime lending so enticing for banks was the fact that they could lend money to high-risk borrowers at exorbitant rates of interest. If a high-risk borrower defaulted, as was likely, the bank could repossess the house, sell it at auction and pay itself back most (if not all) the imaginary money it had lent to the borrower. The bank also got to keep the buyer's down payment, along with any principal and interest the buyer had paid against the loan before he defaulted. It could then turn around and lend all that money it had "earned" to a brand new buyer.

Because the high loan origination fees (two to three percent of the mortgage dollar amount) on sub-prime loans were so juicy, while the long-term risk of carrying such loans on their books was relatively high, the bigger banks began to package up those risky loans and sell them off piecemeal to unsuspecting investors. That earned them huge brokerage commission fees (another several percentage points) *above* the loan origination fees. It also entitled them to claim an annual management fee for continuing to "administer" those loans on behalf of investors, which created for them a steady revenue stream. To make matters worse they purchased cheap insurance (mainly from AIG) on the loans in case the buyers defaulted, insuring *themselves* against the potential losses they'd just pawned off to investors. That meant they were betting *against* the investments they'd sold to the general public as almost risk free. They then turned around and re-lent all that money to brand new high-risk borrowers.

Once they ran out of "easy prey" borrowers to feed their profit-making engines, they created imaginative new loans offering low "teaser" rates, interest only payments, loans where the dollar amount owed grew bigger instead of smaller (negative amortization) and so forth. By lending out the same principal time and time again through creating a loan, selling it off and using the proceeds to create a brand new loan—while charging fees to all of the players every step of the way—banks found themselves able to earn incredible rates of return taking almost no risk.

The game worked amazingly well so long as housing prices kept going up, which meant the banks could sell repossessed inventory for at least the value of the outstanding mortgages. The game collapsed only *after* a majority of ordinary people became so debt-strapped they could no longer afford to pay outlandishly high prices for their homes. At that point the banks turned to the federal government (the elected representatives of the very same families they'd just turned onto the streets) to bail them out of this mess of their own creation. Their claim—that they'd go "under" if we didn't give them a massive infusion of cash, no questions asked—was based on accounting concerns. They still held most of the money they owed to other institutions. What they didn't have any longer was an inventory of *collectible* I.O.U.'s and/or collateralized loans with a high enough market value to equal nine times the dollar amount they held in their vaults, which was necessary in order for them to comply with federal reserve requirements.

That, in a nutshell, reveals the immorality of the modern monetary system we've all embraced to "help" us buy our houses, cars, home furnishings and so forth. Is it any wonder most real people struggle beneath the crushing weight of bank debt?

The banks that operate this way are the very same institutions that cry poor and complain they'll go out of business if the government tries to regulate the late fees, service charges and interest rates they charge us—their customers. Yet we are the very same folks who *lent* those banks their capital to begin with, since the general public is entirely responsible for paying back (via federal taxes) all the principal and interest due on the government I.O.U's (treasury bonds) that have been sold to the Federal Reserve to increase the money supply. We ought not be too surprised that our banks are willing to make predatory loans, offer teaser interest rates and couch the truth of what they're doing in complicated terminology to entice us to sign agreements we don't understand. They already know that if most of us knew the truth about how our monetary system works, we'd revolt against its obvious unfairness.

Why should citizens be required to borrow imaginary money at exorbitant interest rates from a private for-profit bank, when the cash the bank uses to collateralize that debt has already been borrowed (by the United States government) *on behalf of* those very same people, with interest costs to the public already attached? Why can't we just forgo the middleman and borrow it from ourselves at the same rate of interest the government charges *us* to lend it to banks? Better yet, why not just create all the money we need to fund our national economy, and forgo paying interest on it altogether? Why are we borrowing money from our own cookie jar and burdening ourselves with interest costs to do so?

In a letter to John Taylor, dated May 28th, 1816, Thomas Jefferson stated, "The system of banking we have both equally and ever reprobated. I contemplate it as a blot left in all our constitutions, which, if not covered, will end in their destruction, which is already hit by the gamblers in corruption, and is sweeping away in its progress the fortunes and morals of our citizens. Funding I consider as limited, rightfully, to a redemption of the debt within the lives of a majority of the generation contracting it; every generation coming equally, by the laws of the Creator of the world, to the free possession of the earth he made for their subsistence, unencumbered by their predecessors, who, like them, were but tenants for life."

This quotation reveals Jefferson's negative sentiments regarding private banks, as well as his desire to place the burden of debt solely on the generation that originally conceived it. Consider the fact that the United States' public debt presently stands at thirteen trillion dollars. That's debt our children and grandchildren will inherit. They didn't approve of it nor ask to be burdened by it. It's a modern form of slavery, all the more insidious because it holds every citizen captive to forced labor under the theory we must pay off what is in effect an unmanageable and ever-growing mountain of debt. Since ALL modern money is a debt on some ledger, the more of it we must borrow—with interest owed—in order to pay off our past debts, the deeper into debt we inevitably will sink. Yet in a system that requires us to pay as we go for whatever we need to survive, there's no real way to avoid debt, since we're all born with basically nothing in our pockets.

Prices will continue to escalate beyond the ability of most people to pay cash for what they need because indebtedness serves the profit motives of businesses and banks. People will be forced to work longer hours for lower wages because they desperately need *some* income—even at starvation rates—to live. At the same time productivity and technology gains render human labor less necessary for businesses to manufacture their products. Wherever human labor can't be replaced by machines—non-living equipment that doesn't demand either benefits or wages—jobs will continue to be transferred overseas to locales where desperate people are willing to work for even less money than the citizens of countries where the cost of living is higher.

Where does it all end? Perhaps it ends like a game of Monopoly®, where one corporate entity owns the entire world and everyone else goes bankrupt. Perhaps it ends when so many people are starving, homeless, jobless and hopeless that a violent revolution becomes a reasonable option. Perhaps it ends in some great natural cataclysm brought on by our inattention to the things we ought to be doing to ensure our own survival, because we didn't find them "profitable" to attend to while we still had time. Or perhaps, if we're very lucky, it ends when enough of us wake up to the absurdity of what we're doing to each other and come together to envision a new way of doing business; one that reveres life more than money, values the environment over mindless mass production, and chooses brotherly love over destructive competition. That our financial system is collapsing and that we're fast approaching a debt crisis point cannot really be disputed; what *can* be argued (at least until we go extinct from a lack of action) is how we're going to deal with these growing problems.

A NEW WAY THROUGH

Clearly our private banking system is broken. We know intuitively and experientially that allocating power and privilege to a few individuals based on (proxy) wealth alone hinders the capacity of most human beings to flourish and to be able to contribute the best of what they have to offer to this world. Still, blaming the banks for all our problems is misguided at best and delusional at worst. The trouble with arguing over the origins of a crisis or pointing fingers at who's doing what to whom so we can try to affix some blame for the mess we're in is that oppositional sides form up, the arguments crystallize into political power struggles and we all get stuck in the middle of a debate while our systems crumble around us. It really doesn't matter who caused the crisis we presently find ourselves in. What matters is that we're in one, and that we need to find a way beyond it quickly.

The question to ask ourselves then, is this: What can we personally do to change the way we're exchanging our labor, creativity and wisdom, since we're still embedded in a system that requires money to make it all go 'round? How do we begin to change the monetary paradigm, when that paradigm—insane as it may seem—is the primary program that controls our entire social operating system? While we'll look at some potential in-depth solutions more deeply in the final pages of this book, for now let's look at the ways we're choosing to be in relationship with money.

It's been said that insanity is doing the same thing over and over again and expecting different results. The reality is this: our society won't change unless we change our views about it and act accordingly. We can't keep tweaking the same old computer program and running it on the same old operating system while praying for our computer to magically offer us brand new applications with better ways to do the things we're doing. We must *all* take some responsibility for upgrading our hardware (our economic, political and social systems) as well as for writing the new software (our ideas about how to build a win/win world) by shifting the way we think and feel about who we are and what we're doing here.

Where we each have the most control is over our own internal software. As individuals we may not have the power to reconfigure the entire national or international infrastructure, but we *can* change our internal programming and thereby influence how things are being done at the local level. Collectively, if enough of us opt to change our beliefs, we'll overload the larger system with persistent demands that it offer us something new, which will require a total retooling of the system's hardware. At first the system may not support that request, and it may even try a few "hard reboots" to rid itself of the glitches caused by the general public's new demands, but ever increasing incompatibilities between what the system is creating and what we actually want to experience will continue to generate more and more glitches until the system has no choice but to accept human input and retool itself to meet our collective demands.

Obviously, changing the entire global economic structure isn't going to be easy, since we're all presently dependent upon it for our survival. There are ways, though, that we can begin to reduce our personal attachment to the system. For starters, we can engage in selective acts of moral protest to demonstrate to the economic powers that we're no longer interested in playing games that are stacked against humanity. For example, one recent campaign, inspired by articles written in *The Huffington Post*, encouraged Americans to move their savings and investment accounts away from the large multinational banks that triggered the financial crisis of 2008 and deposit them into local banks and S&Ls that weren't involved in the scandal, and whose policies were more people- and community-friendly. By March of 2010 it was estimated that nine percent of all American adults had done exactly that, resulting in a major reduction in assets controlled by banks that were previously considered "too big to fail." This is an example of how small personal choices, when aggregated, have the collective power to make an enormous impact.

Moving our money is one way to show our displeasure with the banking system, but that's still a surface protest against what is a deeper, more fundamental problem. What would help even more is if we could each begin to release our attachment to money as a form of genuine wealth. To accept that money is only debt and at best is a *proxy* for tangible wealth (things like food, shelter and clothing) enables us to let go of our obsessive need to hoard it, as well as helps us release our fear that we might not have enough of it in the future.

One way to begin the process of monetary detachment is to practice giving away and sharing our *real* wealth with each other, bypassing the need to exchange proxy money for human creative expression. The more we let the system know we're not interested in hoarding money so much as we desire a clean environment, a healthy and happy population, better educations for our kids, an opportunity for everyone to discover and bring forth their inner creative genius and so on, the less power the system can wield by forcing us to act as its servants on behalf of monetary profits for corporations.

Whatever we can craft with our hands, utilizing our own re-sources, creative talents and skills, can be gifted away, taught to others, or shared without the need to charge money in exchange for it. Candle or soap making, sewing, home-canned foods, the abili-ty to build a deck or install home plumbing—all can be passed on to others at no charge.

Remember that wisdom too is indeed a form of tangible wealth because it can improve people's lives in the here and now, which is why, historically, elders were so revered. We've unfortunately lost touch with the value of elder wisdom in our crass material culture that worships youth and beauty over knowledge and life experience. The result is we're losing large blocks of multi-generational wisdom every day, as we shunt our elderly into nursing homes and retirement villages and away from our children who could learn from their past experiences. To reclaim that wisdom may one day be crucial for humanity's survival, the way it is for elephants who—in times of deepest drought—trust their elder matriarch to guide them to the watering holes she dimly remembers from the droughts of *her* long ago youth.

Recently we've seen an increased sharing of wisdom across the Internet. People yearn to share their truths and many have begun to post their creative efforts, insights, thoughts and bits of wisdom there for free. Businesses, of course, have been fighting free sharing and have sought ways to block it for fear it will cannibalize their precious profits, but the floodgates are already open and it's unlikely the for-profiteers will be able to close them, no matter how many hard reboots they may attempt. The concept of net neutrality—which promotes the right of all parties to access and/ or broadcast across the Internet freely and equally—seems to be one we've acknowledged as a right and not a privilege, although attempts to stratify the net in favor of the highest bidder have been gathering steam. Still, our insistence so far that access to the net remain open and equal for everyone is good news for humanity going forward.

It also helps to realize we're all in the same predicament. The mind-boggling debts that have been accumulating all around our planet are holding every one of us hostage to the need to pay them back. It therefore seems likely that at some point in the not-too-distant future our rising debt load will crush so many of us that poverty will spread around the globe. The middle class will continue to vanish and privation will become the norm if we continue to permit the continued concentration of wealth. That mass suffering, as hard as it may be for us to endure, will at last expose the underlying insanity of our present system. We can accelerate the realization without needing to suffer the hardships of global poverty by talking honestly to each other right now about the nature of debt, and by sharing our understanding with those who don't yet comprehend how the system works.

The more we talk about these issues, the greater the likelihood we'll collectively hit upon potential solutions that have the power to change our world in a really big way. For instance, in ancient times certain cultures used to hold what they called a "jubilee" every fifty or so years. On the chosen date all outstanding debts would be forgiven, so everyone would be freshly empowered to start their life anew. Just imagine what a glorious day of celebration it would be if we declared a global jubilee day and wiped out everybody's debts: the public and private, the national and the global. Why don't we at least begin to publicly and openly discuss the possibility, and see how the majority of people feel? We can presume that the one percent of the population that already owns forty percent of the world's assets may not rally behind the idea of forgiving the entire world of its debts. But since a good fifty percent of us have been fighting over a mere one percent of the world's assets, we can safely assume those people are far more likely to get behind the concept, followed by perhaps another thirty or forty percent of people who also grasp the value in shifting the system. Were seventy or eighty percent of the world's population to rise in concert and refuse as a block to play the money game, the system would fall. It is only as strong as our willingness to embrace it as our conceptual economic model.

Were we to hold a jubilee, no one in the entire world would owe anybody anything anymore. Everyone would be permitted to keep whatever he or she already had, so the collective focus of First World nations could naturally shift to helping those in need in the Third World countries. Imagine all the human creativity that would be freed up to help the poor. Rather than being stuck doing mindless jobs to produce sub-par goods for thoughtless consumption so we can pay our bills, we could instead focus our attention on providing green housing, clean water, quality foods, higher education, medicines to eliminate preventable diseases and so on. Once we'd met the bulk of those needs worldwide, we could then turn our collective attention to where we want to go as a species and what we hope to achieve to support *all* the life that exists on this planet. Sustainability, efficient recycling, renewable energy processes, space exploration—all those things would be within our reach if even *part* of the energy we're now expending to pay for our own survival were free to be applied to the vision of exploring our dreams instead.

The mindset, or level of consciousness, necessary to support this new attitude is an internal realization of the interconnectedness of all things. To *know* that to keep a child in sub-Saharan Africa starving, uneducated, homeless and exposed to all kinds of life-threatening illnesses is to cause tangible suffering to myself reflects an awareness that many today have already reached, but many have not. That isn't because most people don't care about the needs of other people. We're *predisposed* to love, to desire happiness and to enjoy giving of ourselves to others. We know that because it *feels* good for us to do those things, while it doesn't feel good to turn our backs on someone who is suffering.

The reason so many have yet to shift their way of thinking is because for several millennia our economic system has programmed us all to play the win/lose game. We opt to help ourselves and our families first, our countries, tribes or faith groups next, and to remain deeply suspicious of all those scary "others" who may eventually rise to best us in this win/lose world.

While we can't *make* other people change their minds or force them into the realization that no one truly profits off another for personal gain, we can at least begin to accept that truth for ourselves. To love and help others; to give what we can; to inspire, support and engage other people so as to aid them in bringing out the best of themselves in service to the best in us all—*that* is something each of us can do right here, right now. How we do it and how much we do is a matter of personal choice, but it's the only sure way we can start to shift the collective human consciousness toward building a win/win system that reflects our highest nature instead of continuing with one that subverts it.

FROM SUPPLY AND DEMAND TO INTELLIGENT DISTRIBUTION

I REMEMBER AS A CHILD BEING TOLD RATHER STERNLY TO EAT my lima beans, and to be grateful for them since the poor starving children in some faraway place called "Biafra" had no food at all. More than once I was tempted to ask my mother to pack up my lima beans and send them to those hungry children, but fear of her reaction kept me silent. Still I wondered why my parents forced me to eat food I hated, but that somebody else could use. And what kind of a world was it anyhow, where something as random as birthplace determined who ate and who starved? Last but not least, how had the odd belief that "this is just the way life is" come to be accepted by so many otherwise caring and loving people? To my simple, childlike mind those things didn't make sense.

That terrible famine in Biafra was soon followed by famines in Ethiopia, Somalia and Bangladesh, to name but a few. Obviously the global demand for food was continually high, yet for some reason the supply of food consistently failed to reach those most in need. Only later did I learn that while people might clamor for items like rice or milk, their demands wouldn't be met unless they could afford to pay for the things they needed.

The theory of supply and demand is an economic concept. It's based on the belief that what we produce and consume can be decided solely by monetary methods. The presumption is that when people are allowed to bid for items they want in the open market, how much they're willing to pay will efficiently determine what gets made and how much of it is needed. Prices will rise and fall based on demand in relationship to supply, which will drive production until we reach dynamic equilibrium, where everyone is theoretically satisfied. Unfortunately, this theory is a mechanical approach to a very living reality. It fails to honor the best part of what makes us human beings—our hearts and minds. To understand *why* the supply and demand equation (the so-called "free market system") devalues human life, imagine the global economy as a giant seesaw, with all the people of the world standing on one side and all the products we've created stacked in boxes on the other. The more of us who need a product and clamber onto the seesaw to try to get it, the more weighted down our human side becomes. That causes the product side of the seesaw to rocket into the air, sending the boxes up and out of reach of most folks. The other side then crashes under the weight of all the people, maiming or killing those folks hanging on for dear life.

Remember that businesses earn profits one of two ways. They either set high prices so they can earn more money per item (a high profit margin) or they sell lots of items at a lower cost per item (a low profit margin). Capitalistic logic says that if enough people *really* want something, some company somewhere will eventually figure out a way to make more of it more cheaply. When supply becomes inelastic, however—which means more of the item can't be produced at a profit if sold for less—the price for that item must rise until it suppresses the public demand. Eventually, or so the theory goes, enough people will decide they can't afford to buy a particular product and will climb down off the seesaw, bringing the supply side back into balance with the demand side. Of course, when that product is something vital, like rice or water or precious heating oil, people don't decide they don't *want* to buy it. They're forced by their poverty to survive without it, or perhaps even die, courtesy of our mechanical market system.

If supply *is* elastic and the item *can* be made more cheaply, a new manufacturer will stack a bunch of brand new boxes filled with cheaper versions of the item on the product side of the seesaw, weighing down the supply side. Consumers will then be able to buy the item for less money than before. As demand for that item decreases, the price of any still-unsold goods will drop even lower over time, until all the people who earlier were forced to climb off the seesaw empty-handed can get back on and purchase the item they need. After all that bouncing around, eventually the two sides reach a state of semi-permanent equilibrium where steady new demand is met with a constant fresh supply of each item at a price that provides a profit to the manufacturer.

Presumably this process trains businesses to make more of what we demand and less of what we don't need. Theoretically at least, that creates a dynamic balance between products and personal needs and forges a stable market economy.

A THEORY UNSUPPORTED BY REALITY

As horrific tales of global famine illustrate even today, our mechanical free enterprise system is in truth an inefficient, unintelligent—and dare I say, even *immoral*—way for a society to set the prices for its goods and services. That's because the free market system—like the mechanical seesaw in our example—is a nonliving entity. Yet it holds absolute power to refuse to meet the demands of the living, breathing people who are in need of goods and services. In a free market economy, if you can't afford to buy electricity the utility company has the power to turn off your heat. Freeze to death or not; it isn't the economy's concern. Money alone wields power, not love, compassion or even what's in humanity's best interests in the long run. There is nothing "free" about such a market for the living people involved.

Every new business in a free market economy comes into being primarily for the purpose of making money by satisfying a human need or want, whether genuine or invented. Most of us happen to work for those companies, and if we can't provide them with what they want at a price they're willing to pay, another person out there will replace us on the job. Only through government regulation, which attempts to address the complaints of both downtrodden workers and frustrated consumers, have we managed to curb the worst, most inhumane of modern corporate behaviors. Child labor laws, OSHA regulations, minimum wage laws and so forth were all designed to force businesses to act with a modicum of human decency. Still, we mustn't forget that during the latter decades of the 20th century, professionals hired by businesses relentlessly lobbied government officials to lift those oh-so-burdensome restrictions, often with disastrous results. The steady erosion of the Glass-Steagall banking regulations that occurred between 1980 and 1999 comes immediately to mind, as it culminated in the global financial collapse of 2008.

Of course, those who get richer under the free market system are living people too. Wealth, though, is corruptive of human nature. It grants the wealthy access to more things than most people can afford, thereby pandering to their egos instead of appealing to their hearts and highest natures. By catering to every single whim and desire of those who have the money, the system that disempowers most people keeps itself in business.

Corporations and products don't die if they can't meet the needs of the people. People, on the other hand, definitely *do* die if their basic needs aren't met. Corporations may get bought, sold, downsized, expanded, reconfigured or even dissolved. But a corporation doesn't suffer when those things happen. It experiences no guilt, no shame, no fear, no remorse, and—most importantly— no gratitude or love for the miracle that is life. Certainly those who work for corporations *do* feel such things, but as individuals they remain trapped by the restrictions that are imposed on them by the system. As soon as the workday is over and workers have finished making more of the things others need (or have been trained to believe they need through advertising) they must shift from being a day laborer to a consumer, then go out and spend money so they can continue living for another day. No wonder we're all perennially stressed and exhausted.

Corporations are neither good nor bad. They're just machines that do what we've programmed them to do. Unfortunately, some time ago our ancestors ceded control over people to these corporate machines. Perhaps they did so from a mistaken belief that a mechanical system could do a better job of controlling and directing us than we could do ourselves. Whatever the reason, we've set up a system where our businesses *can't* relate to our needs as living beings, because they're forced to obey the rules we've established to determine their success. Since we presently tell our companies they *must* make money if they wish to remain in business, that's precisely what they do. If we chose to reprogram them by informing them they must do only those things that benefit humanity and serve the greater good of our living planet, they would do that instead.

Back in the late 1970s, during the OPEC oil embargo, had we risen to the challenge of becoming energy self-sufficient instead of allowing our oil and auto companies to control the dialogue around their fears, we might have demanded that all auto manufacturers design and build only fuel-efficient cars, and that our energy companies invest a large portion of their profits into designing new technologies. Electric and solar technologies would have rapidly advanced and many nations would be much closer to energy independence than they are presently. Instead we allowed the corporate demand for profits to outweigh society's need to tackle the challenge of excessive oil consumption. The root problem, it seems, is that we've lived under our current economic programming for so long we've forgotten we hold the power to rewrite the rules.

When reality becomes awful enough for enough of us, we'll likely decide to reclaim our power. Remember, reality always trumps our false beliefs. Sadly, as long as we cling tenaciously to the belief that a free market economy is the best way for us to allocate our planetary resources, more of us will be made to suffer until the rest wake up to the need to rethink the way we're doing business. When enough people find themselves homeless, starving or dying of preventable illnesses, the rest will have to take note of the havoc being wreaked by our system. That's especially true if the one who is dying is our Aunt Mary, our cousin Bob, or a beloved son or daughter.

WINNERS AND LOSERS

Only the wealthiest individuals can always afford the best a free market system has to offer. And who controls the nonliving entities that comprise our free market system? Who decides what's "best" for the general public, and to where the bulk of our natural resources go? The wealthy do. The wealthy have *always* wielded the power to dictate what gets produced and what doesn't.

The wealthy travel by private jet while the rest of humanity jams together in coach—assuming they can afford to travel at all. The wealthy relax in five-star hotels and bask on tropical beaches, where they sometimes even purchase vacation homes. The rest of humanity scrimps to take their kids to a nearby town for a couple of days. Most are lucky if they own *one* house, and even then a bank holds their mortgage while they work to make monthly payments.

The wealthy wear designer clothes and carry five-thousand-dollar handbags because they can. The rest of the people wear clothes made in Third World countries by a cheap, exploited labor force that they purchase from Wal-Mart and Target, or they go without. When the wealthy need surgery they opt for the best doctors at the finest hospitals. The rest of humanity prays their local hospital won't charge them thousands more dollars than their insurance— assuming they have it—has agreed to pay. The children of the wealthy attend top-flight private schools. The rest of the world's children attend under-funded and under-served public schools, drop out early to work in a low paying job, or remain illiterate.

The above is *not* a tirade against the evils of being wealthy. They're people just like everyone else, and are legally reaping the benefits of a system into which we've all been born. Rather, the above is an attempt to illuminate the inherent unfairness of our win/lose economic system. What renders one person more *worthy* of quality treatment as opposed to another? Don't *all* of us deserve to be treated with respect, compassion, thoughtfulness and concern? Why do we blindly embrace the belief that it's fine for money to buy some of us higher quality goods, better service and more humane treatment, while the rest of us must make do with the economic crumbs?

It seems we accept it because that's the way it's been done throughout the ages, from ancient aristocracies to modern capitalist meritocracies. We allow it even though most of us are not (nor ever will be) wealthy under this system. Most days we overlook the indignity of it because we've forgotten we have the power to change how it works.

Ultimately, though, any system based on institutionalized inequality undermines the very upper classes it's designed to serve. As wealth contracts over time into the hands of fewer and fewer people (usually those with enough power to ensure the ongoing concentration of obscene wealth) the majority rebel and overthrow the upper class. Those who seize power then set up a new ruling class, so they in turn might reap the benefits that come from controlling the economic system. Human history illustrates a constant succession of just such "us versus them" imperial upheavals, during which the concepts of power and privilege are reduced to "things" to be coveted by the angry have-nots. Mass suffering inevitably results from these constant struggles over concentrated power and privilege.

Over time we humans have grown clever enough to "tweak" our economic systems just enough so we can't be accused of doing the same thing twice. We like to believe these marginal changes will enable our institutions to survive without the need to totally redesign them. The deeper impulse behind tweaking, of course, is that the people who are implementing the changes usually do so in ways that enable them to retain the bulk of their privileges. The disadvantage of tweaking is that the retention of class privilege always comes at the expense of the rest of humanity—no matter how clever or helpful each movement toward "social fairness" might seem to be on the surface.

These days, what determines the success of a minor economic shift isn't whether more of us are able to live in ways that make us more comfortable; it's whether those in power retain their privileges as the changes unfold. The material comfort of the public certainly carries weight with those in power, but it does so mainly because over time the masses have evolved from the easily controlled illiterate peasants they once were to today's more knowledgeable working and middle classes. While a higher education is mandatory for today's serfs to run the system's more complicated modern machines, it also means the mass illusion that "all is well" must be powerfully seductive enough to convince even the most educated serfs to believe it. We've all been indoctrinated since birth into the fable of the "American Dream," which represents the belief that everyone can succeed with a bit of hard work and sheer determination. The thing is, retelling that myth to young, impressionable minds is the only way the illusion of fairness and freedom has been able to propagate down through the years. It's rather like teaching young children that the volcano gods need virgins when they get angry. Surely the facts don't prove it out—we know there are many people who have struggled and been determined and who haven't been able to succeed financially—but the belief anyone can do it retains a powerful psychic grip on all of us. That's exactly why we try to blame those who fail for their lack of success. In the face of a mountain of evidence that directly contradicts our cherished belief, our only out is to rationalize away all the evidence by placing blame on something other than the system. If it can't be the system's fault people fail, then the fault, we reason, *must* be with the people.

Because knowledge is power, the punishments meted out to those who rebel against the system have had to become more nuanced over time. That explains in part why we no longer have mass hangings, burnings and beheadings. Instead, these days we put our Robin Hoods and Jean Valjeans to "social death" by draping a felony record around their necks for the rest of their lives. Gang members, bank robbers, burglars, drug dealers—one thing they all have in common is they've refused to play the game by the system's rules. They refuse to play because they've realized early on that the system is stacked against them, in most instances far more so than the average person who also struggles mightily to get ahead. Hard as it might be for an ordinary middle class child to rise and become the CEO of a major corporation, that path is a thousand times more arduous for a minority child born in the inner city to a single mother living below the poverty line. For that kid, crime often looks like the only available avenue to success. If we want proof that the free market system is a win/lose game with many more losers than winners, consider that the most obsessively capitalistic nation, the United States, houses more prison inmates per capita than does any other nation in the modern world.[12] Why? Because our insistence on elevating the American dream to the status of national myth, while simultaneously making it nearly impossible for most people to attain it, motivates people to commit crimes out of frustration and desperation.

---

12   International Center For Prison Studies, World Prison Brief, 2003

When we consider the rise of the middle class, many people assume that capitalism is working, gradually pulling people out of grinding poverty, although as we face the still-unfolding ramifications of the 2008 economic collapse, much has been written about the decline of this segment of our society. Even so, we're still not ready to acknowledge that the problem might be the system instead of the people. We presume this downturn is temporary, and that as soon as the recession ends the middle class will come roaring back, along with economic good times. What we're failing to consider, however, is the growing stress and anxiety most middle class people are feeling, or the fact that many are living but a paycheck away from disaster. Basically all we've really done throughout our centuries-long transition from a royal class based on blood lines to a money-based royal class is crack open the door of privilege an inch or two wider, so a few of the smartest peasants could slip inside. We never changed the *nature* of the win/lose game.

The fact is, all is *not* well in our economic system, especially if we use happiness for our yardstick. Today, more people must work harder to pay their bills. They struggle under bigger mortgages and more credit card debt, and more babies are placed in daycare so parents can work. More advertisements bombard us to convince us to buy more stuff. Meanwhile the majority of people around the world are struggling to live on less than a dollar a day. Even so, we've been trained not to let the suffering of others interfere with our personal dreams, particularly when our dreams include the possibility we might someday be one of the lucky ones for whom the door to money-based privilege opens.

Reality is the proving ground where our evolving values occasionally come into conflict with inherited dogmas. When reality proves our dogmas wrong—as it does with the notion that a free market system is the best way to allocate global goods and services—the answer isn't to blindly ignore the truth. Far better for us to learn from our experiences and recraft our system until it mirrors our values.

SHORT-TERM GAINS VS. LONG-TERM COSTS

When a corporation decides to produce goods more cheaply and sell more items at lower prices to increase its profits (think Wal-Mart here), consumers end up replacing those cheaply made products more often. Ironically, that *improves* the bottom-line profits for the manufacturers because they make additional sales, but it winds up costing society far more than it would have if everyone made quality goods all the time. If you have to buy a new four-dollar hammer every three years or so because the wood handle splinters or the metal head falls off, over the course of a lifetime (and with inflation factored in) you might wind up spending as much as two hundred dollars on replacement hammers. In the long run wouldn't it have been cheaper for you to invest in one, high quality, twenty-five-dollar hammer designed to last a lifetime? Wouldn't it also be easier on our landfills, forests and mineral deposits not to waste our limited natural resources in service to short-term profits?

The labor and natural resources dedicated to the creation of inferior hammers could surely be allocated in a more useful way elsewhere. Multiply that by the countless cheap vacuums, microwaves, refrigerators and home furnishings we've all thrown away in disgust, and we begin to see the enormity of the waste. Clearly our shared human experience with "cheap" goods manufactured under the free market concept of supply and demand in a profit-based world informs us that the "cheapest" solution to meet the needs of the poorest individuals in the short run is rarely the most resource efficient or best solution for society over the long run. It's not even good for the individual, who winds up eventually paying more for inferior hammers than he'd pay for a really good one that lasted a lifetime.

When a product can't possibly be made cheaply enough to meet the demand for it, the problem only gets worse. For example, the pent-up demand for items like solar panels and windmills, fuel-efficient cars, high-quality furnishings, long-lasting electronics and organic foods are immeasurable. Millions of people would love to run their homes off solar power or wind energy and avoid the mess and pollution of fossil fuels. In the long run we all know we'd be saving resources, not to mention sparing our ecosystem from destruction and generally improving the well-being of our planet. In the short run, however, the corporations that hold patents on those technologies can't yet make those items at a price most of us can afford. One of the reasons that they can't is that new technologies are often undercut by government subsidies that support the corporations who own the preexisting technologies.

For example, in 2009 the United States government subsidized its farmers to the tune of between six and seven billion dollars to grow corn for ethanol production. Meanwhile it had placed a stiff tariff on sugar cane ethanol imported from Brazil.[13] That policy was misguided for several reasons. First, it diverted food (corn, grain) production away from the global market, where it was sorely needed. At the same time it hindered the importation and use of abundant Brazilian sugar cane ethanol. The policy benefited American agribusiness corn growers because they were able to sell corn to ethanol producers at relatively high (federally subsidized) prices. Although it takes more energy to produce corn ethanol than corn ethanol delivers—while sugar cane is a most energy-efficient feedstock for ethanol manufacture—the subsidies stimulated corn growing for ethanol use. Growers converted their fields away from other staple food crops to capture the federal subsidies[14], thereby reducing the overall global food supply. The results were tragically predictable: higher-priced, energy-inefficient ethanol for the American consumer and a massive shortage of feed grains throughout the world. This decision, designed to "protect" the incomes of American farmers, most of whom were actually large agribusiness corporations that hired lobbyists to promote their agendas, carried a price tag paid for by people all over the world. The irony is that the United States Government initiated all of this, using the public's money to screw the people.

---

13   Jeff Cox, "Sugar Cane's Not-So-Sweet Future," *CnnMoney.com*, August 7, 2007

14   Brian Reidl, How Farm Subsidies Harm Taxpayers, Consumers And Farmers Too, *The Heritage Foundation,* June 20, 2007

As the above example demonstrates, corporations alone are not to blame for what they do. The government also has a hand in the mess, because it often rewards them for behaving in ways that run counter to the public welfare. Corporations respond in predictable ways to the promise of financial rewards, because the biggest challenge they face is the need to show their investors quarterly profits. It's becoming more and more obvious that the long-term financial costs to humanity and the environmental costs to our planet for delaying the implementation of new and renewable resource technologies are incalculable, yet our businesses remain hamstrung because we demand they turn a profit in the short run. Companies like General Electric, DuPont and Ford are expected to provide stock and bondholders with a positive return on their investments. Nowhere in the supply/demand model have we taken into account how these companies might make the products necessary to improve our lives or upgrade the condition of our planet if those products can't be made and sold to the public for immediate profit. We're gradually becoming more aware of this challenge and some industries have begun to invest more capital in research and development, but the bottom line remains the bottom line. If a positive financial return can't somehow be achieved, the product doesn't get made, no matter how pressing the problem it might solve.

Of course, once a problem becomes acute, the costs to produce a response to it may move within reach of a short-term corporate profit, because the amount the public is willing to pay to resolve the crisis rises—and whatever the amount grows to be, it is most often realized in the form of government spending. The ongoing privatization of the prison system is a good example of how a public crisis converts into a profitable private business enterprise. When overcrowding forced the early release of prisoners and increased the odds of criminal attacks on the public, the public in turn agreed to allow governmental funding of for-profit prisons to ensure overcrowding would be alleviated. Regular prisons don't generate a profit, so by definition a private prison is more expensive to operate than a public one, but at least there are fewer criminals on the streets. However, hidden and dangerous social costs abound in these kinds of reactionary approaches. For instance, when we turn the warehousing of criminals into a profitable enterprise that increases economic productivity, we're providing incentives to corporations to detain more criminals for longer periods of time—perhaps longer than would be justified in a non-profit prison system. In October of 2009, for example, the Pennsylvania Supreme Court overturned the convictions of over sixty-five hundred juveniles after determining that the sentencing judge had accepted millions of dollars in bribes from private detention facilities in exchange for those convictions. The facilities were collecting state money to incarcerate juvenile delinquents on a per-capita basis, so the more kids they warehoused the higher their revenues rose. Once incarcerated, many of these children subsequently had their sentences extended without recourse for minor or imaginary infractions. That enabled the facilities to collect many more millions in extra fees for the unwarranted detention of these minors.[15] Taxpayers in Pennsylvania now must

---

15   Frank Mastropolo, Lauren Pearle and Glenn Ruppel, ABC 20/20 News Story: "PA Supreme Court Throws Out Thousands of Juvenile Delinquency Cases," October 29, 2009.

face the prospect of paying out enormous cash settlements on civil lawsuits filed by families protesting the unlawful incarceration of their children, not to mention the artificially high costs they've already absorbed for having incarcerated these children overlong in the first place. On top of all that, we have no idea how much emotional harm has been done to these children as a result of their abuse at the hands of the judicial system, and what the ultimate cost to society will be for that. What becomes clear, though, is that when we try to perform public services more cheaply by contracting the work out to private enterprise, what we often wind up with are consequences that cost the public far more to repair in the end than if the public had paid a fair price and managed the task correctly to begin with.

Not only is our waiting for the arrival of a crisis to fund its solution a dangerous and often inefficient approach, it also assumes that in the meantime the crisis hasn't moved too far out of reach of our ability to address it. If it gets too expensive for us to protect our planet from global warming, will we let the place heat up—no matter how many species go extinct or natural habitats get destroyed? Will we continue to argue endlessly over who is at fault—is it a manmade problem, or part of the natural cycle?— rather than actually *do* something about it? Climate change is occurring all the time, manmade or not. If we hope to continue living here, we'd best start thinking now about how to respond to these noticeable changes in the weather.

THE ENEMY ISN'T "THEM,"
IT'S ACTUALLY "US"

One bizarre outcome of the modern supply/demand system is that we've unwittingly turned our corporations into enemies of humanity by setting them up to profit at the expense of living people. By empowering corporations to deny us what we need if they can't make money, we've disempowered ourselves for the sake of the system. We *expect* our companies to profit off us; in fact, we *demand* they do so. We demand it without fully understanding what that means, or insisting that they in any way connect their short-term successes to the long-term survival of our species or our planet.

Efforts *have* been made in recent years to create pools of investment funds to encourage corporations to behave in socially responsible ways, most notably through mutual funds and exchange traded stock funds (ETFs). As a whole, however, socially responsible investment funds typically limit themselves to avoiding investments in the "big three" areas of moral taboo: they refuse to purchase the so-called sin stocks (gambling, tobacco and alcohol companies), weapons manufacturers, or companies that test their products on live animals. Only recently have fund managers begun to screen for corporations that are reinventing themselves as environmentally and socially friendly businesses. Even then it's still too easy for companies to meet the screening parameters that merit their inclusion into such funds while behaving irresponsibly in ways that fall below the screener's radar. Also, we must remember that none of the so-called socially aware funds are exempt from the need to generate a profit for investors. That places pressure on fund managers to exclude from their portfolios those high-quality start-up companies that have a powerful social vision but which are, as yet, unprofitable operations. The irony is they may be the very companies most of us would love to see succeed, but because there's no short-term profit in it we're disinclined to invest in them.

Occasionally some of us become so angry with our corporations that we boycott them and attempt to expose their dark, immoral underbellies. What we forget is that genuinely moral people run most of our corporations—people who are daily confronted with terrible Hobbesean choices. Most, if given the option, would choose to do the "right thing" by others, but they get paid and promoted to do what's best for their company's bottom line. Since being paid is crucial for every person's survival in our system, to denounce our own company's policies can amount to suicide. To do what's best for me, or to do what's right for everybody else? It's not an easy choice to make and most of us, if we're honest, have struggled with it at one time or another. Why we continue to support a system that requires us to even *ask* that question of ourselves is a question worth examining.

We *are* the people who make the decisions—the corporate leaders *and* the general workers. We are not, however, bad or immoral creatures. We're more frightened than we are wicked or heartless. Afraid of what will happen to us if we don't put our company's aims above our personal moral values. We fear our own ejection from the system that keeps us alive. After all, what possible help can we be to others if we wind up starving or homeless? Rationally, then, for most of us it makes more sense to remain in the system and do our best to tweak it from the inside out.

None of this is anyone's fault. Nor are our parents to blame for teaching us to embrace our system as the best this world has to offer. We need to remember they desperately wanted to see us succeed within the only system they knew, rather than watch us reject it and, by doing so, risk getting cut off from the things we need to survive—and who can blame them? They love us, so they taught us what they believed we needed to know in order for us to "make it" in this world.

HOW SYSTEM SELF-PROMOTION LEADS TO GRIDLOCK

How can we change the rules of the game when the rules are designed to keep the game in place? It's a real challenge, in that a primary aim of any institution is to promote itself. That people initially support an organization provides it with positive feedback that confirms its usefulness, so the urge to self-promote becomes imbedded in all institutions. Something to consider, however, is that once an organization achieves a certain level of power it may grow tempted to *coerce* positive feedback rather than earn it. Organizations are infamous for rewriting the very rules that enabled them to spring into existence so they could then carve out a permanent home for themselves in the power structure.

Consider, for example, the way politics in the United States has changed over the years. America's Founding Fathers didn't belong to political parties, and nowhere in the U.S. constitution are political parties mentioned as necessary power bases for democracy to flourish. One wouldn't know that, however, based on the way the entrenched two-party system works today. In many states, including my own home state of California, voters are disenfranchised from even *voting* in primary elections if they fail to join a specific political party, and once they do join they may vote only for the candidates put forward by their own party. These rules were deliberately designed to prevent unaffiliated and independent voters (of whom there are many) from interfering with or "tainting" the electoral input of the party system. If unaffiliated and independent voters were allowed to vote for whomever they wished in every primary, the partisans fear they would opt for the most thoughtful, intelligent and moderate candidate out there, regardless of his or her party affiliation. That would, of course, lessen the two-party power grip on the political agenda. It might even hinder the parties' ability to control the political environment by rendering them irrelevant to the democratic process.

The end result of allowing our parties to write the rules for our public elections is that primaries tend to attract the most rabid supporters from each political party, while disenfranchised moderates stay home. The two major party candidates who support the most radical viewpoints (of either the right or the left) are then offered up for the general election. General elections, in which the previously disenfranchised voters are at last permitted to vote for whomever they like, then send the winner to Washington. By that time, though, at least for many voters who don't adhere to the two-party system, the so-called "free and democratic" choice they're being offered is between two equally disagreeable party candidates.

Imagine how different the government would look if primary elections used the system known as "preferential voting." That would provide all registered voters with a single ballot listing every candidate vying for every office, with each voter invited to pick their top three choices for each position. The top two vote getters would then engage in a run-off in the general election. While individuals would have much greater influence on the electoral process if elections were conducted in this way, it's possible that in some districts (particularly those that have been gerrymandered to favor the political party in power), one party or the other might not have a candidate on the general ballot. That's the real reason we don't see voting rules changed to favor the will of the people: it isn't in the interests of either party to offer us a true democracy. Their ability to manipulate the system and thereby seize and hold power is too tempting for our parties to ignore.

It's interesting to note that when mathematicians are asked to vote for officers or directors of their internal organizations, they use preferential voting for their elections. They do so because they've *done* the math, so they understand it offers them the highest degree of input in the most democratic fashion.

A preferential voting process would encourage voters to pay closer attention to the actual *positions* of each candidate rather than focus solely on the letter, D or R, beside the name. That might actually serve to reduce the political gridlock we've suffered from over the years. Elected officials—who currently pander to the will of party bosses and lobbyists to ensure their reelection—would instead tend to vote based on actual input from their constituents. What an idea!

The need organizations have to self-promote explains in part why the conservative elements in the United States Congress have successfully fought against health care reform for nearly forty years. Any attempt to reform health care requires government intervention, and one of the core beliefs of the conservative movement is that private initiatives always work better than government intervention. That's because conservatives promote the supply (business) side of the supply/demand equation. They believe corporate profits eventually flow into the coffers of the most intelligent, talented and industrious among us, who then rightfully get to decide—by virtue of money granting them the ability to purchase power—the future direction of our entire nation. Many conservatives believe that when people fail in life (unless they suffer some physical or mental impediment beyond their control) it's indicative of a moral weakness in the individual. They support entrepreneurship and believe *everyone* can achieve success if they put in enough hard work, even though—given the nature of our win/lose system—the dogma they're promoting represents an impossible dream. We mustn't ever forget that monetary wealth is relative, not absolute. That means the more you earn, the more I need to earn to be considered successful—even if the things I do cause harm to others.

Liberals, as opposed to conservatives, throw their support behind the demand side of the equation—the people side. They claim compassion for those who suffer from the inequities inherent in the system, so they try to pull money from the pockets of the wealthy and put it in the pockets of the people who don't have enough. All that does, however, is keep the poor clinging desperately to their government-inflated monetary life rafts: those leaky social boats called welfare, Aid to Families With Dependent Children, Social Security, Medicare and Medicaid, to name but a few. The difficulty here is that most participants in such programs aren't offered *enough* money or social support to empower them to self-educate or advance themselves so they can become contributing members of society. The rich therefore get strong-armed by liberals into "trickling down" just enough cash to keep the bulk of these folks barely breathing…year after year.

This lack of appreciable forward momentum among the poor fosters deep resentment in those providing the money without seeing any substantive results, as well as in those forced to accept what little they're grudgingly given. The poor must contend with the added insult that they're supposed to feel *grateful* to the rich for being permitted through charity to barely survive.

Either political party can point to the failed policies of the other to make a potent case for their own entrenched beliefs. What *neither* side has yet embraced (because it would threaten their ability to self-perpetuate) is that the entire model we're operating under is based on a false belief: the idea that EVERYONE can somehow win while playing a win/lose game.

We're witnessing institutionalized political gridlock today because there's plenty of evidence to support the accusations being made by either side against one another, since both parties are operating under the same false assumption. For instance, for a decade or more we've been observing the shrinking of the American middle class. Republicans blame the problem on excessive governmental intrusion into the free market system, claiming business's capacity to create good jobs has been hampered by federal regulations and excessive taxation. Democrats blame the problem on a lack of government oversight, and claim we need higher taxes to empower the government to stimulate the economy where that's needed. The truth is, what we really need is a system that doesn't require us to mindlessly, relentlessly consume, exploit and waste our precious and finite natural resources in exchange for printed money that fools us into believing we're "successful."

The absurdity of all this is that if we set aside the supply/demand game and instead designed a win/win system to replace it, we wouldn't even need opposition parties. All we'd need would be an intelligent analysis of what works best and why, along with new ideas that might work better. The sad truth of all this is that by giving us what we genuinely need, our political parties would put themselves out of business. And if there's one thing we humans need to remember about the way we've structured all our organizations, it's that they have zero incentive to do such a fine job we won't need them anymore!

Each employee of every organization needs to eat. The self-interest inherent in the human drive to survive encourages each of us to do whatever we need to do to keep our income flowing. That means we're encouraged to promote those systems that employ us instead of render them obsolete as we outgrow them. Perhaps that explains why drug companies invest so much energy promoting symptom alleviators instead of cures, or why energy companies oppose home solar panels so families can go "off the grid" and cease paying those burdensome monthly utility bills. It may also explain why some religious institutions demand their followers attend regular weekly services. If the only thing saving believers from hell is a weekly confessional, then the system has built into its own design its necessity for the rest of human existence.

Many of us take dogmatic positions *not* because we've examined and analyzed our beliefs, but because the organizations with which we've affiliated ourselves have instructed us to embrace their dogmas as our own unquestioned truths. This holds whether the institution is economic, political, social or religious. To challenge an organization's dogmas implies they aren't already perfect, which necessitates change. Change upsets an organization by asking that it expend energy to create something new and different, when it would rather invest its energy in promoting itself and expanding its power base. On the other hand, once we've become convinced that a system's ideologies are absolutely correct, we're likely to support that system forever—just as it is.

One thing we *do* know for certain is that our world inexorably changes. This means every aging organization eventually reaches a point where it no longer meets humanity's shifting needs. When that occurs, an institution can survive only if it gently adapts to reality, or else becomes so rigidly controlling that it terrifies its members into supporting it if *they* wish to survive (or perhaps get to heaven).

We can either love our systems or fear them, but we can't do both. Knowing that, and because we are both the creators *of* and the participants *in* all our systems, it's time we each decide which emotional bond we prefer: to love or to fear.

ENDING STRUCTURAL GRIDLOCK

We observe adaptation all the time in our changing biosphere. Weather patterns shift and an afflicted species must either adapt or die. For years now we've been witnessing the tragic loss of polar bears as the Arctic seas warm and the ice they rely on to access their food supply melts. Conversely, every species alive today is alive because it's managed to adapt to its environment. Adaptation also occurs in the business world. For example, once enough people embraced the convenience of cellular technology, the phone companies had no choice but to support it instead of stubbornly clinging to their existing landline models. Digital cable likewise replaced our analog television broadcasts. Those businesses that made the shift to the digital format survived, while those that didn't eventually disappeared. In time, the same will hold true for all our economic systems, religious institutions, judicial structures, schools and political processes. Adapt or die is a truth we can't ignore if we hope to survive.

If we'd like to evolve without experiencing overly chaotic collapses (violent revolution) or painful periods of ideological fascism (oppressive stagnation) we'd be well served to progress in a way that encourages gentle evolution within a reasonably stable system, which nature manages to accomplish all the time. In a dynamically balanced natural system things change constantly, but everything else pays attention to the changes taking place and makes its own adjustment in response to them. If the squirrel population explodes in a given location, denuding the landscape and damaging the health of the larger ecosystem, eventually coyotes and hawks will take notice. They move into the area, breed and thrive by preying on squirrels until eventually the balance is restored. This is not only good for the system, it's good for the squirrels. If their population went unchecked they'd eventually destroy their own capacity to survive.

We humans, unlike squirrels, have the ability to notice our own negative environmental impact and change our behavior before the world changes it for us. Unfortunately, the more dogmatic among us sometimes grow so fearful of potential change that we try to force continued compliance with our outmoded social systems. Political dictators like Kim Jong-il of North Korea and Bashar al-Assad of Syria are ruthless suppressors of individual freedom within their countries. That's unfortunate, since social oppression often leads to the very event rigid thinkers most fear will happen— a revolution. The populist uprisings in Egypt, Tunisia and many other Middle Eastern and African nations in early 2011 demonstrate how readily the people can overthrow even the most ruthless of dictators once their anger and hopelessness rises beyond their fear of physical reprisals. The most dangerous people in the world are those who feel they have nothing left to lose. When such people rise in force to challenge their oppressors (who stand to lose a great deal and aren't in most cases willing to personally die for their cause), the people usually win.

Even when it's a massive populist uprising met by official resistance, a social revolution need not result in violence and destruction. In the early 1940s, the peaceful independence movement in India was met with fierce brutality from the British Army.

Mahatma Gandhi's exhortations to his supporters to stand firm (but remain peaceful) in the face of escalating British violence exemplified for the world the moral superiority of intellectual reason over the need to resort to violence to achieve a particular end. Eventually the rise of a free and independent India proved to the world the strength and power of peaceful resistance to forcible oppression.

Humanity's innate desire for freedom being what it is, our passionate rejection of tyranny will eventually overcome even the most violent and oppressive of our political systems. Sometimes the change is inspired from without, as with a powerful wave of populist resistance. Other times, though admittedly more rare, the rulers voluntarily give power back to the people as happened in the Soviet Union under Boris Yeltsin in 1991. Either way, when a system isn't beloved by its citizens, those people—being for the most part clever, imaginative and resourceful—will do their best to "game" it to their advantage, which weakens the system.

We witnessed exactly that in Germany, which was split after WWII into a totalitarian sector (East) and a democratic sector (West). The most obvious iconic proof that the East Germans disapproved of their new government was the notorious Berlin Wall. A beloved social order wouldn't have needed to build a wall around itself to box its people in, but that's exactly what East Germany did to prevent an exodus to the West. Yet despite the potential risks to life and limb, for years East Germans tunneled under it, scrambled over it and generally did what they could to "conquer" the wall. Finally, when the sheer oppressiveness of the political system led it to turn on itself, the wall came down. We witnessed a similar occurrence with the fall of the Soviet Union. Though it seemed like an invulnerable, mighty totalitarian nation, it collapsed on itself in a matter of just a few months.

As both totalitarianism and fascism have taught us, ideas and values can't be forcibly imposed on humanity. Values must be freely embraced if they're to be willingly practiced and explored. Likewise, what capitalism is teaching us is that mechanistic systems can't squeeze the energy out of people without bleeding the lifeblood out of the participants.

THE JOY OF CONTINUOUS CHANGE

The irony of anyone standing firmly resistant to change is that we awaken into a brand new world every day. We call it the universe, and it's never the same place twice. In our universe, though, the changes happening all around us are either so constant we take them for granted or so slow and imperceptible we fail to notice them.

Indeed, we use alarm clocks and artificial lighting to "conquer" the limitations of our planet's daily movements, and as a result we've lost touch with our own circadian rhythms. We import fruits and vegetables from all around the world, so we've lost sight of the seasonality of foods that are locally grown. We look to calendars to define our days and have lost our awareness of the movement of the sun, the moon and the stars. In short, we've "smoothed out" many of the variables inherent in our reality to better suit our mechanized industrial needs, to the point we're ignoring the ever-changing nature of this amazing world we live in.

One day we may all suddenly wake up and realize our world has changed dramatically while we weren't paying attention. We already know a volcano like Montserrat can erupt and in an instant wipe out two-thirds of an island. A hurricane can decimate a seemingly permanent city like New Orleans, and a virus like AIDS can arrive on the scene and threaten our survival. We don't argue for long with the powerful forces of nature, and we certainly don't ignore these events when they happen. Reality always marches on, not caring whether we'd like to ignore its existence.

To move joyfully into alignment with what is—to honor the nature of the ever-changing cosmic organism of which we are all part—is to love the world that has created us, and to live in accord with the changes it inspires. Then only can we step into our role as conscious beings with the power to *activate* change. What a wonderful gift we've been given: the ability to *observe* universal change along with the power to *understand* it, coupled with the *capacity* to bend the world in ways that might best serve the needs of the whole. What a shame we've managed to squander that gift for so long.

So far most of our attempts to bend reality to humanity's vision have been for short-term personal gain rather than long-term social or planetary benefit. In fact, most of the changes we've made so far have been designed to advantage a few of us at the *expense* of the planetary whole. For example, we've carved up the land into artificial chunks and sold them to the highest bidder, depriving countless living creatures, as well as other, less fortunate humans, of their natural right to a place in this world without our explicit permission.

We've decimated whole species with our clear-cutting, strip mining, oil drilling and so forth in service to our economic interests, with little concern for the impact those extinctions have had on our planet. We've polluted our oceans, rivers and seas and urbanized large swaths of land, reshaping, scarring and paving over nature to construct our idea of how a human world "should" look. We've done so from a place of separation consciousness. Separation consciousness is the perspective that we were somehow set apart from everything else, and that what we did for ourselves in the short run was more important than the consequences of our actions in the long run. We behaved this way not because we were purposefully trying to destroy the Earth, but out of a complete lack of awareness of the heaviness of our own footprint on the neck of our mother planet. Even as recently as fifty years ago we might have noticed the problems we were creating were getting bigger but assumed they would fall on another generation to manage, that we could personally escape from the need to change or suffer a social collapse. Now though, with our problems looming ever larger in the span of our own lifetimes, it would be disingenuous (and maybe suicidal) for us to decide we've no choice but to continue along the path of "business as usual" because we've created a machine that's too big to fail and too cumbersome to change. That may have been the fate of the dinosaurs, but it needn't be ours...unless we shrug and surrender ourselves to it.

THE WORLD IS HUMANITY'S STAGE— BUT WHO WRITES OUR SCRIPTS?

Shakespeare wrote, "All the world's a stage." That line is more than simple metaphor. The Earth *is* a stage, albeit a living one, having been constructed over some four billion years of planetary evolution. The land and social environments that constitute our local sets are ever-shifting, and the dramatic, individual life and death stories being acted out upon those many stages are ever-changing. We're the actors and actresses, some of the many creatures who enter this cosmic field of play through the doorway of birth. Each of us will act out our personal story, as well as perform supporting roles in the personal stories of others, until commanded by life (our cosmic director) to exit, which each of us will do through the doorway of death.

Actually, that's only part of the truth, not the whole truth. For at heart we *are* life. We are inseparable from it, thus from each other and from all other things. Life blows into and out of this world through the countless forms it creates, but underneath them all it remains eternal, infinite, formless. No matter how hard we try to pin life down it can't be isolated, dissected or put back together by us, as can a machine. When we *do* try to understand it, for instance if we dissect a dog to learn more about how it functions, we have to extinguish the dog's life essence in our quest for some objective truth.

Life is energy in its purest form, a miraculous dancer that animates every atom, molecule, cell, plant and creature in this world.

Life is the creator of the magic and the source of the light that flows into the cosmos. Some of us call that light of life the soul, while others call it divine energy or God. Whatever we call it, it exists not only in people, but also in everything that exists around us. We feel it flowing inside ourselves, which is why we're drawn to a notion of "self" that extends beyond the borders of our temporary forms. When we finally learn to sense it in everything else is when we'll shed our feelings of isolation. We are *not* alone; we never were. We just lost sight of the life bursting out all around us.

Once a majority of us let go of that false sense of separation by noticing the eternal dimension of life that binds the entire cosmos together, we'll be that much closer to healing the wounds created by our feelings of isolation. Humans won't become *less* special by granting the status of "living" to all other things. Instead we'll be *honoring* all things in existence so they each become *more* special, thus sacred to and beloved by us all.

What makes this change so hard is that the scripts we're currently following promote isolation and human separation. They were written thousands of years ago and given to us as children, before we could think about whether the ideas in them made sense. We were taught at an early age to be patriotic citizens of our respective nations, which means we "like" some countries and rush to do battle with others. We were taught that our God is the "right" one while everybody else's God is the "wrong" one. We were taught to embrace our country's economic policies, which means we must support our corporations and promote their continuation, no matter the cost. At no time were we offered the chance to write a modern script that better defines who we believe ourselves to be in the here and now, or where we think we're heading as a species. Certainly we've not yet seized the opportunity to write "the end" on the chapter that details the mechanical/industrial era, so we can begin telling our story from a new and living perspective.

Though it's really our choice to rewrite our human story, our planet seems to be setting the stage for just such an opportunity as we leave behind the first decade of the third millennium. For the first time in modern history, with a majority of institutions groaning beneath the weight of global change, we're being invited to rise to the occasion. And it's not just the wealthy who are being invited to this party, not just the disenfranchised who are being invited to this revolution, but *all* of us…together. We're being offered the chance to create something more beautiful, compassionate, loving and more *alive* for ourselves than the mechanical win/lose system that runs us now. We're being invited to construct healthy, whole systems that more accurately reflect our understanding of humanity as a living organism on a living planet, imbedded in a living universe.

Our world is inviting us to create a new vision for humanity by accelerating the global rate of change. In less than a hundred and fifty years humanity has gone from horse-drawn carriages to space travel, from letters delivered by Pony Express to instant communication around the world. Twenty years ago if we walked into a coffee shop our choices were limited to cream or sugar. Enter a Starbucks today and we're confronted with a nearly limitless number of choices—all around a simple cup of coffee!

Clearly, human imagination is expanding its capacity to create by leaps and bounds. The question is this: do we want to continue building more and more complex mechanical systems that suck the lifeblood out of us, or is it time for us to breathe life into what we're creating? When we create with *human* values and needs in mind instead of focusing only on what will keep the business machinery running, what we create will begin to reflect the best of what we are.

Whether we survive this present evolutionary shift depends on our willingness to let go of our old ideas and eliminate the practices that no longer serve us. But first we must identify and agree about what needs changing. How long our planet will wait while we quarrel is anyone's guess, but as our challenges mount we'll surely be pressed into responding to some very real events. We've already been pressed hard to respond to devastating earthquakes and hurricanes, a terrible tsunami, record flooding in Asia and Australia and diseases that are devastating the people of Africa. How well we've done so far is open to question, but the challenges just keep on coming with little time in between for us to regroup. Things will likely go much easier for us if we consciously make time now to reflect on what needs to be done and then begin gently to change our ways.

If we insist on waiting for some dire emergency to force us to blindly, unconsciously react we're likely to fall back on our animalistic survival instincts rather than to use reason to make more grounded moral choices. Remember that on the evolutionary time scale we're still a very young species when it comes to our ability to use our sense of reason. We need more practice before reason becomes our default tool when we're confronted with immediate danger. Our tendency is to fall back on our old standby, the fight, flight or freeze reflex, which is rooted in fear and often creates more

suffering than it averts. We observe this when we witness a riot-
ing mob. Fear generates anger, which feeds reactivity, until reason
and values get shunted aside and the energies of instinct become
overwhelming. We've seen furious mobs in the streets of Palestine
attacking armed Israeli soldiers with rocks and sticks; acts those
same individuals would never dream of committing on their own.
Unfortunately, when people get caught up in a mob mentality they
briefly lose touch with their higher sense of self.

FROM SUPPLY AND DEMAND TO RESOURCE ALLOCATION

One of the core problems we must address sooner rather than later
is the question of how best to allocate our planet's limited resources.
When we examine the highest priced products we're making today,
we find many require detailed craftsmanship. Since labor is one of
the highest costs a producer must recover when he sets his prices, such items are generally produced in lower numbers. They're
therefore reserved as a privilege for the wealthy. Yachts, custom
mansions and luxury cars all fall into this category. Still, since the
profit margins on luxury goods are quite high (the wealthiest can
afford to pay much more for items than they actually cost to produce) the resources necessary to make these goods are allocated
with little regard for their scarcity or how they might be better put
to collective social use.

Inefficient resource allocation is a direct effect of the free market system paradigm. The biggest problem with allowing our resources to go to the highest bidder instead of the most worthy cause is that it perpetuates human misery. Global consumption statistics for 2005, the most recent year for which this information is available, inform us that the richest twenty percent of the world's population consumed more than seventy-six percent of all products manufactured during the year. The middle sixty percent consumed almost twenty-two percent of all the goods, while the poorest twenty percent of the people consumed a mere one and one-half percent of all goods produced.[16]

Consider the United States. It houses five percent of the world's population but consumes nearly thirty percent of its oil[17]—not because it needs to, but because it can afford to. Our thoughtless over-consumption of oil creates scarcity among the rest of the world's population, even more so today when previously unindustrialized parts of the world are joining the rush to industrialize. While the United States may need more oil to operate its economy than do natives living in the Brazilian rainforest, inarguably we squander a lot of fossil fuel simply because we can.

Additionally, the wealthiest nations consume and destroy far more than their fair share of pristine land and sea. For example, since the 1950s the world has seen a proliferation of plastic clogging its landfills and leeching damaging environmental toxins into the soil and air. The problem has only accelerated since we began marketing bottled water as a preferential substitute for tap water. The

16   World Bank Development Indicators, 2008, *http://data.worldbank.org/indicator*.

17   The CIA World Factbook, US Central Intelligence Agency (updated bi-weekly).

current attitude is that our wealth makes it OK for us to use and discard such items at our convenience, and that as long as we're willing to buy another bottle it's nobody's business but our own what we throw away. The crucial question that attitude ignores is this: when we discard something, where, exactly, is "away?" What we're learning is that when we dispose of something improperly, eventually we're going to meet it again—and not on good terms.

On the surface, at least, our distribution and consumption agreements may seem plenty fair to the privileged people in the United States. After all, we have the capacity to pay for all that oil we're consuming, at least so long as other nations remain willing to accept our paper dollars. But we can hardly blame the remaining ninety-five percent of humanity for feeling bitter about our wasting our planet's oil. What we need to remind ourselves is that no amount of money will be able to produce more global oil once it's gone. Not only that, but the dollars we're using to pay for oil (which *is* real wealth) are only proxy wealth substitutes, a fact most of our trading partners are starting to grasp.

American dollars are fast becoming the hot potatoes of the world. In 2006 alone the United States imported nearly sixty billion dollars more in goods than we exported every month.[18] That means U.S. citizens acquired nearly a trillion dollars' worth of real wealth produced by the rest of the world, while the rest of the world got our proxy wealth in exchange.

The United States's trade imbalance has grown so large that foreign nations are growing eager to spend their cash before the

18   Steven R. Weisman, "U.S. Ran a Record Trade Deficit in 2006," *The New York Times*, February 13, 2007.

dollar's value falls farther. The problem is, if they spend their dollars too fast they'll crush its value and collapse the American economy, and under the global monetary system they still need us to consume what they're producing. Eventually, though, once the Chinese, Indians, Latin Americans and Russians have created large enough middle classes and developed enough capacity to consume their own goods internally, they won't need American consumers anymore. The value of the dollar will likely plunge then as an international rush to unload dollars accelerates. In the not-too-distant future, then, the newly impoverished and desperate citizens of the United States may ironically become the cheap, exploited Third World laborers making products for sale to the wealthy in China and India. That's the trouble with playing a win/lose game. Since the game never ends, nobody wins it forever. Meanwhile, losers must always exist for new winners to rise. And so the cycle of human suffering continues—it just changes faces and places.

Another major problem is that the United States historically has—by sheer force of its monetary power and its perceived position as the wealthiest nation on Earth—flexed its monetary muscles and driven up the price of resources (like oil) beyond the financial ability of most nations to compete. We've consumed what we purchased without wondering whether we were putting those resources to best use. The thinking was that the oil was ours to do with as we pleased—even if we chose to squander it at the expense of the rest of the world. Who cares what happens to the poor if we get what we want?

Had the United States been a poor nation when we were all born we'd hardly consider the arrangement "fair," humane or even very smart. One advantage to being born into the winning side of the game is that we can avoid asking ourselves the more uncomfortable questions, at least for a little while. In the long run, though, our shortsightedness will catch up with us, as we're now beginning to notice.

The trouble with profiting through economic force rather than through a compassionate system that supports global sharing and intelligent resource allocation is that we flex our muscles at somebody else's expense. Since those "somebody elses" are living human beings, we'll eventually be forced to face the consequences of our own selfish behavior. Americans sometimes wonder why we're not well liked by the rest of the world anymore. The answer is plain and simple: we have shoved our own economic script into the hands of the world and strong-armed its people into acting out life our way, when all most of them really wanted was to live in ways most suitable to their own cultures and local resources. Sure, some have observed our privileged lifestyles by watching our television programs and reading our magazines and now want our same "good life." And who can blame them? The challenge, however, is that the American lifestyle wasn't designed to be sustainable for the entire planet over the long run—not even for us, and certainly not for seven billion people. As it stands, current thinking says we'd need five more planet Earths to bring the world up to the standard of living as it exists today in the U.S.[19] The more people who therefore strive to achieve the American lifestyle, the sooner we'll have to acknowledge an obvious truth: There's not enough stuff for everyone

19   Take the challenge and play the game if you dare: *http://sustainability.publicradio.org/consumerconsequences/*

to win while playing this win/lose game, at least not the way we're presently distributing what we have.

What's even more disturbing is that populous nations like China and India have recently embraced the American ideological script and are now beginning to compete with us for resources like oil. Since they're following our lead, they're not placing a whole lot more focus on intelligent consumption and resource distribution than we have, so they too are squandering much of what they buy for the sake of profits. The likelihood that our planet will run out of resources sooner rather than later is accelerating, even as demand for resources is exponentially escalating.

TOWARD MORE EFFECTIVE RESOURCE MANAGEMENT

In centuries past, the limited number of humans combined with a lack of global regulation meant people had the ability to migrate away from areas where scarcities occurred and to resettle in "lands of plenty." The idea of intelligently allocating natural resources didn't occur to us back then, because we hadn't experienced *planetary* scarcity. When a shortage occurred we could go someplace else and discover more of it. Now, however, with our burgeoning population and the unfettered growth engine that is driving modern, global capitalism, we need to shift our perspectives around our planetary resources.

In the past we were ignorant as to the limits of our resources and it mattered little to us whether we produced cars that got eight miles to the gallon or forty. Now it's time to admit it's stupid to continue to ignore the global cost of excessive oil consumption. The "we'll just go get it somewhere else" approach won't help us any longer, because soon there will be nowhere else to go. We're already drilling thousands of feet beneath the ocean floor in search of oil, disturbing areas we don't know how to manage if we cause a problem. The recent tragic explosion and sinking of the BP Deepwater Horizon rig and the subsequent spill it caused in the Gulf of Mexico revealed to us the terrible risks we're taking to slake our thirst for ever more crude.

Not only have we circumnavigated the planet to exploit its resources, we've expanded into areas never meant by nature to support the populations they now support. Our planet is, in many locations, groaning beneath the strain of too many people for the local resources to handle. We've overrun and destroyed many delicate ecosystems, and we're continuing to wreak more planetary havoc every day.

Humans have upset the dynamic natural balance across the entire continent of Africa, with disastrous results. The famines and widespread diseases African nations often suffer result from failed attempts to Westernize native cultures that for millennia maintained a dynamic balance in relationship to their resources. Westerners imported diseases from other countries and encouraged urbanization and mechanization among previously tribal cultures. When too many people move to industrialized cities that contain too few resources to support the people they need to run their machines, suffering is the inevitable result.

The destruction of the world's rainforests, which has been taking place at the alarming rate of 2.4 acres per second,[20] is another example of the exportation of Western capitalism into areas not conducive to industrial-scale activities. Deforestation is justified to make room to grow new crops, many of which get imported to the United States for personal consumption. How much better might it be for all if the industrialized nations supported the indigenous peoples of Africa (as well as those of the rainforests) by providing them with all the food, water, shelter, clothing, education and medical care they needed in exchange for their ongoing commitment to act as loving stewards of this planet's priceless habitats?

Take areas like Brazil, for instance. Rainforests cover less than six percent of Earth's landmass,[21] yet scientists estimate they contain more than half the world's plants and animals and produce forty percent of our oxygen.[22] Consider too the Arctic wilderness ecosystem. Its fragile balance of tundra, tussock plains and spruce boreal forests are easily damaged. They take years to regenerate due to permafrost and a very short growing season, yet business interests continue to push for oil drilling in the Arctic tundra. Last but not least we've been gifted the great African plains and highlands, which contain some of the largest surviving species of wildlife. Endangered rhinos, lions, tigers, gorillas and elephants are being poached to the point of

---

20   Data provided by the World Resource Institute, Washington D.C.

21   Rainforest Facts; Raintree Nutrition Inc, Carson City, NV, last updated March 20, 2010, *http://www.rain-tree.com/facts.htm*

22   Tropical Rainforest; *http://www.blueplanetbiomes.org/rainforest.htm*

extinction for their skins, body parts, tusks and horns, because their parts fetch astronomical prices on the black market.

How much more intelligent would it be for the wealthiest nations to freely provide whatever is necessary to encourage human life to flourish in our overpopulated, impoverished areas? How much saner would it be for us to provide birth control to the poor rather than impose a fundamentalist Christian morality on those who don't have enough resources to keep their children alive? Twenty-two thousand children die each day from hunger or disease in Third World nations. That amounts to eight million, one hundred thousand dead innocents every single year.[23] Those are real live children experiencing genuine pain and suffering—now. Consider that tragic statistic in light of the religiously-based aversion to the prevention of conception. It's wickedly hypocritical for us to fight passionately for an *ideological* right to life by denying grownups birth control, while ignoring the needs of live children after they're born.

The right to life applies first and foremost to those already alive. Only *after* we've proved we give a damn about how to nurture the already born who are—right now—suffering and dying from starvation and disease, will we have perhaps earned the right to protect the rights of the as-yet unborn. Until then, our efforts to force childbirth upon those least capable of caring for their offspring without regard for those innocent lives or the suffering that ensues is deeply misguided.

---

23   Anup Shah, "Today, Over 22,000 Children Died Around the World," Global Issues: Social, Political, Economic and Environmental Issues That Affect us All, last updated September 20, 2010.

It's important to note here that preventing conception does not mean supporting abortion. Activists who clump them together in the mistaken belief they're protecting the "sanctity of life" by opposing both would be well served to embrace contraceptives if they genuinely desire a reduction in global abortions. Where human life has not yet come into being, no human life exists to require our protection. Trying to control the mere *possibility* of conceiving a life by demanding that people either abstain from human sexual intimacy or be intimate without protection falls well beyond the scope of "sanctity." It's a paternalistic intrusion into somebody else's right to choose their destiny. By contrast, the nearly forty-two *million* abortions performed globally[24] (as of 2003) speak to the pressing need for free and accessible birth control. This is a prime example of how the rigidity of a dogma causes more real-world suffering than it imagines it prevents.

By helping impoverished segments of the population practice better methods of birth control and by offering their existing children food, clean water, shelter, healthcare and a better education, we could contribute to the well-being of *all* the children parents choose to bring into this world, instead of unwittingly contributing to the suffering and deaths of those babies nobody can care for. Since we're talking about resources here, let's not forget that children *are* our most precious resource, and to squander their lives from a lack of care is the most tragic waste of resources we can commit.

---

24   Liz Olson, Infoplease, A Part of Family Education Network, "Global Abortion Rates," Pearson Information, 2007. *http://www.infoplease.com/science/health/global-abortion-rates.html*

FREE MARKET CONSTRAINTS ON CREATIVITY

As we've seen in the examples above, an incalculable amount of human suffering results from allowing the monetary might of the supply and demand model to determine natural resource distribution. The problem grows even more acute when we consider individual creativity. Take, for instance, an item like a simple paintbrush. To the average person a paintbrush might be worth a couple of dollars at most. But to someone like Vincent Van Gogh—or to any young artist who has not yet been discovered—that paintbrush is priceless. Yet we regularly deny paintbrushes and canvasses to potential future Van Goghs because they haven't yet produced the magnificent paintings they could sell to acquire the supplies they need to paint. How backwards is that? What we've created is a system where we can't *afford* to create so we can contribute to society rather than be a constant drain on its resources!

While most of us appreciate the arts, art programs are usually the first to go when we need to make budget cuts. Human beings love art, literature and music and we know the arts feed our souls, but most budding artists can't afford to create art if it can't be turned into a marketable commodity. Imagine if the Egyptians had taken that approach with the pyramids, or the French with Notre Dame or Chartres Cathedral. Some of the most magnificent creations of humanity were built *not* to stoke an economy, but to offer up a creative, artistic statement about a particular culture's worldview. What statement are we making about our modern worldview by limiting the arts to only those products that prove financially profitable?

It's insane, yet our system stifles creativity at its source. It's based on a delusional (but shared) dogma that says we must produce *before* we acquire, and we must exchange *before* we create. But how is a person supposed to pay for resources *before* she can be allowed to apply those resources creatively to achieve her full and productive potential? What does she have to exchange *before* she produces something of value? Whose resources are we selling anyway? And why isn't the wonder or insight humanity stands to gain through supporting those who strive to bring new visions into this world payment enough?

As always we can look to nature for a better blueprint for living, since nature has survived much longer than humankind. For years nature will provide a seedling peach tree with enough water, soil, nutrients and sunlight so it can grow to maturity, at which point it finally bears fruit. Those peaches are then distributed throughout the natural system. Birds, animals and even worms benefit from the tree's bounty. If nature demanded a "pay-go" fee from the tree in exchange for the resources it needed to survive, the sapling would have to surrender all it had—its green leaves, tender new shoots and protective outer bark—in exchange for the water and sunlight it required. It wouldn't be long before the poor little seedling died, and the entire world would be worse for the loss of its peaches.

The tree makes an easier, more cooperative bargain with nature. It willingly surrenders its dead leaves every winter. Those leaves, which the tree no longer needs anyhow, replenish the earth and enable the soil to nourish the tree (and many other plants surrounding it) come spring. The tree also agrees to play host to the birds, ants and bees who make their homes in its branches. Those animals and insects may chew a few of its green leaves or burrow a bit into its bark, but not usually in a way that does the tree real harm. Later they'll eat its fruit and spread its pollen and seeds throughout the locale, which helps the peach tree propagate its kind.

These cooperative arrangements benefit the *whole* of nature, as well as create more abundance for all participants. If a natural system falls out of balance, say when a parasite shows up and devours an entire pine forest, the living matrix of the planet temporarily loses some of its creative power. Those parasites will either die or move on in the short run, but in the long run they pay a price for their appetites. Black locusts, for example, are required to remain dormant in the ground for as long as seventeen years, because if they emerged more often the plant world would soon be decimated. They're surely a necessary part of the cycle of life/death/ rebirth, which is why they still exist, but the tradeoff they've made is not one we humans should envy. Should we follow the pattern of the locust and continue to consume our planet without concern, we're not likely to wind up spending seventeen years buried underground. We're likely to witness the complete decimation of human civilization as our reward.

RESTORING PLANETARY HARMONY

Humanity, like locusts, has engaged in unthinking, almost parasitic behavior toward our planet through our money-is-power idea of supply and demand. We must forgive ourselves for our past consumptive behavior, since we were operating from ignorance and from a fear of lack. Now, though, it's time we paid more attention to living examples of how symbiosis works, and less to our economic dogmas of the past.

In symbiotic relationships, the word "mutualism" describes an arrangement between individuals where both eventually derive some benefit from the relationship, which can in turn be described as a form of enlightened self-interest. Rather than allowing our lives to be controlled by the laws of supply and demand, which are designed so some can profit at the expense of the many, we'd all be far better served to rework our economy around the practice of mutualism. The clear advantage of mutualism is that—unlike the present for-profit system—it offers us all a win/win opportunity. Mutualism can be practiced between people, between mankind and other species, and also between mankind and the planet itself.

What might a mutually beneficial exchange look like as opposed to a for-profit exchange, and how might we begin to go about forging such relationships? Let's consider some simple ideas as a place to start. Say for instance, that I have an empty bedroom and a friend who's in need of housing, I might offer that room to my friend in exchange for his willingness to perform some basic handyman skills around the house when the need arises. If I know someone who loves to garden but doesn't have land to do so, yet I have some unworked soil and a very brown thumb, perhaps I could offer her the use of my land in exchange for some of her harvest. If I love to make jam but don't own any fruit trees, yet I notice a neighbor's trees are going to rot, perhaps I could offer to pick some of their fruit in exchange for a couple of jars of my homemade jam. The key here is that both parties eventually win and the lives of everyone become enhanced by the novel connections they're making.

When we consider the possibilities of resource allocation through the lens of mutualism, we discover that what today seems scarce may not be scarce at all. If everyone who had an extra bedroom (or second and third houses) took in a homeless friend or family as part of a mutually beneficial relationship, we might not need to build nearly as much new housing as we think. If everyone who grew extra produce shared that bounty with their neighbors in exchange for an occasional homemade dish, we'd probably need to import less food and would benefit richly by eating healthier meals. Mutualism says, "share with me what you can spare right now, and later when I have something to offer I'll give it to you in thanks for your support." It's a loving, highly generous system, and it honors the various stages of life through which we all must pass. Adults help children, who in turn help the elderly, who were once parents and helped their children without getting any immediate return. It's a cyclical flow instead of a direct exchange.

The antithesis of the for-profit approach (selfish self-interest) would be to increase our charitable giving (altruism.) However, while charitable giving may make a donor briefly feel good about his ability to help someone in need, the charity recipient typically gains nothing of lasting value. Charitable gifting can thus be disempowering to the human spirit. It leaves the poor dependent on others while offering the donor nothing in return, beyond a brief feel-good moment that can quickly shift to unhealthy feelings of superiority. The underlying problem with charity is reflected in the statement that when we give a man a fish we feed him for a day, but when we teach a man to fish we feed him for life. The teaching, then, is clearly a better way to solve the problem for the long run. It's also a win/win scenario, because when we teach a man to fish we have the opportunity to share our own skills, which makes us feel good, *and* we're empowering another to be able to care for himself, which makes him feel good. Other than when people—due to illness, mental incapacitation or physical disability—are unable to care for themselves, outright charity serves humanity no better in the long run than does the for-profit economic model.

For each of us to give as much or more *to* each other than we demand *from* each other, while graciously accepting whatever another can give us in return when they have the power to do so, will pave the way for our system to evolve into something far more sustainable than our present model. Such a model will lead to greater future abundance for all living beings. Mutualism is one way we can ensure our system will always be greater—therefore have the power to give back to each of us more than we contribute—than a simple sum of the parts would indicate. This form of fluid sharing, pure and simple, creates far more health and abundance than a system where a few people hoard almost all of the money and then dole out barely enough to keep the impoverished people alive but not productive.

WHY SHARING WORKS
BETTER THAN SELLING

WHEN I FIRST BEGAN TO PUT THESE WORDS TO PAPER, I REAL-
ized any person who writes a book in today's society is, in a very
real and tangible way, accessing the skills and talents of all the
people who have ever come before him. Without the physical inventions of paper, ink, printing presses, keyboards, computers and
so forth, I could never have written this book. I also must take
into consideration the scientific research I'm utilizing that has
been painstakingly collected by others, along with the hundreds
of imaginative ideas I'm compiling that others first conceived. Last
but not least I must give credit to the myriad social innovations
that have fostered my ability to write: things like our public schools,
a steady food supply, decent housing, the Internet and a reliable
energy grid. Everything I've accomplished then is clearly a collaborative effort. That those with whom I'm collaborating may be long

dead doesn't free me of my obligation to recognize and honor their achievements.

This is not just a phenomenon experienced by writers. Any individual's creative output will *always* be grounded in the insights, talents and skills of all others who have come before him. Therefore, to assign ownership of any human output to a single person is to devalue the prior, countless, human endeavors that empowered that person to achieve his or her own creative potential.

The concept of personal ownership of intellectual and creative output is founded on the faulty belief that an individual's output is indeed the product of a lone individual. In truth, everything in this world exists in relationship to everything else, as well as to the past and to the future. Buddhists refer to this phenomenon as "interbeing." How far, we must ask, would Hubble have gotten in astronomy had not Galileo first invented the telescope? Would Descartes' philosophies have ever come into being without the teachings of Socrates, Plato and Aristotle to provide him with a foundation? Would the Beatles have ever existed had it not been for those first primitive tribal songs and dances around some long forgotten campfire?

How did humanity reach a point where we now deem it perfectly acceptable to claim credit for what we produce, and even go so far as to charge others money to access it? What events in our history caused us to move away from collective sharing to such a self-serving approach? Once again we must peer into the mists of the past to seek our answers.

THE HISTORY OF COMMUNICATION AND ITS EFFECT ON HUMAN CONSCIOUSNESS

Many thousands of years ago, long before the invention of writing, our ancestors shared their understanding of the world through oral communication. Tribal elders and shamans gathered around campfires and told stories to wide-eyed children, who then passed that wisdom from one generation to the next. While the story details may have changed on occasion because the storytellers liked to keep things entertaining, the recipients knew the message was the point of the story. This process differs greatly from modern teaching, where facts are cherished and students are expected to focus on and memorize the details.

The storytellers of old were wisdom keepers, not instructors of fact. Neither can tribal members be viewed as students who simply received information and didn't help create it. The stories being told were all about the exploits and foibles of various tribe members, so the listeners were living contributors *to* as well as recipients *of* their ongoing compilation of human wisdom.

When a splinter group migrated somewhere new, the tales they told around their own campfires evolved over time into a different set of stories more applicable to their new environment. Still, tales from the old tribe would likely have remained part of their heritage, though the details may have changed greatly though retelling over the years. This explains in part why historians have uncovered hundreds of different mythologies across dozens of cultures that carry many common mythological threads. The key to understanding oral traditions, then, is to realize the stories themselves were constantly evolving. No one claimed authorship of these stories and none of the details were deemed to be absolute truth. The underlying message, *not* the details, was the purpose behind all oral communication. At its heart, the intent of storytelling was to unite a specific group of people around a shared worldview so they could successfully function as a community. (Note that "community" and "communication" both spring from the root "to commune.")

Historically, it was humanity's free distribution of information—along with an open sharing of innovative ideas—that enabled our early ancestors to evolve over hundreds of thousands of years. Sharing wisdom aided our progress and instilled in us community and direction. The notion of individual ownership of a story would have been alien to the earliest humans, because to them community was everything and awareness of the self as a distinct individual was only a dim realization. Their existence was defined in terms of their relationships with their gods, the Earth, the stars and other living creatures, as well as with each other. At that stage in human evolution people were too busy surviving and contextualizing themselves in relationship to the larger world to reflect upon the nature of themselves as individuals.

Oral communication sustained humanity for eons in the same way as did bartering, until the earliest forms of writing emerged on the scene sometime around 4000 BCE.[25] Not coincidentally, that was approximately the same time humanity first began using shells and other items to represent wealth. Clearly, some shift was occurring in human consciousness that inspired people to take their

---

25   Steven Roger Fisher, *A History of Writing*, Reaktion Books Ltd., 2001.

mental constructs and convert them into formalized (material) representations that could then be physically exchanged with other people. Over the next several thousand years, what had begun as loosely woven oral communications—concurrent with the loose social bartering of human goods and services—gradually morphed into both the far more scholarly, detailed and solidified printed word as well as the more mathematical formulation of money we understand and utilize today.

At the present time we are entering a third major shift in our communication methods, since the printed page as primary teaching tool is just now giving way to the more highly interactive, multi-sensory communication processes of the modern digital age. Money, too, is shifting rapidly away from its purely coin and paper forms to a much looser digital format, more abstract and less bound by prior physical constraints.

It's crucial for us to recognize both the strengths and the weaknesses inherent in each of these three methods of communication if we are to grasp their impact on human evolution. We must therefore ask ourselves what effect each of these shifts may have had (or will have) on the development of the collective human psyche, and vice versa.

We've already noted that the oral tradition encouraged community building and interactivity. The pool of human knowledge grew steadily based on new experiences, and the messages in the stories were a fluid blend of both practical wisdom and evolving social values. Whenever people relocated, they told different stories to enhance their ability to survive in their new environment. If over time their old stories (say a tale about how a tribesman had bravely slain a lion) lost relevance (because lions did not exist in the new locale), certain stories would be forgotten or adulterated over time. Whole cultures were thus born out of the different stories told by people to support their survival in each unique environment. Oral communication was ever a social experience, one that served to unite humans around a shared worldview.

The invention of writing changed all that. For the first time, humanity was able to "fix" onto a tablet or scroll the specific details of any given story. While permanently fixing language onto a surface enabled the various cultures to create a richer, more detailed and longer lasting record of their history, it also caused many individuals to erroneously assume that if someone had taken the time to permanently "fix" those words onto a surface, they must be true, and therefore could not be questioned.

Even today, certain fundamentalist Christian sects teach their adherents that the gospels of the New Testament contain the unvarnished truth about Jesus' life and works. In truth, most scholars believe the gospels were written between A.D. 65 and 110, many years after Jesus' death, and were anonymously compiled from stories that had previously been orally transmitted (therefore subject to embellishment and/or changes) before they were affixed to the page. In the last century alone archeologists have uncovered dozens of other gospels written around those same time periods. Some were recorded even earlier than the four gospels approved by the Council of Nicaea for inclusion in the first official biblical text, which itself was compiled in 397 A.D.

The gospels of Thomas, Judas and Mary, to name but a few, brim with information about Jesus' life that differs greatly from the stories in the modern Bible. They also offer alternative interpretations of Jesus' teachings. While there is no scientific or historical reason to reject *any* works that might open a new window onto the richness and fullness of Jesus' life story, these new books are denounced as heresy by Christian fundamentalists, many of who remain steeped in the print era consciousness that is marked by the worship of "the word" as immutable truth. Not surprisingly, people holding that worldview also consider money the most important "resource" to obtain. It's a worldview that cherishes the *abstraction* as it has been manifested in a representational form, rather than views *reality* as the thing to be explored and cherished.

The belief that "the word" *must* be inerrant and therefore *must* be worshipped sprang from the respect our ancestors paid to the emerging minority class of literate "experts." It was assumed such individuals had investigated their subjects in depth and recorded their factual findings to teach the masses. That such people might be capable of errors, deliberate omissions or even the imposition of their personal biases was not as apparent in ancient times as it may be today, where literacy is far more common and people can do their own research if they choose.

What's apparent is that the invention of writing caused humanity to split into two new classes of people—the literate, who became the gatekeepers and disseminators of a tightly controlled body of information; and the peasants, who were forced into a childlike state of dependence on the so-called experts due to their illiteracy. Before the written word, anyone who wasn't deaf or mute was free to repeat any story he'd overheard. Once writing became popular, however, only those with the power to read were able to transmit a story in all its richness and colorful detail. Respect for the wisdom of shamans and tribal elders dimmed as hierarchical religious institutions sprang up around the need to protect and preserve the sacred integrity of "the word."

With the emergence of religious experts who then became the instructors, the campfire stories of the wisdom keepers, the dialogues of philosophers like Socrates and Plato and public challenges to the existing social order by spiritual teachers like Krishna, Buddha and Jesus eventually gave way to this highly one-way form of communication. If a controversy arose as to what was true and what was potentially untrue, the dominant power structure of the time—which in most nations became the Catholic Church—settled all questions by determining which work adhered most closely to their previously accepted dogma. These powerful, literate factions coerced the mainly illiterate public into accepting their decisions by banning all disapproved works from circulation. Death quickly became the penalty for circulating banned material or creating new works that defied the approved written teachings. We still see the residue of this oppressive and intellectually condescending policy in modern China, where Internet access is tightly controlled and monitored by the government; and in North Korea, where the punishment for accessing the Internet is death.

It didn't take long for religious institutions to discover they could wield political power as well as spiritual dominion over their followers. By controlling the flow of information they held the power to dictate what the peasants would believe about the world. That empowered them to turn the people against even their own emperors or kings in the name of God, particularly if the king or emperor angered the Church hierarchy. Sooner or later, the ruler of virtually every kingdom was forced to forge an economic alliance with one spiritual faith or another to protect himself from the risk of religious insurgency. Hundreds of thousands (perhaps millions) of wisdom keepers—particularly the shamans, spiritual leaders and elder tribeswomen to whom people had historically turned whenever they needed assistance or information—were condemned as heretics and crucified or burned at the stake. That horribly inhumane chapter of human history, the crescendo of which was apparent in the brutality of the Spanish Inquisition, literally forced our reluctant transformation from an oral culture into one that worshipped printed information. What was lost during the process was a vast amount of human information that had been painstakingly passed down through generations. Some of it has been lost forever; some of it we're only just beginning to recover, understand and appreciate today.

It was their observation of the dangers inherent in mixing church and state that led the founding fathers of the United States to insist on separation in the new republic. They understood that any religion's agenda—to protect and preserve the "words" of its God(s) against all heresies—did not necessarily coincide with the evolving values of a free and democratic society, and that it was dangerous to grant a religion the power to restrict the flow of information or set rules for those who were not its willing believers.

Humanity's subjugation of its own sense of reason to the infallibility of the written word continues today. Modern schoolteachers impart to their students data compiled by the so-called experts. Students are then expected to regurgitate it, unaltered if possible, onto a test paper to be viewed as "successfully" educated. Some-where along the way critical thinking and the joy of stamping our own individual imprint onto the collective wisdom of humanity was shunted aside by a growing obsession to transmit—as inerrant-ly as possible—the word.

On a higher note, the invention of writing birthed our embrace of the right to privacy and fostered a more distinct sense of the individual as a unique and complex person, one worthy of love and respect simply by virtue of *being* human. While in the era of the oral tradition choosing solitude or viewing oneself as sepa-rate from the tribe had been looked upon with suspicion or even considered a sign of mental illness, during the print era solitude became a mark of intelligence. People preferred to sit alone and read so they could absorb information without having to deal with the confusion caused by external sensory stimuli. Later, once fic-tion came into vogue, readers learned to lose themselves in a story and to empathize more deeply with the rich interior lives of other people by placing themselves in circumstances far beyond their limited life experiences. It then became obvious to many that dif-ferent experiences made for vastly different ways of looking at life. The notion of an individual perspective on reality and the realiza-tion that there was some validity to every person's singular point of view began to emerge.

Unfortunately, readers rarely had the opportunity to ques-tion written material or discuss their competing worldview with a book's author. What had, during the oral era, been an intimate exchange and shared agreement between storyteller and audience became, during the print era, a formalized and far more distant teacher/pupil arrangement. Indeed, the very idea of a "separate creator God" who no longer mingled with the characters of his creation may have been born out of our transformation from a socially intimate, oral community to a peasant class who received "the word" from an on-high expert instructor. This worldview also coincides with our meek acceptance of physical money as an omnipotent means of controlling our collective creative exchange.

During the earlier oral era, goddess figures were revered as highly as were male gods and all deities were viewed as omnipresent—alive in all things and participatory in the lives of all people. Once writing replaced the oral tradition, however, God became an isolated, disembodied entity who existed somewhere "out there." While God occasionally stepped forward to dictate some refined expression of "the word" to a chosen individual or two, He just as swiftly retreated to His heavenly domain to await humanity's dutiful submission to those newly delivered teachings. This new God was wholly male (as were virtually all the literate experts of the earliest print era), so it's not surprising He possessed the masculine trait of aggression, demanded respect and felt a need to maintain dominion over all others. Instead of being God's beloved playmates, as they'd been in the oral era, humans became God's unruly children during the age of print. Religious believers began to view life itself as a test that measured how well they embraced God's written lesson plans, with Heaven or Hell as the eternal pass/fail mark.

THE EFFECT OF INDUSTRIALIZATION
ON THE PRINT ERA

It was only *after* the invention of the printing press that the
Church's rigid stranglehold on the flow of information began to
diminish. For hundreds of years before the printing press was invented, religious institutions were the primary educators of the
young. The Church didn't charge for the education of its disciples
but it did control the lessons being taught. Students, if they wanted a copy of a particular manuscript, were required to transcribe it
by hand, while monks created hand-illustrated copies for distribution to the various parishes. Information was still mostly free, yet it
remained largely inaccessible due to the lack of books, the general
illiteracy of the masses and the systematic elimination of anything
that challenged or opposed the Church's dogmas.

It wasn't until the merchants of mass production found a way
to automate the packaging of data that information began to cir-
culate more widely. It's not surprising then that the very first book
published was the Gutenberg Bible. For Gutenberg to enlist the
Church's support of the very invention that would eventually break
its stranglehold on information was a stroke of inspired genius. Not
coincidentally, it also marked the watershed moment when education likely began to command a price, since the advent of mass
market printed books meant people had to purchase them in order
to obtain their information.

The printing press heralded the beginning of the end of the
Dark Ages, which spanned the fall of the Roman Empire around

400 AD to the Modern Renaissance period that began in the 1400s. The so-called "darkness" of that age is often viewed as a direct reference to the Church's imperial and tight-fisted domination of the printed word, which created such an information bottleneck that it reduced most of humanity to a collective state of ignorance. The restriction of information, coupled by a general lack of literacy and the suppression of oral traditions through means of torture and murder, hobbled human advancement for centuries. While the transfer of control over information from the Church to the merchant class represented an immense opening of the information bottleneck, it also created yet another split into two different classes of people: those who could afford to buy knowledge, and those who were forced into ignorance because they didn't have money. If information was self-empowering and it took money to buy information, by default we moved to a worldview where money WAS power.

INFORMATION: A BUSINESS OR A BIRTHRIGHT?

Selling knowledge has long benefited those who can afford to buy it and those who stand to profit from its sale in the short run, but it hinders human advancement over time. Just as limiting the distribution of knowledge to those who were both literate and who unquestioningly adhered to the Church's worldview hindered the advancement of wisdom in the Dark Ages, our modern commoditization of information limits our collective capacity to achieve greater things. In the long run that limit diminishes us all.

The first caveman who discovered and harnessed the power of fire didn't hide his newfound knowledge from his peers; he shared it with the realization he was gifting to his fellow tribesman an insight that would aid them all with survival. Tool making, cave painting, hut building, crop growing—all are examples of the myriad ways mankind collectively shared its insights throughout the millennia. We can still observe this behavior today among our closest living relatives, the apes. Whenever a chimpanzee in the wild creates a new tool or learns a skill that benefits him or her, other chimps huddle close to observe and mimic the behavior until they too have mastered the technique. That's how intelligent species evolve their culture over time.

Humanity might once again take a valuable lesson from nature, which seems to intuit the importance of intraspecies cooperation. When geese fly in formation, for example, they do so out of regard for the entire flock. The strongest birds make their way to the formation's front, where they generate wind drag that enables the birds farther back to "coast" on the current created. When the geese at the front grow tired, they fall toward the back, and the more rested birds come forward to take their place. None has the power to purchase the most comfortable spot in the formation for the duration of the journey. Nor are the poorer or weaker birds sent to the front to suffer consistent hardship for the benefit of wealthier, stronger birds. Their system resets itself constantly to maximize the survival of as many geese as possible because on some innate level the flock knows it's in everyone's best interest if they all survive.

Contrast that practice to what we consider "success" in our free market system, where each of us struggles to attain and maintain a position of dominance and privilege relative to the less fortunate among us.

The collaborative approach can also be observed among the emperor penguins of Antarctica. The males spend months huddled against freezing storms while precariously balancing fertilized eggs on their feet. Once a male warms himself up near the center of the huddle he heads to the outer ring. The penguins that earlier bore the brunt of the cold then waddle in toward the warmth of the huddle's center. Under this system, survival is once again maximized and a new generation of penguins comes into the world.

As the old saying goes: "a house divided against itself cannot stand." Any species that pits self against self to preserve the individual's short-term survival at the long-term expense of the collective *must* go extinct unless it adapts. With the creation of public schools, libraries, public radio and television—and more recently with the emergence of the Internet—we humans have gradually been letting go of our harmful dual-class worldview that pits the knowledgeable against the ignorant and the wealthy against the impoverished. We have a long way to go, however, to ensure every human being has unfettered access to the entire library of human knowledge so all can pursue their deepest passions and exercise their greatest talents for the benefit of us all.

For example, we're still wrestling with the last vestiges of print era consciousness. During the time when control over the flow of knowledge meant power over the masses, the masses were trained to submit to the masculine authority of the keepers of the word by the very men who'd formulated "the word." The modern word keepers—our churches, institutions of higher learning, media sources and political propagandists—are not surrendering their domination lightly, any more than the storytellers of the oral era voluntarily surrendered their rights to communicate with the people. Likewise, the modern moneychangers—the banks, financial service corporations and government agencies—are not willingly releasing their grip on the distribution of resources and the flow of goods and services between people. The most recent example we have of this is the ongoing struggle for net neutrality. Businesses have tried to argue that they ought to be able to create a two-tiered system, in which companies that can afford the price can send their traffic through the web at higher speeds, while small businesses and individuals would be forced to use low speed transmissions. That system would provide large and well-capitalized businesses with an unfair competitive marketing advantage. Their Internet pages would load rapidly, while small companies would lose customers who got tired of waiting for their web pages to load. This would effectively allow big business to control the flow of information to the public. Yet as human history teaches us, granting any single group the power to control information is a very dangerous thing.

Totalitarian governments rely on the rigid control of the word. They use imprisonment, torture and murder to impose their will. Modern economic systems use our perceived dependency on money—a dependency they've actively fostered to guarantee ongoing profits—to instill in people a fear of starvation and death should they "rebel." Meanwhile our religious institutions continue to instill an even greater fear of eternal damnation in those who would challenge *their* highly controlling worldview. With the fear of God's wrath having been more strongly indoctrinated in people than the mercy and grace of love for many centuries, religious doctrine represents a significant challenge for us to overcome. It requires of us a huge investment of courage if we are to evolve beyond these self-limiting beliefs.

In many countries today, religious institutions are still inserting their worldview in the political arena, often with disastrous consequences. Terrorism, genocide, fatwas, religious wars and tribal wars are all remnant behaviors caused by either print-era or—in the case of certain tribal conflicts and genocides—oral-era consciousness. Meanwhile, many seemingly intelligent people continue, as a result of their religious indoctrination, to surrender their birthright to think critically for themselves. They don't know how to even *begin* to discover what they genuinely believe might be true, because they've been instructed for so long to embrace "the word" as something more precious and true than their personal moral compass, or their ability to feel, reason and experience life as it is in the here and now. Sadly, we've substituted an *enlightened* faith in ourselves to learn, grow and evolve for the *blind* faith that somebody else, many thousands of years ago, figured out everything we'll ever need to know and wrote it down. We've allowed a few so-called "experts" to tell us what to believe, and the whole of humanity has grown poorer for it. This doesn't mean the print era was evil or wrong or bad; it means we're outgrowing the need for a powerful few to control our minds and hearts. It's time for us all to contribute our truths and shape a new, more democratic worldview, so we can tell a more evolved story about who we are and why we think we're here.

Unlike the past transition from oral to print era, this next shift does not require bloodshed to unfold. It requires only that enough of us to decide to *ignore* the abstract controls and rules being imposed on us by the dominator structures. We already have enough new systems in place to enable us to exchange both information and human creative output *freely* and *directly* without the need for middlemen to control and dominate us, and while doing so slice a large chunk of power and wealth off the pie for themselves.

This is where the coming digital age begins to shine. It's a messy medium, to be sure, yet it enables us to connect directly with each other across inconceivable distances. It allows us to share, to express, to negotiate, to observe and think and feel. With the click of a mouse we can communicate with typhoon victims halfway around the world. We can witness people protesting injustices in nations too dangerous to visit. We can learn about other cultures, witness life in other environments, observe how other modes of thinking are changing the way people live in all kinds of places. Though at the moment we may still be reliant on the for-profit middlemen like Google and Microsoft to create, maintain and control the technologies we're using, eventually we may reach a point where the vital importance of achieving full digital freedom overwhelms the old for-profit worldview the same way the printing press overcame the Church's domination of information.

Won't it be fascinating if we eventually develop a more sophisticated form of communication that enables us to tap into the larger universal broadcast system? What if other highly intelligent species on other planets in other star systems are already communicating with each other via wireless transmissions through outer space? While stellar distances may be impossible for us to traverse in person, wireless communication may enable us to meet other species and learn about them from the comfort of our own armchairs inside our homes, the way we're now learning more about our home planet. Adding our own voices and experiences to that intelligence pool and drawing upon the collective experiences of other life forms would surely propel us into an accelerated transformation!

TALENT ISN'T A BUSINESS, IT'S A GIFT MEANT TO BE SHARED

In my opinion the rock band U2's album *Joshua Tree* was one of the greatest musical efforts ever recorded. I love it so much I've purchased it on vinyl, cassette and on CD twice, and have also attended U2 concerts to hear them play live on stage. Bono, the band's lead singer, is an amazing, loving and compassionate human being; by doing well in the music business he's empowered himself to do great deeds for the whole world. He, along with many other celebrities and philanthropists, illustrates how often those who rise to the pinnacle of material success find that acquiring more stuff is no longer enough to fulfill them. Such people wield tremendous power to help us change our system from within, but only individually and only by so much. Sadly, billions of people will never have the chance to hear U2's wonderful music because they can't afford the price of a CD, can't pay to download it from iTunes and certainly can't afford the equipment on which to listen to it.

If Bono couldn't earn another dime singing, but was granted the opportunity to freely share his music with every being across the cosmos who clamored to hear it, I suspect he'd keep on singing since that's what he loves. Don't all of us crave the opportunity to have our voices heard and our talents appreciated instead of stifled by that barrier to success we know as money?

There's nothing wrong with any of us working within the present system, since our capitalistic system is all we've got. Once we recognize its limitations, though, we begin to realize we're *all* being shortchanged—even the most successful among us, like Bono. Capitalism doesn't empower us to share our talents with everyone who desperately seeks or could appreciate our gifts. Even if Bono longed to give himself away, he's got fellow band members, roadies and a corporate recording label all lined up behind him. They expect him to help them earn money in exchange for their efforts and support. Talent, therefore, gets commoditized and packaged in ways that enable businesses to sell it. If talent can't be sold, it isn't valued in our modern economy. That doesn't mean our talent has no worth; it simply proves that money is not the most efficient method by which to match the fruits of human talent with those who might most benefit from whatever is being created. What suffers when we depend *solely* on money to provide the conduit between artisans and their potential patrons is artisanship and creativity itself. We're all poorer when we fail to value art for its own sake because we've been trained to place a price tag on its worth.

THE EXPANSION OF HUMAN INVENTION
THROUGH DISTRIBUTION OF INFORMATION

One of the most insidious consequences of continuing to deny information to those who can't afford to pay for it is that we're relegating the poorest among us to a life of future suffering by depriving them of intellectual growth. While some may profit in the short run from the selling of information, in the long run it will certainly hinder collective human progress. Even in the short run we may be denying information to the very people who have the capacity to re-imagine how we do things. They may be just the people we need to help us create the kind of work we'd love to do, or to help us find more enjoyable ways to do the jobs we have. Unfortunately, through selective selling of information (i.e. the college tuition system), we've chosen to advantage the wealthy few over the many, many gifted people among us. While it's impossible to calculate the effect of that choice on progress, the cost must be high.

Even when, against all odds, inventors do make a breakthrough, they're often thwarted by lack of available funds. The sad truth is many of our most gifted inventors died penniless, though some eventually made other people rich. Nikola Tesla, a brilliant man who invented the AC transformer, fluorescent light bulb, neon light, car ignition system and the speedometer, to name just a few, didn't have enough money to bring his inventions to market, so wealthier men reaped the benefits of his work. In that regard Tesla wasn't unusual. As many as ninety percent of all would-be inventors die broke, their work discarded or stolen by those who could afford to bring it forward (or who suppressed it) for personal gain.

Consider the tragic case of Antonio Meucci, the original inventor of the telephone. A poor and sickly man in 1860, Meucci was unable to afford the ten dollar fee the government was charging for him to renew his telephone patent. Meanwhile, Alexander Graham Bell registered his own telephone patent shortly after Meucci's sketches arrived at the Western Union laboratory where Bell worked. Meucci tried to sue Bell and requested the return of his original sketches, but his sketches had somehow strangely disappeared. Coincidence? Or a case of outright thievery driven by greed. We can only wonder how many brilliant individuals like Meucci and Tesla failed to achieve as much as they were capable of accomplishing because they lacked enough funding to support their creative endeavors. Having a wildly creative idea is no guarantee a person can get that idea in front of someone with the clout to fund the venture, since access to wealthy capitalists is notoriously hard to gain. And most inventors aren't known for their ability to wow investors. (Thomas Edison was a notable exception; he often invited investors into his lab to view his experiments.)

When creativity is suppressed due to lack of funding, the result is both a social poverty of ideas and an actual experience of poverty for creatively hampered individuals. The poor, the people most commonly deprived of creative opportunities within our economic system, begin to feel frustrated, and the crime rate eventually rises as a result of that frustration. For example, in 2008, shoplifting incidents in one county in Indiana climbed ten percent above the previous year.[26] That rise mirrors a national increase in theft as the economic recession hit the United States.[27] Just two years earlier, shoplifters were mainly young people stealing expensive items they could sell privately or auction away on eBay. By 2008, the demographics of criminals had shifted. Shoplifters were more likely to be mothers and fathers, the elderly or the homeless. They were caught stealing simple, relatively inexpensive items like food, baby formula, toothpaste and soap—necessities they could no longer afford to buy.[28]

Most people wouldn't steal or cheat if they weren't driven to it out of desperation. It's also true that resentment and rage around a social order that institutionalizes inequality can cause people to behave in ways that are contrary to their better nature. In the Bible, for example, we encounter the story of Cain, a farmer who killed his sheepherding brother Abel after God rejected Cain's sacrifice of grain in favor of Abel's offering of a newborn lamb. Why God rejected the heartfelt offering that sprang from Cain's hard labor the Bible doesn't say, but we *do* know this: Cain's resentment of God's favoritism drove him to murder Abel out of jealousy. Perhaps that explains why God allowed Cain to live and ordered others not to harm him once the horrible deed was exposed; God belatedly realized he'd treated Cain unfairly.

Fulfilled people don't resent other people's successes. People don't steal from others unless they fear a future of lack. Once we

---

26   *http://www.indy.com/posts/crimes-of-desperation*

27   Bruce Crumley, "Recession Sparks Global Shoplifting Spree," *Time* Magazine/ World, November 11, 2009.

28   *http://www.indy.com/posts/crimes-of-desperation*

know we're loveable and realize we have everything we need, the natural beauty within us finds space to flower.

Knowledge has always been a key component of human self-actualization. That's why the Internet has become so powerful in such a short time. With the dawning of the digital age, anyone with access to a computer now has access to a great deal of information that used to be accessible by only the very wealthy. That isn't a trend that'll reverse itself anytime soon. As more and more people discover the power of information and realize how much they can do with it, there'll be no turning back toward a world of ignorance.

WISDOM CAN'T FLOURISH WITHOUT HUMAN NURTURING

Our son Bryan and his best friend James have known each other since the second grade. I often refer to James as "my son by another mother." James is an amazing young man who comes from a broken home marred by difficulties with alcoholism, intermittent poverty and physical and emotional abuse. For years he's wandered in and out of our lives depending on his level of need, and has even lived with us from time to time. My husband Dave and I have done whatever we can to support James's development over the years—not because we've had any expectations of getting something in return, but because we noticed a child who was suffering and felt lovingly called to support him. James is now a bright and confident young man of twenty-four, and the love he feels for us and we for him graces us all immeasurably.

Offer a person unconditional love, and rather than continually take from you he'll likely gift you more than you could imagine. Dave and I just became "grandparents" because James and his wife Janelle recently gave birth to their first son. Being invited to share in their experience fills us with joy.

If you doubt that offering love without expectations results in receiving love beyond your expectations, look to the experiences you've had with your own parents for insight. If your parents were kind, loving and nurturing people, you likely held them in high regard and did what you could to repay them for gifting you life. If they were selfish, brutal or cold people, you likely had a more distant, socially "obligatory" bond with them, or no relationship. It isn't "blood" that binds people together then—it's the energy and love they invest in each other. Besides, if blood were all it took we'd all be effortlessly bonded, because at heart we're all the offspring of the same first humans to ever walk this Earth.

Clearly it's in our enlightened self-interest to love and support each other to the best of our abilities, and to give greater consideration to nurturing the limitless creative potential inside one another. In the long run we'd all be more successful if we freely and lovingly gave others whatever they thought they needed to become happy, creative contributors to our shared world. According to biblical scripture, Jesus died on a cross to make that point. Out of his deep love for humanity it's said he willingly surrendered his own life to demonstrate that loving each other is a better way to live than to cower in fear of the "other" or battle against him. Perhaps, after two thousand years, it's time we embraced the message behind that story.

EVOLVING THE MODERN INFORMATION SYSTEM

The great news for mankind is that our shift from the print era into the digital age is already well underway. That shift is bringing about profound changes in the way we both communicate and disseminate information. In the digital age we're experiencing a greater democratization of expertise since everyone with a computer, a search engine and a passionate level of curiosity can learn as much as he wants about virtually any topic. Information is also no longer "fixed" to pages, making it difficult to change, but can be updated instantly with a few simple keystrokes whenever we learn something new.

Consider the vast difference between how the Encyclopedia Britannica has traditionally been compiled versus the constant beehive of energy behind Wikipedia. Just a couple of decades ago it was a mark of economic status for a family to invest in a set of encyclopedias. Door-to-door salesmen convinced grownups to purchase a set on a financial installment plan to provide their children with an educational boost. My father recently confided that his parents had only managed to purchase volumes A, B and C before they could no longer afford to pay the installment bill, so his childhood access to information was limited to whatever those three letters covered. Today, any child with access to a computer can instantaneously find multiple current sources on any topic. Most schools and public libraries provide free Internet access, so information is more widely available than ever before. The musty encyclopedia, on the other hand, became outdated the moment it went into print.

Communication is no longer unidirectional (top down) but has become an interactive conversation between multiple parties. This sometimes triggers conflict as people argue in support of their own worldviews, but eventually these conversations help shape popular opinion and enable those with narrow viewpoints to develop a richer, fuller perspective on the world.

Human thinking has also gone non-linear, far different from the way it evolved in the old print era. When we read words on a page line by line, everything seems to flow neatly from everything else and the cause/effect relationship between things seems obvious. In a three-dimensional reality, however, chaos and synchronicities enter the mix. We see that events can happen simultaneously and that any given event can have multiple unrelated causes, and we begin to realize that life is more complex and messy than a simple cause/effect linear thought process implies. Every child who has ever played a computer game knows that events don't happen one after another after another in a visual 3D field, but are often simultaneous occurrences, and that it's not always easy to discern what went wrong if their character gets killed by a group of attackers.

Another major shift we're observing is in the way young people perceive the distribution of information via the Internet. When information can be transmitted at the push of a button and no physical goods must be produced to move it from place to place, it's harder for us to rationalize why we have to pay for it. Before the advent of the digital age, copyright and patent laws, which protect and privatize information for financial reasons, were established to guarantee the profitability of businesses that printed information and/or invented new products. Because products like books needed to be printed and distributed at some expense to the manufacturer, it became crucial to their creators that people pay for the right to access the information. Thus the purpose of copyright and patent laws was to punish people for using information, accessing artistic output or building on existing designs without first paying the creator for the privilege. Because books and manufactured materials were a huge part of higher education, it too for the most part grew restricted to only those who could afford it. At the same time, exposure to the performing arts, which in modern times demanded the construction of complex sets and paid actors, grew limited to those who could afford the price of a ticket. Most museums, which found themselves competing with one another and paying exorbitant prices to acquire works of art, also began to charge the public for admission, and even most national parks today charge public entrance fees to cover the costs of maintenance and oversight.

This modern demand that we pay for access to nearly everything of value has created an ongoing division between the "haves" and "have nots." It's a social carryover from the ancient split between the literate upper classes and the illiterate peasants that occurred when writing first came into vogue. The question we must ask ourselves now is whether it truly serves humanity to continue to charge each other for access to the arts, to nature and for the use of information, and whether we should continue to enforce these policies simply because that's the way we did things in the past.

If the answer is no, the next question to ask is how might we begin to loosen the stranglehold our ancient laws have had on the distribution of information and on public exposure to the arts and nature? We could start by drastically reducing time protections on patents and copyrights, so the information that they protect can move into the public domain more rapidly. To limit control over or ownership of information to perhaps no more than a two-year window would speed up humanity's ability to distribute data and benefit collectively from information in a much more meaningful way.

Providing free global Internet access, distributing low-cost computers to the poor and encouraging children to use search engines to pursue their individual passions aggressively would also be most helpful. Drawing children away from the passivity of television and into interactive electronics stimulates the brain rather than sedates it. Allowing them to follow a train of thought into the spider web that is the Internet and pursue their curiosity down whatever roads it leads them will teach them the value of critical thinking, as well as how to make more conscious choices. Encouraging them to be responsibly active on social networks like Facebook helps them learn about people from other walks of life, and teaches them to empathize with other cultures and different points of view. Expanding the perspective of the next generation in this way will become crucial as we attempt to solve our rising global problems.

Where the arts are concerned, sidewalk arts and craft exchanges can be easily arranged in any community. These events create opportunities for local children to give away their creative endeavors, from soaps to woodcarvings to paintings to hand-made jewelry. Local schools could be invited to participate, and each classroom could choose an age-appropriate product to make as a group. Such projects ground children in a real-world under-standing of how to make the items we presently take for granted. Churning butter out of milk, forming new candles from the scraps of old ones, drying local wildflowers and turning them into bou-quets—all are examples of inexpensive projects that children can readily do. Each classroom would then bring their offerings to the fair for gifting, and each child would be invited to choose one item made by another group to take home free.

Likewise school drama productions, for which government funding has been drastically reduced in recent years, could be sponsored and supported by local residents and business owners. Adults who love the arts might volunteer to produce and direct these productions, while parents who enjoy artwork or have some construction skills might volunteer to coordinate the sets and cos-tumes. Local stores could donate the needed materials, and local musicians could create and provide the music. Perhaps the school could sponsor a competition for local writers to submit their per-formance pieces. Seats for the shows would be reserved in advance, but tickets would be free to all members of the community. The number of performances would depend on the level of community interest, not on how much the people could afford to pay.

Local book exchanges are also a great way for us to more free-ly share information. So many of us buy books, read them and then allow them to gather dust on shelves or pack them away in boxes. Inviting people to come together and take whatever books they wish to read from those who have already read them allows print information to be more fully disseminated. Readers can then return the books to the pool when they're finished so others can read them. Leftover books can be donated to the local library, public shelters or schools.

When it comes to nature, it's time we placed greater attention on ourselves as natural, living beings, and likewise encouraged our children to view themselves as life forms acting within a living matrix. The best way for children to become attuned to themselves *as* nature in the flesh is for them to spend quality time *in* nature, experiencing themselves as integral parts of the larger cycle of life. If we can't convince our local governments to eliminate fees at public parks, we can at least facilitate outings to local spots where our children can romp freely in natural settings. Seasonal walks in the woods invite children to take notice of the changes happening around them, and prompt their curiosity about nature. When we take the time to encourage our children to notice the phases of the moon, the different types of plants that grow during different seasons and the migratory patterns of the local animals, it also reminds *us* that we are embedded in an awesome web of life—and that we too *are* life, not economic automatons in some corporate machine.

These are simple but meaningful ways in which we can begin to consciously practice sharing our creative abilities and the information we've communally collected without demanding financial reimbursement in exchange for access to human wisdom or the wonder triggered by artistic creativity and exposure to wild nature.

LETTING GO
OF THE "STUFF
EQUALS HAPPINESS"
WORLDVIEW

FOR YEARS WE'VE BEEN ENCOURAGED TO BELIEVE THAT THE more stuff a person consumes or owns, the more comfortable, safer and happier he'll be. It's not a hard concept for us to embrace because on a fundamental level we know it to be true. Given a choice between homelessness and having a comfortable place to sleep, most of us would choose to sleep indoors. If we have a choice between starvation and satiation, being content is preferable to feeling hungry. These are universal human preferences that relate to our survival. Since we're all living, breathing animals that need food, water and protection from the elements if we are to survive, and since the desire to survive is programmed inside every living creature before its birth, it's important we recognize and honor these imperative drives in us all. On the level of survival every living creature is the same.

Once a certain level of material comfort has been attained, however, owning more things does *not* seem to increase a person's happiness or sense of security.[29] In fact, the more possessions we own the less comfortable we may feel over time, because at some point our satisfaction with having achieved a certain status turns to fear that we might not be able to hold onto the things we possess— we might lose our present status and become someone "less than" we currently are. That's precisely the fear capitalism both stimulates and preys upon in order to facilitate the short-term growth of corporate profits. On the one hand we're constantly told we don't have enough—we *need* the bigger television screen and the brand new touch pad cell phone—and on the other hand we're told we must do whatever is necessary—be it borrow ourselves into endless debt or work so hard we don't have time for our families—to preserve and protect the stuff we've already accumulated.

THE HAPPIEST PEOPLE ON EARTH

Contrary to what we might expect, according to the World Database of Happiness, using studies that span the entire first decade of the third millennium, the happiest people on Earth don't live

---

29   Dr. Ruut Veenhoven, World Database of Happiness, Distributional Findings in Nations, Erasmus University Rotterdam, 2009.

in the United States. Surprisingly, the United States doesn't even rank among the top ten nations when it comes to general happiness. The countries that did make the list are these, in descending order: Costa Rica, Denmark, Puerto Rico, Iceland, Switzerland, Canada, Finland, Mexico, Norway and Sweden.[30] While most of these nations (the exception being Mexico) aren't struggling with high levels of poverty or crime, neither do they possess the most powerful global economic engines. At some point then, a nation's economic success no longer seems to factor into who feels happy and who reaches for Prozac to get them through the day. What, we must therefore ask ourselves, differentiates those who feel happy from all the rest of us?

INTERNALS VS. EXTERNALS

Another study conducted in 2003 by Dr. Robert A. Emmons[31] revealed that people who feel and express deep gratitude about their lives are twenty-five percent happier than most others. Grateful people express more optimism about the future, felt better about their lives and even do more exercise each week than those who focus on their problems or personal troubles. Something about gratitude, then, whatever our financial situation may be, empowers us to open our hearts more fully to the world and spread our happiness to those around us.

---

30   Ibid.

31   http://psychology.ucdavis.edu/labs/emmons/

It's also true happiness isn't maintained in a vacuum. Over the centuries the wealthiest among us have gradually been growing more aware of the suffering experienced by others in comparison to ourselves. It's one thing to read dispassionately about the effects of poverty, but quite another to deal with the graphic images of suffering and privation that are prevalent in our modern digital age. Witnessing the misery of countless others makes it harder for those who are wealthy to feel happy about their good fortune. Documentary television programs, commercials for children's charities and even feature films demand we notice how many children are dying from war, poverty, disease and malnutrition around our planet. These days it takes a conscious act of will to ignore the reality with which we're currently being confronted. We can hardly turn on the news without seeing somebody suffering, grieving or dying somewhere on Earth.

While those of us who have been blessed with much may be inclined to feel relieved that we're doing OK compared to the suffering and deprivation we observe, it's a bit more difficult for us to feel blissfully happy about our good fortune when we realize that not everyone has been as blessed as us. It's also true that the poorest among us often manage to feel grateful for things that have nothing to do with material wealth and possessions. The beauty of a budding rose, the wonder of a crimson sunset, witnessing a child climbing a tree—anyone can feel deep joy from any of these experiences, and all of them are free to the beholder.

How much harder it is to feel grateful about the things we own when what we possess is often accompanied by a fear of loss and a nagging sense of guilt that we might have more than our share.

The Buddha referred to this as the suffering of external attachment, and noted it as one of the primary causes of human unhappiness. For example, the couple that "owns" a six-bedroom, five-thousand-square-foot mansion with an infinity pool and its own private movie theater may seem like people worthy of admiration according to our capitalist way of thinking, but unbeknownst to the rest of us they may be living under the constant stress of wondering whether or not they'll be able to make their monthly mortgage payment. Perhaps this explains why so many of the world's religions exhort people to "leave behind" their worldly possessions. They're not necessarily suggesting we live in poverty because it's somehow nobler than leading a comfortable life. They're simply reminding us we need to let go of our emotional *attachments* to our material possessions, because emotional attachments bind us to our possessions out of fear of loss. They prevent us from gratefully opening our hearts to the miracle of life that's unfolding all around us. We tend to get so busy protecting our possessions that we lose touch with what matters—life itself—and miss out on the joy of loving the people, creatures and ecosystems that share our space with us.

As Jesus is reputed to have said so eloquently in a conversation about how human beings should treat each other, "Truly I say unto you, as you did it to one of the least of these, my brothers, you did it to me.'" When we consume massive quantities of "things" *because we can*, while our brothers and sisters around the world are suffering, starving or dying from the lack of basic necessities, the undeniable part of each of us that is compassionate, loving and knows itself to be inextricably interconnected to the entire web of life feels sorrow and guilt at the plight of the human race. Intuitively we know we ought to do *something* about poverty, hunger, preventable diseases, pollution, natural resource depletion and homelessness, but mainly we've been raised to accept that life isn't fair and it's just the way things are. It's easier, then, for us to shrug sadly and do nothing, because humanity's problems seem too big for any one person to manage.

Are they, though? Perhaps the root problem lies not with the immenseness of the tasks we're facing, but in the smallness and stuck-ness of our personal thinking. If, for example, we each committed ourselves to taking one small step at a time to enhance the quality of life on Earth, collectively we could rise to meet our challenges. What's needed isn't necessarily a monstrous labor-intensive effort or huge sacrifices; what's genuinely needed is a massive shift in our individual mindsets. Were each of us—or even a large minority of us—to make a thriving future for *all* life on Earth our highest priority, the entire world would begin to change today.

THE TRAGIC HISTORY OF REVOLUTION

History teaches us that whenever the distribution of wealth and power between the "haves" and the "have nots" becomes too extreme, the "have nots"—fearing for their very survival—will rise up and destroy the "haves," typically through bloodshed and a radical upheaval of the social and economic structures that favored the few over the many. We must remember—whenever starving and oppressed people are forced to choose between doing whatever they need to do to survive or blindly obeying the rules set down by a rich and powerful few, the survival drive behind life itself will take precedence over politeness or social values. We needn't go too far back in time to find well-known examples of where the suffering caused by extreme unfairness trumped society's beliefs about who deserved to have stuff and who did not.

For starters, we can turn to the guillotine-happy French revolutionists of 1789-1799, as well as the Russian Bolshevik revolutionaries of 1917. The leaders of both rebellions demanded redress for the frightful plight of their respective under classes, but their governments ignored the needs of the people. The rebels then used that lack of political will to fuel a boiling anger in the masses over the injustices created by their unfair social systems. The swelling rage of the masses, multiplied a thousand fold by their suffering, ultimately led to the wholesale massacre of both the French and Russian royal classes. Both revolutions were then followed by half-hearted attempts to redesign their economic systems in ways that included partial wealth redistribution, albeit by transferring the bulk of power and privileges to their newly created political upper classes. Neither nation, therefore, addressed the core social problems both societies faced before their revolutions—the collective belief that it was *reasonable and right* to accept a social system in which inequitable property distribution and the use of force against its own citizenry to maintain domination was inevitable; *or* one where granting favoritism to a privileged few through blood lineage, political patronage or financial cronyism was fine, even though most people would remain forever deprived of the chance to live a truly fulfilling life under that system. Interestingly enough, much of humanity embraces these same core beliefs even today. Our collective acceptance of "that's just the way things are" is a reflection of the former, while our acceptance that "life is unfair" is a reflection of the latter.

There's always a higher price to be paid for violent revolution than there is for a peaceful evolution of the social order. The uprising in Darfur (which began in 2003 and is only beginning to show signs of abating as of this writing in March 2011) has cost an estimated four hundred thousand lives and has displaced many hundreds of thousands more. The 1994 Rwandan uprising, which pitted the majority ruling Hutus against the oppressed national minority of Tutsis, led to the deaths of at least eight hundred thousand people, many of them women and children. By contrast, the destruction of the Berlin Wall and the subsequent reunification of East and West Germany in 1989 occurred without a single civilian casualty. The primary difference was that the ruling classes on both sides of the wall gave up attempting to thwart the will of the people. They recognized the futility of continuing to insist that the arbitrary distinction between East and West was just the way things were, and instead allowed change to happen.

Revolt is always painful, chaotic and destructive, while evolution tends to be beneficial, gentler and socially reconstructive. Revolution pits one group against another, creating an "us versus them" siege mentality, while evolution is creative, connective and supports growth and change for the benefit of the whole. However noble the goals of most violent revolutionaries may be, they often find themselves challenged at every turn by the survivors of the preexisting culture, unless they've managed to massacre them all.

At the same time, the citizens on whom they're forcing radical new ideas will often silently (but firmly) resist the policies their new leaders try to implement. This explains why we frequently see a reversion to the old ways whenever a government that imposed itself on a conquered people falls. While it's possible to control a person's behavior through fear and the threat of violence, we can't change the way people think or feel by applying physical force.

THE HAVES AGAINST THE HAVE NOTS

More often then not, revolutions lead to a brand new class of "haves" and a new mass group of "have nots," which speaks to the difficulty revolutions have in successfully changing an existing social paradigm. It took only a few years for the Bolsheviks in Russia, whose original aim was to uplift the impoverished masses by overthrowing the ruling elite, to morph into an equally powerful ruling elite complete with their private shops, fancy cars and luxurious seaside dachas. After a brief seventy years of military governance marked by fear and the violent suppression of dissenting opinions, they too were overthrown. Clearly, we can't presume a conquering militia will automatically create a safer, more equitable society than the one it's overthrowing. Yet despite all the suffering and drawbacks inherent in the revolutionary option, when the downtrodden or the starving feel like revolution is the only choice remaining, they *will* exercise that option. The people in power who ignored the cries of the suffering will then be forced to either surrender their right to hold power or else do battle against their own citizens. We witnessed just such populist uprisings in early 2011, when the citizens of Tunisia, Sudan, Yemen and Egypt rose to protest and/ or overthrow the authoritarian regimes that had for too long oppressed them.

Excessive wealth concentrated in the hands of a few obviously doesn't grant those few a more secure position in society than the impoverished masses around them. In truth, any sense of security the wealthy might feel in the short run is but an illusion. When wealth becomes too concentrated *and* the power to change that dynamic also gets concentrated into the hands of the wealthy, the poor are left with no choice but to strip the wealthy of their illusions and privileges in exchange for the capacity to survive. Just where that tipping point lies may vary from culture to culture, but every culture has one. The greater the dispersal of power, the more likely it is a nation's wealth can become highly concentrated without triggering a violent revolution. The more concentrated a nation's political power becomes, however, the less people are likely to feel hope that things may change in the future, so the more likely they are to rebel against an omnipotent government.

Interestingly enough, the recent concentration of wealth in the United States stands at its highest level since the formation of the nation—higher even than it was just before the Great Depression.[32] Viewed in that context, the economic recession that began in 2008 might be viewed as a harbinger of greater unrest to come if the nation doesn't gracefully choose to repair its predatory economic system, limit the power of the military/industrial complex and

---

32 http://sociology.ucsc.edu/whorulesamerica/power/wealth.html

return the power of self-determination to the people, to whom it rightfully belongs. Attempts to confuse the public by misdirecting its anger at the government rather than at the win/lose economic system will only delay the inevitable, not avoid it.

Excessive consumption of goods and services by a wealthy few always means fewer goods and services remain available to aid with the advancement of the whole. Whenever the many are shortchanged that way, the wealthy will eventually suffer the consequences of the poor's deprivation. While most nations no longer recognize the automatic superiority of a noble class through bloodlines, almost all have substituted the birth merit of family wealth for the birthrights of nobility, to the same effect. A child born to a wealthy family now has all the rights and privileges previously granted to children of the noble class. A child born into poverty likewise suffers all the misery and deprivation of a child once born to peasants, slaves, serfs or untouchables. While we like to believe capitalism allows for greater mobility between classes than did the old peerage system, we must ask ourselves which child is more *likely* to gain the necessary tools to succeed, to fulfill his or her life's destiny and to contribute something of value to our world—a child born into exceptional wealth, or a child born into crushing poverty?

That exceptions can be found does not disprove the rule. There are always exceptions to every situation, but in general we must acknowledge that under our current system the children of the poor will most likely grow up to be poor. Already they fill our jails, our broken public schools, our homeless shelters and our army barracks. They are our "throw away" children, the expendable ones we ignore or send off to die for the rest of us because we've convinced ourselves we can afford to lose them.

For every wealthy young man who avoided the draft during the Vietnam War by using educational deferments, parental connections and the like, some inner-city mother's son was called to take his place. Quite a lot of them died. Meanwhile the children of the wealthy, men like President George H.W. Bush, used their powerful family connections to avoid combat duty by getting assigned to units like the Texas Air National Guard. Vice President Dick Cheney's family pulled their own set of political strings to get him both student and family-related draft deferments. President Bill Clinton not only received student deferments (which were reserved for those who could afford to pay college tuition) but when his student deferments were canceled he was able to postpone his physical exam for over ten months (compared to an average wait of about two months). He was also permitted to enroll in the Reserve Officer Training Corps to avoid combat, despite being ineligible for ROTC at that time. While we can understand why any young man might feel loath to risk his life in an unpopular foreign war, the fact remains that as that war dragged on, only those men who had family money and powerful connections were able to avoid the draft.

ADDRESSING THE CHALLENGE

An important question to ask ourselves is this: Is it possible we could eliminate the suffering caused by poverty in the span of a single lifetime? Most people seem as yet unwilling to surrender their emotional attachment to individual property ownership, though that would be the simplest (albeit most radical) solution to the problem of unfair asset distribution. If we all willingly agreed to share everything we have out of love for each other, and took for ourselves only those things we needed to meet our daily needs, hone our talents or fulfill our collective dreams for a better world, society would likely function much better and accomplish much more than it's managed to do thus far. That shift, though, requires us to let go of our fear of not having enough by recognizing the astounding amount of life support that already exists all around us. Humanity doesn't really have a poverty problem; what we *do* have is a lack of social willpower to distribute our excess goods more equably. What holds us back from becoming more generous—even though most of us know that giving to others feels better than does hoarding or being selfish—is the anxiety-provoking oppressiveness of the scarcity system under which we've all been operating. In a capitalist economy, feelings of scarcity are deliberately manufactured to foster anxiety and encourage people to spend more on what they fear won't be there tomorrow. That's why we see advertisements promising, "Only while supplies last," or "just ten available at this price." Money is also deliberately kept scarce to keep people striving to earn it. That reduces overhead labor costs for the corporate profiteers. Last but not least, success is kept scarce, yet success is held up as the ultimate brass ring so people will keep on struggling to attain it. The fact is most of us are kept so busy trying to "get there" that we don't have time to notice that the people all around us are struggling too.

For as long as we've embraced the concept of property own-ership (as in "me" and "mine"), it seems the poor have been with us. Perhaps they'll be here to point to the errors of our ways until we choose to change our beliefs. At the very least, if we began to exercise greater self-discipline and conscious restraint around our personal consumption choices, we might begin to notice the difference between the life-affirming drive for comfort and the fear-based drive of greed.

No one can determine how much another person needs to feel contented. We can, however, cease valuing unfettered consumption and stop celebrating the worth of designer labels. Why is a handbag with a couple of initials on it worth one hundred times a handbag that doesn't have them? Are the materials used to construct the designer bag of such high quality that it will last a hundred times longer than a regular purse would last, or are we simply paying an outrageous amount for "bragging rights" to carry around those let-ters, so others will perceive us as rich and successful?

Thankfully the global recession that began in 2008 has caused people to begin reassessing the importance of conspicu-ous consumption. Less is gradually becoming the sexy new "more." Meanwhile books on how to simplify our lives and make do with fewer possessions are moving into the general public's awareness. We're finally beginning to reduce our attachment to material pos-sessions by practicing voluntary simplicity, and as a result many are rediscovering the deep peace that comes from no longer being afraid of losing our stuff.

We might also begin to lessen our attachment to stuff by setting up local sharing centers where neighbors could offer their creative wisdom to others, along with free neighborhood donation/recycling warehouses (co-opting some of the abandoned or vacant commercial space that seems to be present in every town these days) where we could easily give away things we no longer need to those who could use them. We could also focus on setting up local, organic neighborhood gardens on empty parcels of land, where everyone could share in the harvest bounty. Last but not least, we could concentrate on expressing our humanity in ways that can't be bought or sold, through shared values like friendship, love, compassion, kindness, generosity, patience and peacefulness.

To cease measuring each other's worth (as well as our own) based on how much "stuff" we possess, and to instead discover for ourselves how generous and wonderful we each can be if given half a chance would be a powerful step for us all in the right direction.

7
FOSTERING
ENLIGHTENED
SELF-INTEREST

In 2009 my hometown of Camarillo, California experienced an alarming increase in foreclosures that turned many unfortunate families into the streets. As the number of homeless escalated and people noticed them sleeping in cars or local parks, the homeowners began to express some safety concerns. Complaints rose around numerous parked cars lining the streets at night and about the health risks of improper human waste disposal. Our city council acted on those complaints by passing an ordinance making it illegal for people to sleep in their cars or in any public space within the city. By catering to the homeowner's complaints, my city proved itself to be less concerned with the welfare of the suffering than it was about the fears of those who were financially OK. Our elected officials pushed the problem of homelessness out from under the immediate view of the locals, but where did it go?

It moved to our riverbanks, the local flood plain and the rugged swatches of chaparral in the mountains surrounding our town. The homeless camped beneath the underpasses, on the beaches and in the Wal-Mart parking lots. During the day they now show up on our freeway off ramps and by the exit to every strip mall shopping center, holding up cardboard signs and begging passersby for spare change, work or food.

Although we support a population of nearly seventy thousand, our city provides free shelter beds for fewer than three hundred people on any given night. And we're not alone in our lack of attention to the growing plight of the homeless. In a nation where the "right to life" is considered fundamental, why don't we notice the hypocrisy of denying people the right to live because they can't afford to pay for a place to sleep? How long, we must ask, can a person survive without space in which to exist?

What we're discovering as a species is what happens when our abstract worldview falls out of alignment with our actions in the real world. We Americans, for example, love our constitutional ideals in principle, but we tend to fail to exercise them in practice. Let's at least be honest with ourselves and admit that these days we're placing property values, corporate profits and our desire to avoid dealing with the consequences of our selfish economic policies above the fundamental human values we supposedly hold so dear.

Although many people have likely never given it too much thought, the notion that we each must pay for what we need to survive is an entirely human construct, one that benefits just a few at the expense of the rest of us. The concept has no foundation in natural law, nor is there any moral justification for the suffering that arises from its self-infliction. By virtue of being children of Earth we *all* deserve to live here and share in our planet's generous bounty. Every one of us has an Earth-granted birthright to occupy a bit of natural space and to go about the business of thriving freely. That we've been socially precluded from doing so because human rules and regulations inform us we're not *allowed* to do so isn't our planet's fault. It's ours. It's as if we've all been lobotomized into meekly supporting an unfair system we didn't design and can see isn't working for most of us.

Sure, we support our system in principle by saying things like, "America, love it or leave it!" In private, though, many of us strive to get around the system we publicly claim to love so much. We do that by paying as little in income taxes as we can, taking advantage of every legal loophole we can find, and abusing the system by gaming it in every conceivable way. It's important for us to realize that people who genuinely love their system don't try to game it; they work tirelessly to support its continuance. Yet as many as twenty percent of us regularly pad our tax deductions and/or underreport our incomes[33] to the IRS. An additional 7.3 million of us are currently in prison, on parole or on probation for committing crimes against the system.[34] On top of that, some forty percent of us who

---

33   Andrew Johns and Joel Slemrod, "The Distribution of Income Tax Noncompliance," November 12, 2008 Study. http://graphics8.nytimes.com/images/2010/04/13/business/Tax_Noncompliance.pdf

34   CNN/Justice, 7.3 Million in U.S. Prison System in '07, March 2, 2009.

are eligible to participate don't even bother to vote in our presidential elections.[35] Those statistics speak volumes about the nature of our commitment to what we've created.

Looking at the challenges humanity is facing, examining the flaws in our existing systems and then deciding to *do* something about them is hard work; it's much easier to yawn, turn on a football game, pop open a beer and pretend that nothing is wrong...at least until the foreclosure notice gets posted on *our* door.

THE HISTORY AND IMPACTS OF PROPERTY OWNERSHIP

Planet Earth has been a fine hostess for life. As long as we're willing to cooperate with her, she'll provide more than enough bounty to support the diverse needs of the many life forms to which she's given birth. It's an obvious truth because if the resources necessary to support us didn't exist we wouldn't be here now. The ecosystem of which we're a part would kill us and we'd go extinct. That it hasn't happened yet is less a credit to our own cleverness than it is to the incredible depth of resources Earth has to offer.

For millions of years now the majority of Earth's creatures have engaged in complex cooperative and feedback arrangements when it comes to sharing her bounty—with the single notable exception of modern humans. Humanity stands out as the only species that demands an immediate return from another being for the right

35   Infoplease, National Voter Turnout in Federal Elections, 1960-2008.

to use what our planet provides us for free. Each winter when the bears go off to hibernate in caves, they slumber peacefully without worrying about who "owns" the particular cave they've chosen. Nor do fish block the oceanic rights of way for each other, demanding usage fees in order to pass. Animals grasp instinctively that the freedom to come and go, to eat and sleep and drink what one needs to survive, is a natural right that's been granted to all Earth's creatures. When an imbalance *does* occur, say when a population of ground squirrels grows too large for the surrounding grassland to sustain it, predators will arrive to thin the population and rebalance the system so that *all* its inhabitants may thrive—*including* the squirrels.

The truth is, we're each just temporary houseguests within our planet's large and ancient living matrix. And the fact that the whole complex web of life is a gift to all of us from our *planet*— and not our personal property—is something humanity seems to have forgotten. In these times of environmental upheaval, species extinction and atmospheric distress, it is a fact well worth remembering again.

Human beings haven't always believed in the importance of property ownership. Early hunter-gatherer societies tended to migrate along with their sources of food, which made more sense than waiting around for their food to come to them. Binding themselves to a plot of land would have only made life more difficult. It wasn't until the emergence of the great agrarian societies, which began some ten thousand to eleven thousand years ago, that people discovered the pleasure of settling down in a single spot. Only after humans began to farm could they let go of the need to wander afar in search of their daily meals. They realized then they could at last build more permanent and comfortable structures near their fields, so the concept of housing was born. As houses became more and more common over time, it seemed only fair for the community to acknowledge that if a family went to all the trouble of constructing a house, tilling and planting the surrounding soil and putting down roots in the area, they had earned the right to remain with what they'd built.

Fast forward some ten thousand years later and what we encounter today is a patchwork quilt of individual property lines that literally span the globe. Where just a few centuries ago people could almost always find a slice of unsettled space they could claim as home, today virtually no land exists anywhere on Earth that hasn't already been claimed by a person, private organization or government entity. Fragile ecosystems have been carved up and parceled out without regard to the delicate living relationships they support, and in many cases individuals have been granted the right to do whatever damage they've a mind to cause because the land is considered theirs. We've established only the meekest of laws to protect the environment against the most destructively selfish behaviors.

Rivers and streams have been dammed and diverted for the benefit of a few, while people and animals living downstream must fight for the right to access their natural flows. Delicate wildlife habitats have been plowed over, fenced off or turned under and preexisting plant and animal residents have been exterminated in the name of progress.

This piecemeal division of our planet has led to the wholesale destruction of natural resources and a gradual degradation of the environment. Ironically, while these days most everyone says they want to live on a clean and healthy planet, the majority of us still seem unwilling to embrace what that means: that collectively we'll need to adhere to whatever policies are deemed necessary to protect this planet across *all* property boundaries, regardless of profit motives, personal ownership rights and selfish desires.

If one nation chooses to cut its carbon emissions by twenty percent but another increases its emissions by fifty percent, the net effect on our planet's health will be negative. Unfortunately, while we didn't need to coordinate our efforts to inflict great damage on our environment, we *will* be required to coordinate a serious global human effort to reverse that process and begin to make a lasting positive impact. One nation's thrown-away and forgotten waste, we need to keep in mind, becomes another country's acid rain.

RELEASING OUR BELIEFS AROUND POSSESSIONS

Belief in the "possession" of anything, as we've already explored, is a purely human concept. The irony is we've all become slaves to the concept of property ownership without realizing we've gained very few benefits as a result of it. We each may cling tenaciously to our little slice of Earth (be it rented or purchased) but we hold little or no power to impact the way the behavior of others affects our soil quality, our water supply, the cleanliness of our air and the flow of nature through and within our space. What we're only now beginning to realize is that space devoid of life's necessities is space that we can't use. Once we embrace the fact that our home planet is the *only* space in the vastness of the known universe that we can say with any certainty has the ability to sustain us, honoring it and caring for it takes on a whole new meaning.

The plain fact is we can't even state with certainty that we "own" our physical bodies. While it's true our individual awareness occupies our body for a time, we can't command our livers to stop working, our lungs to cease breathing or our hearts to stop beating inside us. If we can't even control our body's most basic functions, how can we possibly imagine we own it? There's a universe of activity going on inside each of us—entire worlds of bacteria and cells and complex DNA factories and the like—to which we have no access and over which we have zero managerial control. You may be surprised to note that of the hundred trillion or so cells that make up your human body, some seventy trillion of them are not even human! They belong to all the other living organisms that are hitching a ride on your life form, and without which you wouldn't be able to survive.

What hubris it is, then, to presume we *own* anything. Ownership implies full power over something. And even though our minds can suggest the general direction in which our bodies should travel, our bodies don't always comply with those mental requests. Ever try to make a three-point shot, or run a mile in under four minutes? Sometimes we manage to coordinate our thoughts and bodies well enough to accomplish our objectives, while other times our bodies just say "no!" As for most of what's happening inside us, it's being done *for* us, not *by* us, whether we agree with what's happening inside of us or not.

We may have the power to choose the substances we put into our bodies, but if our bodies don't like our decisions they're free to reject them. Eat too much food and your body may vomit it out. Take too many drugs or drink too much and your body may respond by making you feel very ill. Push your body past its limits and your muscles will spasm in pain to discourage more movement. Our taste buds and stomachs rebel against noxious foods, our pores secrete excess toxins and our colons eject any items they find indigestible. If we still persist in putting things into our bodies that they don't like and can't tolerate, they'll outright die on us. Clearly, if we insist on forcing a battle of wills between our body and our mind, the mind is the party most likely to lose that war. Mind over matter is but a mental delusion, created by mind. Try flying sometime or manifesting a pile of gold out of thin air if you doubt it. For us to accomplish *anything* in this world physically, our minds must *cooperate* with our bodies as well as respect and honor their limits and needs.

When our bodies die, our atoms melt back into the planetary matrix from which they emerged to become part of something else, no matter how hard we may try to preserve what's left of ourselves. Though it may take hundreds of thousands of years, even the most expensive lead-lined coffin will eventually break down in the molten heat of Earth's mantle, and the body it contains will eventually return to the whole. At best, then, we might say our personal consciousness holds a long-term lease on the atoms of our body through a mutually cooperative arrangement; although even that's not exact since none of us can be sure we'll live a *long* life. The truth is, we don't even *possess* a life! To possess something implies we can lose it, that what we possess is something distinct from what we are. However, when we ask ourselves the question, "Who am I if I'm no longer alive?"—we come to the realization that life and "me" are not two separate parties, they're one and the same. Put more simply, we *are* life—the One, eternal field of life that's going about the playful business of eternally differentiating, exploring and experiencing itself by creating and occupying an infinite variety of temporary forms. This field of infinite/eternal life is what some of us refer to as God.

We don't really know what happens to our personal sense of awareness when we die. We've imagined some things about it, we've established religions that have told us what to believe and we've birthed hopes and have certainly developed a few fears around that ultimate mystery, but none of us truly *know*. The universe has designed it that way for its own reasons—reasons we aren't privy to. Perhaps it's to help us stay focused, collaborative and in service to *all* of life right here and now, instead of distracted by thoughts of what's going to happen next. If so, it's a clear message for us to pay closer attention to what's happening here and let tomorrow take care of itself.

THE TROUBLE WITH OWNERSHIP CONCEPTS

The trouble with abstract concepts like property ownership is that they train us to reduce reality to a *belief* about what's real, instead of encouraging us to *see* reality. Our ideological worldviews mask the truth and make it difficult for us to function in the most efficient and loving ways as we move through life. For example, let's take the abstract concept of a homeless person. In our rather delusional society, a homeless person is defined as someone who has no place to live; in other words, someone who can't pay for a space in which to exist.

Yet that homeless person *does* exist, and he or she *is* living someplace. That place may be under the freeway, in a park or over a street grate in your city; but it exists just as surely as that person exists. By reducing that person to an abstract concept—i.e. homeless person—we miss what's real and right there in front of us. What's *real* is that we're encountering a living human being, perhaps shivering, suffering and hungry, tired or ill. Any of those challenges are small enough to be addressed by another person, so we could assist that individual if we stopped and took the time. Homelessness, on the other hand, is a much larger and more abstract challenge, not something most of us have the power to solve. So we shake our heads in dismay and walk on past, feeling guilty for not helping, sorry for the other person and perhaps even a bit irritated that they interfered with what had been a personally happy day before they appeared. Too often we'd rather they not show up at all, shoving their homelessness in our faces and upending our worldview of how things are *supposed* to look. We might even start to blame them for their very existence. Perhaps the little voice in our head makes up a story about them: they must be an alcoholic, or crazy, or maybe they're on parole for some terrible crime.

That's the danger behind conceptual thinking. It enables us to fictionalize what's going on all around us so we can remain mentally detached from all the reality we observe.

In *reality*, a homeless person is someone who hasn't been successful in the ownership-society game humanity has constructed. This holds true for the poor, the imprisoned, the financially duped, the ignorant and the mentally ill among us. Since in *reality* there seem to be quite a large number of homeless, sick, imprisoned and impoverished people, perhaps the problem isn't with those people at all. Perhaps the problem lies in the larger narrative itself.

The *reality* of the daily suffering we encounter trumps our beliefs about the perfection of the system we've created, whether we accept that truth as our own worldview or not. As much as we may wish to cling to our mental delusions about the wonders of our capitalistic system, we can't entirely ignore the suffering it causes. Americans who consider themselves patriotic are often quoted saying silly things like, "We live in the greatest country in the world, and if you don't like it you're free to go somewhere else." Not only is it offensive to other nations for us to proclaim ourselves the greatest country in the world (whatever *that* means!), most of us are also *not* free to move wherever we'd like if we're unhappy. There are immigration rules, work restrictions, land and language barriers and financial considerations built into the larger global system that inhibit our movements, and all of us know it. Yet people say such things so they can dismiss the ideas of those who wish to criticize the system constructively.

A person who loves his country doesn't willfully blind himself to its flaws or its need for improvement. He acknowledges them, because his aim is to do whatever he can to improve his nation's health. The more we deny that those flaws exist, the greater the suffering we'll meet through poverty, crime, mental illness and homelessness. Those are all flaming symptoms of the systemic flaws we've pretended not to notice, problems caused by human exploitation, selfishness, callousness, jealousy, greed and fear. All are an outgrowth of property ownership attitudes. They begin with the attitude of "I want" and end with us doing whatever it takes to seize what we desire.

WHAT MOVES OF ITS OWN FREE WILL CAN'T BE POSSESSED

The oak tree which stands on your property will grow, put forth leaves and nuts and eventually die without concerning itself with your views about possession. Perhaps your property will be bought and sold several times during the tree's lifecycle, none of which will affect the tree unless one of the property owners chops it down. You can't insist that "your" tree put out more leaves or nuts on your behalf if the conditions to do so aren't right, no matter how possessive you may feel. The tree will also return to the Earth when it dies. No document stating you own it can force it to stay where you'd like it to be once its time to die is upon it. In *reality*, the only life forms that modify their behavior to conform to abstract ownership claims based on paper declarations are humans. Through the concept of possession we've inadvertently superimposed a set of mental cages onto nature's living matrix, and have allowed those cages to capture and contain us all.

The land on which our houses sit—the land we believe we own—is free to do whatever it pleases, whenever it feels the urge. Just ask the victims of Hurricane Katrina. Land erupts, undulates, quakes and floods every day, yet we still believe we possess it because some contract tells us so. If the land does shift beneath us or our home is destroyed by a natural disaster, we may even feel the world has betrayed us because it violated our contract and upended our world, when in *reality* the world was just being the world. The fault was with our delusional belief that we held ownership over the world, and that ownership gave us the power to control it.

Recently designed GPS systems are now being used to mark human property lines. They're proving how the land shifts over time, sometimes by many feet in a single earthquake. Land that once cradled a mighty ocean now makes up much of the southwestern United States. In other locations tropical rainforests have morphed into hot, dry plains, and once-fertile valleys are now nearly lifeless deserts. Some of these changes are natural, occurring over time. Humans—for good or ill—have triggered others. Given that we have the capacity to either heal or destroy our environment, perhaps it's time for us to shift our views around property ownership to a new worldview that honors stewardship instead. Ownership, which is a me-based worldview, mentally conveys upon individuals the right to exploit Earth's natural resources for personal gain. Stewardship on the other hand, which is an ours-based worldview, conveys upon humanity the responsibility to support *all* the life forms with whom we share this sacred home, planet Earth.

WHEN DISASTER STRIKES

As difficult as it is for us to bear the suffering caused by natural disasters, it's even harder when we learn a disaster was mainly manmade. In a June 2006 report on the Hurricane Katrina disaster in New Orleans, the U.S. Army Corps of Engineers admitted that faulty design specifications, incomplete construction and substandard construction of certain levee segments contributed to the damage done to the city.[36] A report released by the American Society of Civil Engineers in June of the following year acknowledged that two-thirds of the flooding in the city could have been avoided if the levees had been properly constructed.[37] Similarly, in the aftermath of a 7.9 magnitude earthquake that struck Sichuan, China in May of 2008, thousands of children reportedly died when their schools collapsed because of shoddy construction. Likewise in Haiti in January of 2010, an earthquake with a 7.0 magnitude claimed well over two hundred thousand human lives. But earthquakes don't kill people; buildings do. Those deaths were not the

36   Jennifer Hoar, "Katrina Report Blames Levees," CBS News/US, June 1, 2006.

37   American Society of Civil Engineers, "The New Orleans Hurricane Protection Systems, What Went Wrong and Why," June 1, 2007.

fault of nature, they were caused by poverty, greed and cost-cutting efforts designed to generate corporate profits from government building contracts. When businesses place profits and cost-saving measures ahead of public safety, people die.

We humans hold less power over the vagaries of nature than we do over the greedy special interests that exploit it for personal gain. Our belief in our dominion over nature is an illusion—one each of us hopes will survive long enough that we make it through life unscathed by the forces of nature that exist out there. This false belief system sets up a kind of land lottery when it comes to property ownership. Some of us get lucky and our land and homes stay right where we expect them to be, intact for our human lifetimes. Others find themselves suddenly deprived of their land and/or the use of their homes after natural disasters. A single powerful earthquake that rocked central Italy in April 2009 killed more than ninety people, injured thousands and left forty thousand others without a roof over their heads.[38] While we might feel sorry for those who get upended by nature's fury, we often treat disasters like they're not our problem. The victims are the unlucky few who lost the land lottery, having chanced to live in the wrong place at the wrong moment in history. Lucky for us; unfortunate for them. Perhaps they can buy another ticket and try again.

Interestingly enough, when we listen to survivors of a natural disaster being interviewed by the news media, they'll often say how grateful they feel to be alive. They rejoice to learn their family members are unhurt, and acknowledge that their possessions were only things and can be replaced. What we so often term misfortune,

---

38   Fox News/World, "Powerful Earthquake in Italy Kills at Least 92," April 6, 2009.

then, clearly has the power to enlighten us as to the truth about our possessions: they don't really belong to us at all, but instead are on loan to us from the larger world. Possessions, in the end, matter far less to us than the loving bonds we share with our families and friends.

Occasionally our governments will offer low-interest loans to disaster victims to help them rebuild, or perhaps their insurance carriers reimburse them for their losses. Still, many families never recover from the aftermath of a natural disaster. We also know that most insurance companies (which are profit-based businesses, not morally focused enterprises) exclude natural disasters or "acts of God" from their policies, because to cover those risks would cost them an unacceptable amount of money. Somehow it's become more socially acceptable to allow people to suffer than it is to simply *give* them whatever they need to help rebuild their lives once disaster strikes.

While wind damage caused by Hurricane Katrina was covered for those who bought hurricane insurance, the flood damage caused by the surge from the broken levees was mainly excluded. Since the vast majority of the damage during Katrina was related to water and not from wind, most homeowners weren't entitled to nearly enough insurance reimbursement to allow them to rebuild their homes. Of the over two hundred thousand buildings that were either damaged or destroyed in the hurricane's aftermath, some fifty-five thousand had yet to be rebuilt even five years later.[39]

Sometimes we even go so far as to *blame* the victims of disasters for their suffering. After all, we reason, they opted to live in a

---

39 "Katrina, Five Years Later," New York Times Editorial, September 1, 2010.

place that seems inhospitable or undesirable to us. Through these kinds of conceptual thought patterns we're able to invent a cause by using what seems like reason, so we can justify our fear-based desire to deny compassionate assistance to our suffering brothers and sisters. The fear that we won't have enough for ourselves if we give too much to others is always with us, and is often accompanied by the suspicion that others will take advantage of our generosity should we give without attaching harsh conditions. The fact is, though, if we use the power of reason *not* to justify our own fears but rather to examine the real world in which we live more fully, we quickly realize that fire zones, tornado alleys, hurricane coasts, earthquake regions, volcanic zones and flood plains cover the entire habitable zone of human existence. Exactly where on this living, breathing planet does the supposed "safe" region lie? Presuming we could even find a place devoid of natural disasters, how many of the nearly seven billion of us could comfortably live there, and what price might we have to pay to acquire that right?

Globally, most people still typically live where they were born. If they do move, they either go where the jobs are or settle where they can afford the cost of living. The free market system guarantees that places with the least desirable characteristics are the most affordable locations for the poorest among us to settle. Undesirable attributes include lack of a natural water supply, high heat or below-freezing temperatures during much of the year, ultra-low or ultra-high humidity, poor quality topsoil and a greater propensity for natural disasters. All those challenges place further pressures on the already tiny budgets of the working poor, rendering them *more* dependent on business infrastructure and monthly for-profit services for their needs. If that infrastructure collapses—for any reason—the poor will suffer and die in the greatest numbers. We observed that during the great tsunami of December 2004, and we see it whenever an earthquake or typhoon strikes a Third World nation. We witnessed it here in the United States during Hurricane Katrina.

The wealthiest among us own multiple houses. If one of their houses burns down in a wildfire, they move to another while they rebuild the one they lost. It might cause them some irritation, but their lives aren't severely disrupted by natural disasters. The poor, on the other hand, may find themselves living on the streets, in shanties, in makeshift tents or in toxin-tainted FEMA trailers—for which they're supposed to feel gratitude toward the rest of us for providing.

We're getting much better at peering around the walls of our own worldviews into the larger reality and noticing the immorality of what we're doing to each other. That's good news. People all around the world compassionately reached out to aid the victims of Katrina, as well as the victims of the Indonesian tsunami. Haiti and Chile also experienced a massive outpouring of humanitarian aid. What, we can only wonder, would happen if all those who cared so much about the suffering caused by these disasters came together in a more comprehensive way, to *tackle* the deep underlying social problems instead of simply responding to all the emergencies and symptoms? The answer is still anybody's guess; but if the nearly two billion dollars donated by private citizens to support the tsunami victims is an indication, we can feel great hope for humanity's future direction.

FUTURE DISASTERS AND OUTCOMES ARE HUMAN FICTIONS

Just as we can't genuinely possess Earth, we can't destroy it either. We may trash what's currently living here and wreak great havoc across it, but thankfully the Earth itself is resistant to our antics. While we often scare ourselves into believing we have the power to destroy our world, the best we can actually manage to do is destroy our own civilization, perhaps taking down a lot of innocent species in the process. Thankfully, we're not nearly as powerful or in control as we like to imagine we are!

Lately there's been a lot of talk about the meaning behind the mystical Mayan calendar 2012 date, which has led to increased speculation about the possible coming of a biblical Armageddon. More than a few people are wondering if a legendary battle between good and evil is beginning, and how things might turn out.

But truly, what ends? In the world of abstract concepts, perhaps everything comes to an end. A person is born, exists and dies. We *label* that a beginning and an ending. But in *reality*, the atoms that make up a person existed long before that person came into existence. Those atoms temporarily coalesce into a body, which grows and changes; then eventually, they loosen their bonds so they can move on to be part of something else. They don't *end*. The only thing that ends is the intangible collaborative arrangement they've established between themselves to create a person. Once the form dissolves, the atoms themselves go merrily about the business of forging new relationships with other atoms to create new and different life forms.

And what about life, that deep field of awareness that flows through us all and gives birth to our personal consciousness? Does *that* end when the body itself disintegrates? How could it, and why *would* it, when nothing else we observe in *reality* ends? Consciousness is already formless, ageless and infinite in size, so it seems even less likely to end than will our material atoms. What we do know through longstanding observation is that if we watch a body dissolve long enough a brand new life form—or two, or twenty, or a hundred or thousand—new ones will arise. It seems likely, then, that consciousness also shifts forms, to give itself a brand new view and a different take on the world. Pure awareness, which is what all life *is* beneath these temporary structures we know and observe as bodies, might therefore be envisioned as a formless observer who gazes onto and accesses this world through every possible open window—be it a worm, a stone, a tree or a human being. Call it God, if you will, peering into the realm of creation to observe what it is building, to enjoy and engage with all its amazing creations. Whatever the field of consciousness is, it doesn't occupy a physical form in a way that would cause its destruction, any more than an ocean can be destroyed when a wave on its surface subsides.

Once we realize that the infinite field of life animates *all* things, and once we know it to be an indestructible, formless essence that moves seamlessly through the physical realm at will, observing reality and engaging itself through constant interactivity, we understand there is no "us" or "them" in this cosmos, no beginnings or meaningful endings beyond our limited human perspective. Such distinctions exist only in the stories we tell ourselves inside our own minds about the importance of this being we call the "self."

It's helpful, then, to know that our inner narrator, the ego element of what we are, is extraordinarily unreliable.

According to classic definitions, the ego is what gives us our sense of self as a separate individual. Because it's also the way we define ourselves (mainly based on our perception of how we're being viewed by other people), the opportunities for self-distortion are quite high. The ego often tells us what we want to hear: "You're handsome, talented, brilliant, successful, and so on," or else it warns us what others might be thinking about us: "You're fat, selfish, stupid, lazy, etc." All the ego really *is*, however, is a sensory data interpreter, a mental processor that enables us to compare and contrast our personal life experiences with those of other life forms we encounter as we move about this planet in relationship to each other. When our senses dissolve with our body, we will have no more use for the sensory processor portion of our awareness, so it too shall pass. What's left when the ego dissolves is pure awareness *beneath* the level of limited sensory input—the all encompassing I AM.

The human ego, when it doesn't have good answers, makes up all kinds of fictions about the world. It tells stories to explain the seemingly random and inexplicable things in life, because it's confused its true role—which is to serve the greater I AM—with the belief that the I AM needs protection from the world.

Say you get mugged, for instance. The ego will immediately remind you the world is a dangerous place. Or perhaps it will scold you for being so careless you failed to notice the gang of teenagers eyeing your wallet in the parking lot. Or maybe one day you become famous, and your ego starts to whisper to you how much the whole world loves you, and tells you that you must be someone really special. Or it warns you not to trust the others, because people will take advantage of your fame or steal your fortune.

None of those stories your ego tells are the truth about reality. The ego *can't* know what others are thinking or feeling, it can only project its own fears, feelings and experiences onto others. The ego itself is a *fiction*, a mental ghost that wants to think it's real. Are we merely a collection of all our thoughts, sensory experiences and life stories, as the ego would have us believe, because that's what it is? Scary as it may seem at first, when we allow ourselves to think deeply about it, we come to realize that the past is just a bunch of ideas and floating memories; it's not enough to tell us who we are.

If our past isn't strong enough to define us, we might start to imagine the future surely will do so. We humans race passionately toward the future, hoping our next business success, a bigger house or a new spouse or child will fulfill us. The trouble arises when we finally arrive in that special future moment that we hoped would define us, only to discover it has become the present. Before long, it too will be the ghost of a distant memory. So as hard as we strive to get ourselves to the kingdom of the Happy Future, we begin to fear the arriving. That's because we can't freeze frame the special moments in life if they're wonderful, and we can't prevent them from happening if they're bad. We can only observe their comings and goings, like the weather.

Our fear of the future, triggered by constant anxiety about whether our personal life story is going to turn out the way we hope it will, can overwhelm us. That's strange really, when the fact is everyone's personal story will reach the same forgone conclusion: they all end in death! While we might *want* our personal stories to provide us with a happily-ever-after fairy tale ending, underneath we already know the final result. The effect of all that suppressed anxiety is that we strive toward our desired happy ending while at the same time part of us knows that the thing we call "time" will eventually snatch it away. That fear inhibits our ability to relax and fully enjoy where we are and what we're doing in the here and now, which is the only place in *reality* we can ever actually be. The rest of it—all the fears, anxieties and desires for the future, all the depression, regret and bitterness we carry about the past—is in our *heads*, being told to us by the ego-ghost that wants so badly to be important it will say anything to get our attention. Once we step into the realization that we in fact ARE the limitless, boundless and unseparated I AM, and that the individuated ego is its servant, not its master, life gets easier.

This business about humanity destroying the world is a big, collective ego story we've invented, a mental fiction many of us are presently passing around. All we humans have the power to do is damage Earth's ability to support its present collection of temporary life forms, including us. If we do so from ignorance about how *not* to do it, humanity may disappear from Earth, along with millions of other unfortunate species we'll have doomed to share our planetary mass extinction. Afterwards Earth would, over however many eons it took (and Earth likely has billions of years remaining to repair whatever damage we might inflict upon her surface before she dissolves), resurrect anew. If we sever our umbilical lifeline to this planet, our bodies and egos will dissolve. Earth will survive, however, and the formless One life—the I AM—that animates everything in this cosmos will surely survive.

That's my two cents, anyhow. You're free to believe whatever you want to believe about who you are. Just do yourself a favor and make sure that it feels *good*. What's the point in believing awful things about the one person you're stuck with for this whole lifetime—the self that you are? In my opinion, *that's* the hell religious people speak of. Heaven is knowing yourself to be infinitely capable of being the best version of the highest vision you hold about yourself.

PLANETARY RUMBLINGS AND WARNINGS

Climate change is arguably the most powerful warning shot across the bow that Mother Earth has fired our way. That some of us still insist we can't "afford" to address the challenges it presents is indicative of how deeply our fears of short-term lack and our attachment to the fictional need for proxy wealth have imbedded themselves in our collective human psyche.

The concept of lack stems from our attachment to property ownership. We can't lack what we can't own, but we *can* lack what we've been taught to believe we *can* own, but don't yet possess. Our feelings of lack are therefore manufactured, grounded in the fictional human concept of possession. For example, if we gave up the belief that it's fine for a few people to possess huge swaths of land to the exclusion of all other people, there would be plenty of arable land to go around. Every person alive today is already taking up space, so we're surely not out of space to support the life that already exists.

The only question, then, is whether we're going to continue to demand we each pay someone else (the presumed landowner) for the right to occupy space we need to survive, or whether we're collectively willing to agree to declare the right to space an inalienable truth.

We've long been trained to believe we need to go out and "get" things in order to have what we need. What might happen if we started to believe the opposite—that we have everything we need and more, here and now? For starters, we'd empower ourselves to feel the sheer joy that arises from giving to and helping others, without that joy being dampened by the fear we won't have enough for ourselves tomorrow.

The concept of possession, which is really an insidious form of hoarding, may serve the ego-protection needs of a powerful few by enabling them to feel richer than others in the short run, but it does a disservice to us all in the long run by removing from circulation things we could use to benefit all human beings right now. Hoarding means we must create far more stuff than we actually need in the present moment, which in turn demands that we consume our natural resources faster than would be necessary if we manufactured only what we needed here and now, and nothing more. Excess manufacturing can't help but contribute to our waste of fossil fuels. It also adds to pollution and reduces the amount of raw materials available to us in the future, when our creative processes might be better aligned with life, more regenerative and require consumption of fewer resources than they do right now.

To give more attention to the current warming of our planet, whether the causes are human, natural, or a combination of both, would be a most intelligent use of our time if we hope to preserve our species. It isn't about abstract concepts like profits or business cycles or whether humans are good or evil; it's about investigating and answering *real* questions around ongoing human existence and developing habitable places to live. We may discover we need do nothing; it might be our planet is suffering from a temporary fever that will break all by itself. We may also discover we could make a few basic changes to our processes, and in doing so prevent large swaths of land from becoming uninhabitable in the future. However, to ignore the question, or to argue with each other and ignore the observable symptoms, is to remain willfully ignorant in the face of what looks like a very real risk right now. Consciousness in the form of loving, reasoning intelligence—which is the gift humanity brings to life's great feast—has never been rewarded for its willful ignorance.

COOPERATIVE BEHAVIOR IS NATURAL HUMAN BEHAVIOR

As always, we can continue to look to nature itself for cues on how to relate to each other when it comes to material possessions and abstract ideas. Consider loving relationships, for example. We're basically hardwired to need them. That we have two sexes means we've no choice but to connect with each other on an intimate level if our species hopes to survive, and the imperative to survive is hardwired as well. We're each born instinctively gasping for air, and we die clinging to our final breath of life.

So how do we go about getting the relational love we desire? Some men choose sexual assault on women, and female subjugation still exists in most modern cultures to some degree, but we've learned over time that brute force doesn't guarantee men a steady supply of *pleasurable* sex or intimacy. A willing mate, most men will agree, makes a far more pleasant companion than does an angry, fearful or oppressed one. With regards to sex, then, when we offer another person our love, kindness, compassion and intimacy, it's far more likely we'll receive pleasurable sex and a lot of love in return—if not from the person to whom we've offered our heart, then from another who has observed our integrity and kindness, appreciates us for who we are and wants the very gifts we have to offer.

And so it seems that nature has cleverly bonded the physical pleasures of sex to the positive ideals it wants to promote in consciousness, like love and intimacy. Here again, consciousness and matter seem to have reached an agreement surrounding what they each want. The body craves sex while the spirit craves love; thus a bargain has been struck and the deal is on. It's up to us to accept that truth or continue to battle against it, although truth inevitably trumps our false beliefs. If collectively, for example, we all disavowed sex to avoid the risk of being exposed and vulnerable in the act of love, humanity would swiftly go extinct. That's reality, and beliefs won't change it.

It's true we can't insist that another person love us first before we're willing to offer them our love. The mind is always required to give of itself first; then, should we receive physical confirmation from the world around us as to the value of our gift, so much the better. If not, though, what have we truly lost? We've always got the potential of more love inside of us. Love comes into this world through the infinite field that is consciousness itself. Consciousness knows no limitations, finds no bottom in the well of human emotions. To love a single other is to know how to love them all.

Sharing, it seems, also comes as naturally to us as does breathing. It's another one of the countless, unconscious, cooperative agreements that have been struck between our bodies and consciousness to make us feel good while supporting the needs of our bodies. Sharing is also why we sometimes argue; we love to *share* our ideas and beliefs with others. Sometimes we hope to convince others to believe the same as we do, but just as often we're simply looking for answers to our questions or wondering if maybe we've found an answer to somebody else's question that may ease their suffering or solve a problem. Sharing, then, like loving, is an act of enlightened self-interest. Whatever we do to improve ourselves will ultimately benefit the whole.

THE INSIDIOUSNESS OF MANUFACTURED LACK

Where sharing typically fails us is when people start to feel paranoid about not having enough for themselves. That paranoia isn't unjustified. Intuitively, if not consciously, we understand that we live in a world of manufactured lack, where the less secure we personally feel the more likely we are to contribute to corporate profits. "Consider the lilies of the field; neither do they sow nor reap, yet our heavenly father feeds them." Jesus' words weren't fully appreciated when he presumably spoke them, for even then most people were locked in the struggle against the forces of manufactured lack. While the prospect of possessing great wealth and the accompanying freedom that great wealth can buy may be a powerful motivation to participate in capitalism in the short run, in the long run the ongoing buying and selling of goods can only escalate humanity's collective sense of lack. For-profit enterprises are not above using artificial means to frighten people into believing they don't yet have enough, or using strong-arm tactics to retain their grip on financial profitability. Because profits can exist only if a company's products are continually being sold, every corporation must build into its business plan and advertising campaigns a means to extract money continuously from the general public...forever.

That's why we see utility companies charging us for access to the clean running water that humanity took for granted for many millennia. Other utility companies actively lobby against proposals to install solar panels on existing home rooftops; encouraging families to draw free, ample electricity from sunshine may be a wonderful solution for our impending energy crisis, but private utility companies would vastly prefer to build their own giant solar arrays in the desert (potentially damaging delicate ecosystems to do so) so that *they* can retain control of the energy flow and continue to charge their customers to receive power. Any company that actually *solved* a problem by inventing an inexpensive product that could deliver a life necessity to the public for free—be it transportation, energy, food, fresh water or housing—is a company that would never be funded by capitalists! Freeing people from the burden of needing to buy things is not a part of the corporate agenda.

In the short run, we may purchase the latest model television and for a brief moment feel satisfied we've finally got everything we need. But in the long run we're soon bombarded with messages informing us we need to own the bigger, flat-panel screen with HD capability. In case we don't embrace the message fast enough, new technologies are always rendering the old ones obsolete, often making it impossible for us to continue using items that might otherwise still be perfectly operational. Try buying new recordings or a new needle for an old phonograph record player, or finding a replacement cassette tape player these days. Clearly, public satisfaction with what we already have would spell death to the capitalist structure. Dissatisfaction is what feeds the system, but the cost on the human psyche of continuous dissatisfaction is enormous. Stress-related illnesses, crime and workplace violence are all consequences of people hating the system.

By definition, all profits set up a win/lose proposition, since they benefit one individual at the expense of another. In a successful for-profit arrangement, the paying party *always* tenders more cash to the seller than the product he's buying has cost to produce. That's OK if the product enables the buyer to produce new goods or services that defray the cost of the purchase. If, however, the product is used—as so many things are these days—purely for consumption, entertainment or other personal reasons, the buyer has no way to recover the cost. Spending then becomes a steady drain on personal resources, rather than a way to improve one's long-term circumstances.

The fact that resources we must consume for survival are gathered from our planet and sold to us so businesses can profit exposes the dark underbelly of capitalism. It's a system that, at heart, deprives us at birth of our right to a fair share of the natural abundance of our own planet, based on the fictional dogma of human ownership. For us to survive, we're required to work for the capitalist system so we can earn enough money to "buy back" our birthright to land, water, food, shelter and energy from the people and businesses that claim ownership of those resources.

When an oak tree produces acorns, animals flock to it for food. None of them hoard all the nuts and then sell them to the highest bidder the way we humans do. In fact, so many nuts fall from a typical oak tree that the bulk of them rot on the ground. They feed the worms and insects, and then return to the soil to fertilize other plants in the coming years. This pattern of cooperative sharing is the primary means by which life has thrived since it first appeared on our planet. That we humans are still struggling mightily to thrive—after many thousands of years of so-called civilization—illustrates how far we've turned our backs on life's natural order.

There is *plenty* of land, food and water available for humanity to share—were that land not classified as "owned" by certain individuals and nations and thus considered off limits to those in need. We must therefore ask ourselves this: who decided which humans owned what property, and who granted those original decision makers the right to divvy up our vast communal birthplace to begin with? What moral obligation do we modern humans have to honor ownership arrangements that were made by those long dead, particularly if it no longer serves us to view our planet through the lens of private land ownership?

American Indians recognized the absurdity of the idea of land possession, which was why they "sold" Manhattan to the English for a handful of beads. Because they viewed themselves as fully integrated members of a living and cooperative planetary system, they knew no man could own what could only belong to itself. For a person to claim to possess a tree, an animal or a slice of land was an alien concept to them, since those things were alive and obviously governed themselves. How much land, they must have therefore reasoned, did a few white men need to be happy? Obviously the Indians underestimated the avarice as well as the volume of Europeans who would invade them. The tragic result was the marginalization of the American Indian nations.

That Native Americans were forcibly relocated to mainly desolate reservations reveals a terrible irony, in that another of the so-called inalienable constitutional rights upon which the United States was founded is the right to "liberty." While the abstract concept of liberty—like the so-called right to life—triggers a deep emotional response in most Americans, the true meaning of what we *say* we support all too often escapes us. Just as the right to life is meaningless without a physical right to space, a person's right to liberty is meaningless without the physical freedom to relocate. While we no longer force people onto reservations as we did in days of old, we still regularly force them to remain where they are based on financial limitations and immigration policies. To deprive people of liberty is to deny them the right to move…or to stay right where they are if they so choose. How much liberty do we truly have if we're trapped by circumstances in a place we don't wish to remain, either by accident of birth or because we don't have permission or the money to go somewhere else? How much liberty is truly ours if we're forced to leave our family home because we don't have high enough incomes to remain there?

GOVERNANCE (EXTERNAL FORCE) VS. SELF-GOVERNANCE (POWER)

While it's not up to us to decide how much other people should have, we each have a shared and growing social responsibility to become better at disciplining ourselves and controlling our own desires. External governance is a cage we've placed around humanity to ensure the "others" behave in ways we consider reasonable and fair. Over the years we've lost faith in each other to behave civilly should those bars ever come down. We're terrified of the wild humans that might emerge if we dared to spring the locks or open the cages. During natural disasters and in wartime we've seen firsthand what happens when a government loses control of the population. We witnessed populations out of control in Iraq and Afghanistan, when they were invaded by the United States with the help of some of its international allies. As soon as the military invasions toppled their authoritarian regimes, many civilians—absent that authority—reverted to tribal or religious allegiances and began looting, harassing and murdering each other. They also rebelled against the invading forces, miring them in a long and drawn-out conflict. We observed similar looting and crimes against people after Hurricane Katrina and the massive earthquake in Haiti. Clearly, the veneer that is our social fabric is frighteningly thin, and it doesn't take much stress to rip it apart.

Most of us would prefer not to be bound by so many rules and regulations; the problem, we fear, lies in the risk of setting all the *other* guys free. How much harm, we worry, might *they* do if we relax the rules? Fearing the consequences of granting others too much freedom, we opt to remain huddled inside the social cages we've built, resenting the existence of those unruly others. We think it's *their* fault we're now stuck inside *our* cages. If they'd only behave we could all be free. Our bondage, we imagine, has nothing to do with any fault within ourselves. We're forced to live by laws that were written to rein in all those pesky other people.

When we stop to examine those thought patterns we realize the "other guy" isn't the problem. The *real* problem lies in the way we've structured our society at its foundation. Because we deliberately create many more losers than winners with our capitalistic system, we're forced to defend ourselves against the jealousy, resentment, anger and alienation that periodically erupt from that enormous underclass. How tragic it is when that fear cuts us off from our ability to empathize or see ourselves in others, and how much suffering results. To heal even one wounded heart by helping it reestablish a connection with humanity is to bring healing to the whole society—of which we too are part. By reconnecting through empathy instead of separating through judgment, hatred and condemnation we can grow our ability to trust again and learn to govern ourselves.

If our vision for the future is indeed to live in harmony and freedom as a species, we each have an obligation to determine what's truly necessary for our personal happiness and self-fulfillment, and to release everything else we're clinging to that is based on greed or springs from the fear of lack. Self-governance, which arises naturally from a renewed connection with who we truly are, trumps the need for external physical governance based on our conceptual projection of who we think everyone else is. For the record, self-governance isn't the same thing as anarchy, which implies chaos. Self-governance arises from discovering our place in the larger cosmic order and taking responsibility for what we do in *relationship* to all other life forms, as well as in relationship to this entire living matrix we call Earth. Only through practicing conscious self-governance and in turn teaching our children how to self-govern can we hope to create a reality where external controls in the form of force will one day become obsolete.

If we refuse to reassess our values about owning land and having lots of material possessions, we'll need continually expanding external governance to protect us from the wrath and desperation of the ever-growing numbers of "have nots." Even so, our planet may press us into changing our beliefs despite ourselves. Consider the rising sea levels. Scientists are predicting that the increasing glacial melt we're presently experiencing has the capacity to displace billions of those who currently reside in low-lying coastal cities around the planet.[40] It doesn't matter so much *why* it might

---

40   Climate Change and Human Health: Risks and Responses, World Health Organization, Geneva, 2003.

be happening, if it's happening. What matters is what we decide to do about it.

It's started already. The tiny Polynesian island nation of Tuvalu with a population of just under twelve thousand men, women and children, has begun sinking into the ocean, as of this writing. The farmers and fisher folk who live there aren't causing the rising seas, but they're bearing the brunt of the change. At high tide the Tuvalu islands transform into a wet salt marsh. The children wade and play on sodden ground. Houses have been raised on stilts, yet their rotting frames are still covered with fungus. Food is getting hard to find since it's nearly impossible to grow anything there anymore. A few nations, Australia in particular, have allowed some of the wealthiest islanders to immigrate to their shores, leaving the poorest natives behind to fend for themselves. If sea levels continue to rise and Tuvalu finally disappears beneath the waves, how will the rest of us respond? Must the remaining islanders drown because they had the bad luck of being born on the losing side of our world's immense land lotto, and are now being affected by climate change and the steady rise in sea levels we may be causing?[41]

PRACTICAL SOLUTIONS

To rethink the life-devaluing principle of property ownership, to end profiteering off fundamental human necessities and perhaps

---

41   Kim Stewart, Tuvalu Climate Adaptation Report, Friends of the Earth Australia, 2005.

even to surrender the imaginary lines that create restrictive national borders and inhibit human liberty would eliminate many of the present sources of human suffering. No doubt these seem like terrifying notions to some. What, we nervously ask, would happen if we granted everyone in the world the right to go wherever they chose? What would become of *my* community, *my* country, and my comfortable way of life?

The assumption that all our healthy, vibrant communities would be inundated by the impoverished to the point of destruction is fictional, fear-based thinking inspired by the ego. Immigrants, many of whom suffer enormous hardships and leave behind families, language and culture in search of a better life, have been the foundational energy behind every human settlement that exists!

Immigrants go where the opportunities are. They *want* to succeed, and given half a chance they will. When the opportunities in any given place diminish, immigrants shift their flow to a new location. Were we to allow an intelligent and free ebb and flow of human migration the global population would balance itself out in time, which is what we observe wherever animal migration is generally free and flowing. It's why we've begun to create migratory corridors for wildlife around our cities; we recognize how unhealthy it is to keep living creatures penned up in areas that can't support their numbers. If we recognize that truth about other animals, why can't we recognize it about ourselves?

Remember also that migration flows in all directions: toward developed lands where opportunities abound for those who are willing to work, *and* toward undeveloped space where excitement and entrepreneurial opportunities call to the adventurers among us.

Currently we see starvation, misery and deprivation holding sway over people across large swaths of the planet. These problems result from hundreds of years of *unnatural* and unhealthy restrictions on human migration, coupled with the deliberate withholding of basic necessities from those who can't afford them. In states like California, Arizona, New Mexico and Texas, for example, where illegal immigrant populations overwhelm local social services, inundation is occurring precisely *because* legal immigration is so restricted. If the United States granted all who wanted to live within its borders the freedom to travel, settle and work wherever they wished, *and* if current U.S. citizens were alternately allowed to travel, live and work in whichever nation they chose, northern Mexico might eventually begin to resemble Southern California in the same way Southern California has taken on a decidedly Hispanic flavor and cultural influence. As more Americans migrated south, the opportunity gap between the two areas would shrink naturally, and fewer Mexicans would need to leave their birthplace in search of work.

If we embraced human migration as a global natural birthright, the Mexican and Central American immigrants now clustered fearfully in the desert Southwest of the United States would fan out evenly across the United States and perhaps even into Canada, as immigrants did in pioneering days. Canada is still vastly under populated in relationship to its natural resources, and could afford to support a much larger citizenry.[42] More open migration policies would lessen the burden immigrants place on local social services,

---

42   Don Kerr and Roderic Beaujot, "Population Growth and Sustainability: Canadian Considerations," *Entrepreneur* Magazine, November 2007.

as well as offer them greater opportunity to contribute positively to their new locations. As for the remaining repressive totalitarian governments that subjugate and abuse their people, if people could vote with their feet and flee such places of horror, how would a dictator maintain control?

The United States was born out of an understanding of the virtue of unfettered human migration. We once championed the principal of manifest destiny, claiming it our right to perpetuate our culture from sea to shining sea. We also proudly declare on our Statue of Liberty, "Give me your poor, your downtrodden, your huddled masses yearning to be free…." Far from destroying our country's social fabric, immigration *created* this nation's lustrous and diverse social tapestry. It's the bedrock of our strength, not our structural weakness. In fact, were it not for the early practice of welcoming all immigrants to our shores, the majority of us wouldn't even *be* Americans. How then can we deny others the same rights to life, liberty and the pursuit of happiness we so fervently claim for ourselves? Who put a time-stamp limit on human liberty? That's the question we need to ask ourselves as we evolve.

We can begin to loosen the grip of rabid nationalism by ending the construction of border walls and fences. The United States, by virtue of being one of the most desirable places in the world to live, has the power to lead the world on the immigration issue. Individually, we can urge our congressmen to support amnesty for immigrants already here, thereby granting them the freedom to move about the country rather than forcing them to remain concentrated in overburdened locales. We can also ask congress to liberalize our immigration laws, expand the numbers of people allowed to enter and ask other nations to open their doors to United States citizens as part of a fair exchange.

It's highly likely that someday in the not-too-distant future, some as-yet-unknown genius is going to invent a flying car or anti-gravity vehicle. When that happens we'll either have to relax our attachment to boundaries, or we'll need to create a massive police force whose full time job it is to patrol the entire sky and enforce those "borders." Since it's unlikely we'll be able to do the latter, we might as well attempt the former right now.

Practicing intelligent distribution of our shared natural resources and implementing more moderate, self-determined consumption of our Earth's abundant output, combined with the practice of reducing wastefulness—essentially copying the feedback system that has been successfully employed by nature herself for many billions of years—would allow our social structure to grow in complexity and expand in creativity (become regenerative) while remaining self-sustaining over the long run. We don't have to use more to do more; we can instead design products that are longer lasting, made from renewable resources and are beautiful to behold. We don't need to waste more to consume more; we can instead focus on ways to recycle what we don't fully consume and to produce in ways that do little environmental damage. We don't need to hoard more in order to have all we need; we can share many things we don't regularly use and thereby gain access to many more helpful items.

By imitating nature's generous, yet fair, distribution of resources (and by practicing sound recycling) we could eliminate manufactured lack, expand human potential and contribute more of our creative gifts to humanity, while drawing from our system all the resources necessary for our personal comfort, physical well-being, creative joy and continued self-actualization. If we translate our *abstract* values of life, liberty and the pursuit of happiness—the concepts most Americans hold so dear—into the *actualities* of space, freedom of movement and unfettered access to life's necessities, we may finally start to live our truths, not merely say we "believe in" them.

THE BENEFITS OF
HEALTHY COMPETITION

I RECALL THAT DURING MY FIRST JOB INTERVIEW, THE ONLY question that stumped me was when I was asked to describe a past personal failure and how I'd handled it. I honestly couldn't answer the question, because though there'd been many times I'd lost a contest or been unable to accomplish an objective, I'd never thought of myself as a failure. Intuitively I knew I'd gained something of value from all my life experiences. While I got the job, my interviewer later told me he almost hadn't hired me because he was worried I might not be able to "handle" personal failure.

A question that arose in me then, which I've continued to ponder on many occasions, is this: what exactly *is* failure, and how does it relate to winning or losing?

Perhaps the best place to begin to evaluate the concept of failure is to look at the way humanity competes. In our modern world, to lose a competition is considered the same as to fail. Evidence of a cultural bias toward winning abounds; we see it each time the victors of a sporting event receive trophies, attention and accolades, while the losers go home disappointed and on occasion are even publicly humiliated. The truth, though, is that no one can successfully compete by himself in a sporting event. It takes the *co-operation* of worthy opponents for a competition to happen. How many world records, we might wonder, would swimmer Michael Phelps have broken in the 2008 summer Olympics had his competitors not pushed him beyond his previous physical limits?

On a personal level, Phelps's competitors could be labeled losers or failures; on another level, however, they became the powerful agents who challenged Phelps to stretch beyond his comfort zone and set those new world records. And whenever someone shatters past records for speed, endurance or strength, *humanity* wins. We win because we learn that the human body is capable of achieving far more than we'd previously believed was possible. Even the so-called losers can therefore be viewed as winners in the broadest sense of the term, because they too gain wisdom from learning what a human being can do. Post-Phelps, swimmers from every nation will attempt to set an even higher benchmark for excellence, and some will eventually match or break his records.

Competition can be either healthy or unhealthy. The importance we place on winning (and the extent to which we undermine the morale and self-esteem of the losers) determines how healthy it is. Put simply, capitalism tends to promote *unhealthy* competition because it rewards success and punishes personal failure. We've been trained to believe that our personal success as measured by the world's approval is far more important than what we learn about ourselves as a person or species (or even about our world) if we don't succeed. The consequence is we're terrified of the shame, blame and financial failure we'll experience should we fail. A woman who starts a small business that doesn't thrive may lose her home, her future security, her ability to provide for her children and her standing in the community. Those negative possibilities often deter us from taking risks. Meanwhile, when we have no *choice* but to try something new, like when we get booted out of the family nest in our early adulthood, that fear of failure compels us to succeed—at any price. We'll even surrender our dreams and passions, and take on a boring but "safe" career to avoid failing in the eyes of our larger society.

As early as grade school we're taught that success is richly rewarded by our system, and failure is punished. Most of us catch on quickly when our parents respond to our "grades." We become so desperately attached to the accolades, fortune and power we stand to gain from winning that some of us will even resort to cheating to guarantee ourselves a win. Some teachers have even gotten into the act, encouraging students to cheat on standardized tests.[43] (For an excellent analysis of the reasons behind the failure of our modern education system and how we might best reform it, check out this RSA video on changing economic paradigms by Sir Ken Robinson, "Changing Education Paradigms," *http://www.youtube.com/watch?v=zDZFcDGpL4U*).

---

43   Bryan A. Jacob and Steven D. Levitt, "Rotten Apples: An Investigation of the Prevalence and Predictors of Teacher Cheating," National Bureau of Economic Research, December 2002.

Our unhealthy motivations for competing to win, which are unconsciously embraced during childhood and carried through as behaviors into adulthood, help explain why scientists fudge experimental results to make it appear they've succeeded in accomplishing something they haven't truly achieved. In 1989 a huge furor arose when two scientists claimed they'd created nuclear fusion in a jar of room temperature water—a process known as cold fusion. The scientists, however, failed to provide methods that could be replicated by others, and eventually their claim was fully debunked.[44] That same deep-seated desire to win also explains why athletes use performance-enhancing drugs to achieve superstar status even though these drugs are illegal (and often detrimental to one's health), and why CEO's intentionally bury scientific reports revealing their products cause harm or death to their customers. Clearly, competition based on unhealthy motivation (I *have* to be better than everyone else if I'm going to get the reward) places personal behavior on a collision course with social morality.

The trouble lies in the fact that the rewards we offer to winners in our capitalistic society are almost all external. Money and possessions, fame, power over others, public admiration—all cause us to shine in the eyes of *others* instead of in our own eyes. That triggers an internal moral battle between our public persona and our private self that can be downright schizophrenic. What *is* hypocrisy, if not a clash between what one says in public and what one does in private? We wear masks to avoid public ridicule, because we want to be revered by others even if what we say isn't what we believe. It's

44   Malcolm W. Browne, "Physicists Debunk Claim of a New Kind of Fusion," *The New York Times*, May 3, 1989.

why we see politicians and evangelical ministers condemning homosexuality when they themselves are closeted homosexuals. It's why our politicians make laws against bribery and undue influence even as they accept bribes and sell their votes to the highest corporate bidder. It's why bankers chastise their customers for not being fiscally responsible while they gamble irresponsibly with billions of dollars of the public's money for short-term gratification.

We don't encourage and support each other to act out of personal integrity in the best interests of humanity. Rather, we compel each other to *struggle* internally with the desire to do what's right, given the unremitting social and economic pressures to succeed at any cost. Then we denigrate ourselves whenever some hypocrisy gets exposed, claiming it's "human nature" for us to be greedy, selfish, dishonorable and bad. Certainly those behaviors all exist in the realm of human possibility, which is like a vast rainbow of colorful choices we all have the power to express. Being loving and generous, compassionate and kind are all part of that rainbow as well. The question is: why do we make it so *hard* for each other to call forth our most exquisite qualities and express the most beautiful colors in our rainbow? Why do we *reward* ourselves for manifesting ugly colors?

There *is* no such thing as human nature, since our potential responses to life exist in a nearly unlimited bandwidth. There are only socialized behaviors and self-limiting beliefs that we use to self-define. Ironically, by using punishments, judgments and condemnation, and by dangling external rewards in front of each other to try to minimize our usage of the worst behaviors in our human possibility range, we've also inadvertently inhibited our willingness to take risks and call forth the highest and best of behavior. Eliminating the extremes has driven us all toward mediocrity. Ultimately, though, our internal evolutionary impulses—which drive us all to want to be more, do more, know more and love more—compel some of us, out of desperation, to downshift and use our baser instincts to break ourselves out of the prison of mediocrity. The very behavior we're hoping to confine may remain controlled in the short run, but in the long run it reasserts itself with even greater force because the truth is, we're not *satisfied* with mediocrity. Solutions to our challenges don't come from the satisfied anyway. They come from those willing to think outside the box because they feel dissatisfaction with what is. We can't compress the bell curve of human experience into a single giant blob and remain successful. Our mission, then, is to become more like an inchworm. We must gently encourage the center mass of our body ever upward, stretching ourselves toward our highest capacities, and over time pulling along with us even the lowest aspects of our own behavior.

While some businesses stretch themselves this way, adhering to higher standards and acting as quality role models for other companies, many more choose to annihilate their competitors by flooding the marketplace with cheap products or by using aggressive techniques to gain a monopoly. That's exactly the way Wal-Mart and Microsoft have treated other businesses over the years. We're left to wonder how much better our desktop computers might run today if, rather than ruthlessly crushing its competitors, Microsoft had instead encouraged creativity to flourish by supporting better software instead of destroying it. For that matter, what if Detroit automakers hadn't been so quick to preserve their profits by undermining our early attempts to produce electric cars? How much closer to renewable energy vehicles might we be today if automakers had invested heavily in the necessary research to build solar- or hydrogen-powered cars instead of protecting the internal combustion engine for the sake of short-term profits? Where might we be today if we'd continued our early efforts in the creation of mass transit systems rather than allowing private companies to campaign against them and actively encourage their dismantling? At one time the Red Car system in Los Angeles represented the largest electric rail system in the world. Eventually though, it's sale to a private bus company marked its doom. Metropolitan Coach Lines dismantled the Red Car system with the approval of the public authorities and replaced it with gasoline-powered buses instead.[45]

Craftsmanship, creativity, the environment and quality community relationships all suffer for the sake of profits successfully derived from cheaply made, mass-manufactured or monopoly-protected products. Most of us, I'd argue, would prefer to own a beautiful wooden dining table handcrafted with care by a tradesman from our community instead of a flimsy, particleboard "made in China" model. That most of us don't own such a table is because of the pervasiveness of cheap mass-market imports, not due to our lack of taste or our not caring if the table we purchase will last. Not only is this unfortunate for consumers, it's demoralizing to laborers as well. How many workers do you imagine might prefer to learn woodcarving so they could craft quality furnishings from their

---

45   Guy Span, "Paving the Way For Buses-The Great GM Streetcar Conspiracy," www.baycrossings.com, Archives, April 03, 2003

own backyards, as opposed to the present, mind-numbing task of repetitive parts assembly in a sterile factory? Too many of us wind up doing jobs that don't encourage us to explore or express our creative abilities because of the mechanistic production systems we've engineered and have rewarded under capitalism. Mass-market production was beneficial during our time of great expansion, but now that we've reached planetary saturation it's time we reconsider both our motivations and our social incentives.

Over the years, capitalism has unwittingly elevated thoughtless, mechanistic mass-production above thoughtful, creative, quality production by defining continuous profits as the main metric for corporate success. Today, the more inexpensive (and swiftly replaceable) products a company can produce using ever fewer people, the higher its profits inevitably climb. As any parent knows, the behavior we choose to reward is the behavior we tend to see. By rewarding corporations for being careless with our environment and our natural resources, for creating inhumane working environments, for disregarding the well-being and long-term satisfaction of their customers and for discarding loyal employees so they can exploit cheaper labor forces in Third World nations, we're encouraging them to be ever more immoral in their dealings with all of life. Of course, on occasion we punish those companies and the individuals who run them if we catch them behaving so egregiously they actually violate some law, but that doesn't change the fact we've still got an underlying flaw in the system: we *continue* to reward the behavior we don't want.

This clear misalignment between what's good for a person or company and what's good for society *must* be addressed if we hope to eliminate the negative consequences of unhealthy competition, many of which lie at the root of our social ills. Pollution, ecosystem destruction and natural resource exploitation, poverty, crime, widespread preventable illnesses—all can be traced as the consequences of humanity placing a higher value on individual (and by extension, corporate or national) success than it places on our collective long-term success as a planetary species. Redesigning our economic system so that what's good for the individual (or corporation or nation) is *good* for humanity, and what's *bad* for humanity is also bad for the individual (or corporation or nation) seems crucial in fostering personal, corporate and national behavior in accordance with the values we say we hold dear as human beings. It will also make it easier for us to trust people, corporations and nations to do the right thing if we know we're rewarding them for acting in ways that are in full alignment with humanity's best interests.

On an even more fundamental level it would be helpful for us to foster this new mindset in society by encouraging our children to self-reward. Rather than berating them for losing or not being perfect, we can teach them to learn a lesson for which they can be thankful from every competition, and encourage them to apply that lesson to all their future endeavors without shaming, blaming or punishing them for trying to succeed and coming up short. In her controversial book, *Battle Hymn of the Tiger Mother*, author Amy Chua reveals the authoritarian tactics she used, as well as the occasionally abusive levels to which she fell, to ensure her daughters were always first and best at whatever they did.[46] While that

---

46   Amy Chua, *Battle Hymn of the Tiger Mother*, Penguin Press, 2011.

sort of parenting may produce dutiful children with the capacity to fit well into the capitalist structure, what happens to children's creativity, playfulness, imaginative energies and ability to develop core life competencies around decision-making when their parents so rigidly control their lives to achieve a *parental* "success" objective?

The recent problems at Toyota Corporation come to mind as a prime example of where we go wrong with our reward and punishment structure. In 2010 it was brought to the public's attention that Toyota's management had known for some time—and deliberately suppressed—the fact that a number of its cars had problems with sudden vehicle acceleration, and that the problem was leading to accidents and deaths. The trouble appeared widespread across the newer Toyota models, and it resulted in one of the most massive recalls in automotive history. Once Toyota came clean about its problem, the news media savaged it and played up every dramatic human-interest story they could find. Angry consumers lost confidence in the company, car sales declined dramatically and Toyota's stock—a darling of investors before all this happened—collapsed.

Angry as we might feel about the company's deliberate deception, the question we must ask ourselves is this: what *positive* incentive did our capitalist system offer to Toyota to come clean right away, when it first discovered the potentially serious problem? Had Toyota done so, the odds are good they *still* would have suffered a loss of consumer confidence, their sales would still have declined and their stock price would have plunged precipitously. It seems, then, the only potential benefit for them to admit the problem was that they might not have endured quite as much negative publicity as they received *and* they may have avoided a nominal governmental fine. That precious lives might have been saved doesn't count, because that would have made no impact on Toyota's bottom line. In fact it's even doubtful they'd have received much positive publicity for admitting the truth and indicating they did so to *save* human lives, since our media doesn't spotlight good behavior. We're addicted to drama, crime and public humiliation, not to congratulating ourselves for whatever we're doing right. It therefore remained in Toyota's best interests, though it certainly wasn't in the best interests of an unwitting public, to bury the damaging data and hope they could solve the problem before the public found out.

CAPITALISTIC COMPETITION AND THE MODERN ASSEMBLY LINE

With the invention of the automobile assembly line, Henry Ford showed the world it was possible to produce products competitively in higher volume and for much less money by giving up something in the way of quality craftsmanship. (FYI: Ford didn't invent the assembly line, he merely perfected it.) Before Ford's idea came into being, teams of skilled workmen built every car one at a time. That was a slow and expensive process, which meant cars cost more than most people could afford to pay. Before Ford's day, the automobile was a novelty luxury item for the very rich—the same way a private jet has become a luxury item today. The automated assembly line changed all that. Instead of workers gathering around a single car until it was finished, the cars traveled to the workers, who each performed a single task over and over. In this way Ford was able to reduce the completion time for a Model T from twelve and a half hours to less than six without sacrificing too much by way of the finished product. What *was* sacrificed was the fine attention to quality detail, things like handcrafted woodworking and polishing, and the personalized attention each car received to ensure everything was in perfect order before the car went out. Ford thus became one of the first industrialists to exploit the financial profitability that comes from selling a lot of products of lesser quality at lower overall prices. Whether the assembly-line products lasted as long, required more maintenance or generally offered the same long-term *value* to the buyer as the handcrafted products that came before them was less important to Ford than his ability to profit by selling *more* products.

The main thing that got shunted aside during Ford's highly profitable assembly-efficiency experiment was the human aspect of the labor equation. Prior to the adoption of the assembly line, people communed, laughed and learned from each other as they worked. Although pre-industrial assembly lines had long been used for preparing group meals or doing piecework sewing, those workspaces still retained a sense of intimacy. The workers still engaged in conversation, developed new skills and explored creative new ways of accomplishing their work. The mechanical assembly line ruthlessly eliminated the creative and social benefits of communion and replaced them with silent, rapid, physical repetition. Repetition, however, makes a poor substitute for camaraderie, skill development and the exploration of personal creativity.

If we wonder why modern workers experience higher rates of alcoholism, suicide, domestic violence, drug abuse, or obesity than did our pre-industrial forefathers, we need only remind ourselves that human isolation and depression go hand in hand. Studies conducted in 2005 on inmates held in solitary confinement exposed a high correlation between isolation and delusional thinking, panic attacks, anxiety, existential crises and, in rare cases, outright psychosis.[47] The statistical correlation was so high that a group of social crusaders fought to have jailhouse isolation declared a form of cruel and unusual punishment based on the study's results.

Isolation isn't the only problem caused by modern assembly lines. Many people also suffer serious physical injuries like carpal tunnel syndrome or rotator cuff damage resulting from repetitive motions, as well as back and neck problems that result from long periods of enforced immobility. Unfortunately, these mental and physical problems only scratch the surface of the long-term violence being done to human beings in the modern workplace. We also suffer spiritual trauma as well. Just think back a moment to the most beautiful thing you've ever created—be it a painting, a wooden bench or even a child. How amazed were you when you finally saw the results? That powerful response, that deep sense of personal satisfaction for a job well done, is part of our built-in natural feedback system. We're all born with a set of emotions, some of which feel good and some that don't. The ones that make us feel good are *designed* to encourage us to repeat the behaviors that

---

47   Peter Scharff Smith, "The Effects of Solitary Confinement on Prison Inmates: A Brief History and Review of the Literature," The University of Chicago Crime and Justice, 2006.

bring them forward. The ones that feel bad teach us what not to do in the future. When we're reduced to dropping widgets into slots in exchange for a paycheck, however, we find it far more difficult to equate what we're doing every day with feelings of personal accomplishment. Our self-esteem wilts along with our bodies, due to the physical insults we suffer from performing repetitive tasks—from eyestrain to carpal tunnel syndrome to chronic back pain. Combine those injuries with lengthy exposure to industrial pollutants and we can't even *begin* to calculate the long-term human toll our increased mechanization has on our muscles, our cells, our organs and our sense of well-being.

We do know that mental illness has been on the rise since the beginning of the modern industrial age.[48] It expresses itself through increased antisocial and criminal behaviors. The macabre term "going postal" was coined to describe rage-related shootings that have proliferated in modern workplaces since the mid 1970s. A 2008 study on workplace violence reports that, on average, three people will be murdered on the job in the United States each day.[49] According to the U.S. National Institute for Occupational Safety and Health, one million workers are assaulted and more than a thousand are murdered every year.[50] It's also disturbing to note that homicide has become the second highest cause of death on the

---

48 "Society and Self: General Social Trend #8: The Rise in Mental Illness," UCADIA, 2010.

49 Fact Sheet: Violence in the Workplace, North Carolina State University Environmental Health and Public Safety Division of Risk Assessment, 2008.

50 Bureau of Labor Statistics (BLS), U.S. Department of Labor, Fatal occupational injuries by event or exposure and major private industry sector. Revised, April 2007.

job, just below motor vehicle accidents. Perhaps this growing rage against our employers and fellow employees is on the rise because so many of us *blame* our increasingly mechanical society for the steady erosion in our sense of our own humanity.

FOR BETTER OR WORSE?

In its highest form, competition exists to inspire, not destroy. The best forms of competition are *evocative*, not *provocative*. To evoke means to encourage the best out of someone else. To provoke means to put someone on the defensive, which causes a battle that leads to a winner and a loser. Healthy competition creates winners all around.

Not only can individuals engage in healthy competition. A business can also engage in healthy competition by offering higher quality products of greater value than those made by its competitors. Society benefits from this sort of competition, because society itself is enhanced. We must realize, though, that getting a bargain (something cheap) and getting something of value are two different things. We often confuse bargains with values when we compare items on the basis of price alone. A company might advertise its product as a "great value" because it's cheaper than their competitor's product, but the most important question to ask is this: are we actually getting *more* product (or roughly the same amount of it) for a bit less money or for the same price, or are we in fact getting much *less* product at a slightly lower price? If you're my age you can probably remember when coffee manufacturers sold their wares in solid, one-pound cans. Visit any grocery store today though, and it's clear that at some point many manufacturers chose to reduce the size of their cans to twelve ounces and offer those at only a slightly lower price than a sixteen-ounce can once cost. There really is no other reason for coffee manufacturers to sell us a smaller quantity of their merchandise in every package other than to pull this price increase sleight of hand on the general public. This same kind of stealth price increase can be noted when we consider the cardboard tube inside a roll of toilet paper. The tubes used to be only slightly larger than the holder bar on which the roll was hung, but nowadays there's a great deal of empty air between the roller bar and the paper's cardboard tube. That means we're getting far fewer squares per roll than in the past.

A similar effect can be observed when we compare a shirt from Wal-Mart, made in China with one from an American manufacturer. The Wal-Mart shirt may cost a lot less to purchase, but if it falls apart after a couple of washings, while the more expensive shirt lasts a couple of years, who really benefits? Business success shouldn't be based on creating the greatest bargains for individuals or the highest product turnover for corporations; it should be granted to those whose products offer humanity *as a whole* the highest value.

In our driving competition to produce things ever faster and cheaper, over the centuries we've generated massive amounts of industrial waste that we've carelessly dumped into our environment. We see the results in the degradation of air quality, the toxins appearing in soils and the harmful chemicals collecting in marine life. We're also beginning to see their effects on children.

One disturbing result of chemical pollution has been the earlier onset of puberty for our daughters and granddaughters. The environmental estrogen we're all exposed to from deteriorating plastics, from the growth hormones we inject into animals to fatten them faster for market and from a host of other industrial waste sources—including the urine of women who take birth control pills—is staggering. While older medical books say it's abnormal for young girls to show pubic hair or breast development before the age of eight, a 1997 study revealed that a large percentage of American girls have begun experiencing one or both by the age of seven, and in some cases as early as three.[51] By 1997 the average age for puberty had fallen to just under nine for African-Americans and roughly age ten for Caucasians.[52] Older textbooks place the average age for puberty onset between eleven and twelve.[53]

Another study conducted in 2008 by researchers at the University of Italy looked at a group of girls there who were affected by early onset puberty. Of the seventeen girls tested, six were found to have abnormally high levels of mycoestrogen zearalenone (ZEA),

---

51 "Secondary Characteristics and Menses in Young Girls Seen in Office Practice: A Study from the Pediatric Research in Office Settings Network," Pediatrics Vol. 99, No. 4, April 1997.

52 Ibid.

53 "Secondary Sexual Characteristics and Menses in Young Girls Seen in Office Practice: A Study from the Pediatric Research in Office Settings Network," Pediatrics, Vol. 88, No. 4, April 1987.

an estrogen contaminant found in the local water supply.[54] Clearly, rewarding companies for damaging the environment simply so they can make more stuff more cheaply is becoming a problem.

HOW UNHEALTHY MOTIVATION ERODES OUR PRODUCTS AND OUR CHOICES

Choosing between an item that fits into our budget and one that is generally better for society isn't easy. When it comes to product engineering, better or worse is difficult to compare. Bells and whistles, modern electronics and fancy features might make one refrigerator seem better than its competitor; however, if the fancy refrigerator falls apart faster than the simple one, are you better off for buying the bells and whistles? If its drawers break or the plastic shelves crack beneath the weight of a few pickle jars, what does it matter if your refrigerator tells you the temperature at which you're storing your cheeses?

Many products today in the so-called "durable goods" category—items like washers and dryers, ovens, refrigerators, computers, etc.—have been deliberately constructed so their modular electronic components can't be repaired, but must be replaced whenever they go on the fritz. Annie Leonard's delightful Internet video, "The Story of Stuff" (*http://www.storyofstuff.com/*), details the emergence of our modern throwaway culture, beginning in the 1950s.

54 "Environmental Toxins Linked To Early Onset Puberty," Elsevier Health Sciences, February 7, 2008.

The video reveals that in our modern consumer economy, ninety-nine percent of all new products wind up as trash within six months after they're purchased. Why, when we're consuming our natural resources at an increasingly alarming rate, have we become so quick to throw our stuff away? The following quotation from Victor Lebow, a post-WWII retailing analyst, says it all:

> *Our enormously productive economy...demands that we make consumption our way of life, that we convert the buying and use of goods into rituals, that we seek our spiritual satisfaction, our ego satisfaction, in consumption...we need things consumed, burned up, replaced and discarded at an ever-accelerating rate.*"[55]

In other words, we *reward* companies for producing stuff we have to discard very quickly by granting them higher profits for selling more goods! Believe it or not, the predicted lifespan for a washing machine purchased in 2008 now averages between eight and ten years. But when we hearken back to an earlier era, one when local repairmen fixed our durable goods whenever they broke, we might recall that our grandparents owned and operated the same reliable washing machine for twenty or perhaps thirty years.

Consider the average vacuum cleaner, which once had a life expectancy of ten years. Over the past ten years my husband and I have purchased at least four new vacuum cleaners and three electric brooms, along with three new rug shampooers and two

---

55   Victor Lebow, "Price Competition in 1955", Journal of Retailing, Spring 1955

garage shop vacs. What makes that number even more dismal is that for several years now we've contracted with a cleaning service that brings in its own equipment! We vacuum only occasionally between their regular visits, yet still our machines can't seem to handle the workload.

The problem with repairing modern appliances is that the replacement components often cost as much as a brand new appliance. That's not by accident; the manufacturer would much rather sell you a whole new model than a single component that comes from their supplier. If you still insist on buying the component instead of "upgrading" to this year's new model, the company maximizes its profits by overcharging you heavily for that small but crucial component, as well as by tacking on a hefty repair bill for what's often a simple "pop and drop" replacement. That's not only legal, it's considered good strategic marketing practice for businesses today. Never mind the overall cost to society from the waste and purposely built-in obsolescence.

One promising signal that people are finally waking up to the grotesque waste that's been built into the system is the reemergence of the general "Fix It" shop. In the 1950s and 1960s such shops were centerpieces in every local community. Gradually, though, they closed their doors as the sheer number of new products, combined with cheaper construction and growing electronic complexity, made many items too complicated for workmen to repair. Even shoe repair stores seemed to disappear for a time. But since the recession of 2008 began, repair shops are making a comeback in many communities. Repair businesses are able to compete successfully with appliance manufacturers by figuring out ways to repair broken items for a lower cost than the price of replacing the product. The only drawback to their success is we've gotten out of the habit of even *looking* for ways to repair things. We're much more comfortable these days with throwing them away and buying new ones.

When fewer products wind up in our landfills because they've been well constructed and designed for easy repair, even those businesses that might lose some repeat customers stand to benefit—whether they realize it or not. Beyond the limited financial benefit companies derive from selling more products, a whole host of social benefits also accrue to the people who work within companies that strive to produce higher-quality products. None of the employees *want* pollution to hinder their children's ability to thrive. None of them want to see our limited natural resources go to waste. Unfortunately, capitalism itself demands we ignore our longer-term interests in favor of our need to earn a paycheck so that we can put food on the table and feed our children. We can't afford the luxury of worrying about how our kids will fare tomorrow unless we have the resources we need to get through life today.

When a business gets rewarded by the capitalistic structure for *weakening* the system, its behavior causes problems for us all. Any business that wins by contributing lower-quality goods to society (even when doing so at a lower price) offers us nothing of genuine value. The overall quality of society becomes *eroded* instead of elevated, cheapened in every possible sense of the word. People who were once employed by a quality company that a cheaper competitor has driven to fail will lose their jobs, along with their faith in a system where less worthy companies get rewarded for besting their higher-quality peers. Somehow, then, we will need to redesign our short-term reward and punishment system around humanity's longer-term goals if we're going to build a society that thrives.

INSPIRATION OR INTRASPECIES PREDATION?

When we look around at nature we see healthy competition—competition that inspires other creatures to be the best they can become. We observe it in the quest for food, for sexual privileges and for territorial rights. Animal competitions push the gene pools of every species to ever-higher heights, and as such are an integral part of their evolutionary process.

On the subject of destructive competition, it's important to note that animals are *not* motivated to fight to the death for the right to mate or for territorial privileges, although occasionally death may occur by accident. Mainly, our fellow animals put on impressive "shows" of prowess through the use of scents, colors and ritualistic displays of might and/or physical beauty. These displays typically determine which males are most desirable to the females, without the males having to invest a good deal of energy fighting. The strongest, largest and most beautiful males gain the right to pass on their genes to the next generation, improving the viability of the entire species. That benefits even the males we humans consider losers, because they still belong to that species and have a vested interest in its long-term survival.

Most animals, even those for whom fighting has become ritualized into their mating process, aim to conserve their energy as much as possible so they can use it to find food and water, or flee from potential predators. If an animal expends too much energy fighting it becomes exhausted and risks death by some other means. Surrender therefore becomes an important element of ritualistic fighting. At some point in nearly every battle the less powerful animal backs away and grants the victor the rights to his sexual spoils. The weaker animal intuits that he's running low on energy, and realizes he needs to regain his strength if he hopes to see tomorrow.

We humans seem to pose an exception to this animal kingdom rule. We stubbornly fight on—quite often to the death—for access to natural resources, territory and the right to control each other's behaviors and beliefs. Countless millions of us have died at the hands of others; many more than have died from all the animal predation, epidemics or natural disasters we've suffered as a species over time.

In the 20th century alone, it's estimated that humanity's war fatalities range between one hundred sixty million to well over two hundred million people.[56] Compare that to a few million lives lost in earthquakes and floods during the same century, or to the tens of thousands of people killed by sharks, bears, lions, snakes and the like. It seems nature has nothing over mankind when it comes to our own destruction. It's as though humanity's fixation on unhealthy competition, which has morphed into a form of continual intraspecies murder, has turned us into our own worst predator.

---

56   Piero Scaruffi, "War and Genocides of the 20th Century," 2009. http://www.scaruffi.com/politics/massacre.html

Why this fixation on fighting to the death among us? How did the natural, benign competitive drive become so subverted in humans that we grew bent on annihilating each other rather than on encouraging each other to strive harder to improve the survivability of our species? If we're truthful about it, the biggest difference between humans and the rest of the animal world is that we possess a personal ego, while most other creatures apparently do not.

The ego, as we mentioned earlier, enables a person to perceive himself as a separate individual. Unfortunately, that sense of personal uniqueness has been accompanied by our forgetfulness of our deeper connectivity to all things, including each other. This universal (adolescent) evolutionary shift into human ego from our earlier (childlike) state of global connectivity is explored in the ancient mythologies from cultures all around the globe. Virtually every human culture contains within it a story that describes mankind's "fall from grace." Every Jew, Christian and Muslim, for example, knows the story of Adam and Eve's eviction from the Garden of Eden. What *was* the metaphoric fall of which the Genesis myth is speaking, and why does that story seem so universal? Perhaps it's because the expressed longing in the story to return to the childlike state of innocence and deep connectivity with Source that existed before the so-called fall from grace mirrors the often ambivalent feelings adolescents experience once they realize they have to grow up. Growing up can be painful; it requires us to do the hard work of thinking and learning how to make good and moral decisions. The thing is, all creatures—from hatchling turtles to baby birds—experience the trauma of being forced out of the warmth and security of their birth nest. Why should our species have been spared the evolutionary journey all creatures must eventually face?

Not surprisingly, we humans wrote the Genesis story from a place of ego—from the perspective of the baby bird who is suffering fear and anxiety triggered by his "cruel" ejection from the family nest—instead of from the higher perspective of the loving parents hovering above their fledgling, urging it to spread its wings and fly. Maybe our longstanding religious belief that we did something "bad," for which we must forever atone, is based on a faulty, ego-based assumption, the same assumption that fledgling might make if it could wonder why its parents "rejected" it.

Could it be that our human societies the world over have embedded in their mythologies the realization that at some stage in the evolution of our species our minds evolved to the point where we were forced to learn to make choices for ourselves? Due to our inherent insecurities around our competency, perhaps it became more important for our budding egos to believe they were "right" and others were "wrong" in order for us to feel the confidence we needed to act. The fear of making a terrible choice—or worse, having to admit how little knowledge we actually possessed—may have outweighed the cost of doing battle over our beliefs. Might these stories be reflecting our collective shift out of our innocent species childhood, when we accepted all things without question, into our evolutionary adolescence, when we were forced to begin to compile information and grow in hard-won wisdom?

Adolescence, as we all know, is a difficult period often marked by alienation, aggression, rebelliousness, self-consciousness, bullying, and peer group pressures, along with a fear that we'll never be good enough. Could our "modern" social systems actually be carryovers from our adolescent era, reflecting an earlier need to superimpose external parental controls on our confused, separating and emotionally turbulent selves? If so, embracing the *responsibilities* commensurate with the *freedoms* of adulthood seems a logical solution to all our problems.

In *Awakening to Life's Purpose*, Eckhart Tolle encourages humanity to reconsider its belief that the individual ego is the rightful driver for all our human activity. He suggests instead that within us all can be found a deeper access to the truth of who and what we are: one cosmically interconnected and living essence, of which the entirety of humanity is only one small piece.

Perhaps the ego is but a protective mechanism we needed, to shield us as we muddled through life until we developed enough maturation to become competent and successful as a species. After all, geologically speaking, we're still very young. Evolution has a long history of linking crises to the transformation of individual species, and certainly our juvenile self-destructiveness is approaching crisis levels. Whatever the reason, our behaviors have grown increasingly toxic for our species' long-term survival. We now have the ability to annihilate ourselves many times over, both through what we hold the power to do and through what we might fail to do. Bombs don't distinguish between the best and brightest among us versus the most ignorant or violently destructive humans; they're equal opportunity life destroyers. So is climate change an equal opportunity destroyer, at least if we fail to address the impact our behavior may be having on our biosphere.

Clearly, the time has come for us to change the way we competitively interact. Reliance on physical violence and emotional outbursts to impose our views on each other—the behaviors of teenagers and animals who lack the ability to reason and connect compassionately—make it more likely we'll do serious harm to each other, and by extension our whole species. What's needed now is heartfelt debate around competing ideas, with actions grounded in kindness and compassion. We need to acknowledge our self-induced suffering and demonstrate respect for alternative points of view due to cultural and environmental differences. Whenever we validate the needs, fears and feelings of others we discover we're more capable of proposing helpful solutions that can resolve our disagreements. If we can release our individual egos and our personal need to be right about the past, and instead come together around a brand new vision for a better future for all, there is nothing we can't accomplish as a species. We *can* eliminate pollution, reduce our dependence on fossil fuels, intelligently allocate our resources for global abundance, improve the quality of life for all living creatures, protect our water sources and ecosystems, design a sustainable, regenerative society, explore the solar system and beyond. Most *certainly* we can. We simply have to want to do so *more* than we wish to cling to our present behaviors.

THE WRONG-HEADEDNESS OF
SELF-RIGHTEOUSNESS

Whenever we perceive ourselves as right and others as wrong, our ego grows inflated; we may mistakenly perceive ourselves as better than other people who perhaps aren't as clever, informed or powerful as are we. However, the satisfaction we get from gratifying our own ego at the expense of another person is only a temporary high, because sooner or later we'll find ourselves forced to defend our beliefs from others who wish to enhance *their* egos at *our* expense. We must therefore continually fight each other to maintain our ego's status; otherwise we'll experience self-deflation. Of course, we could always choose to release our ego's need to be right and instead make the conscious choice to live in harmony with others, but that requires a radical change in behavior. We're far more accustomed to reacting from anger or fear when we're challenged than we are to responding in compassionate, thoughtful ways. In a capitalistic society that promotes winning at any cost—get straight A's, place first in the sports competition, be better than all your peers if you hope to succeed—is it any wonder we didn't learn as children how to back away gracefully from confrontations?

Literally from birth we're trained to place high value on being right (self-righteousness) and on besting other people at any cost (unhealthy competition). That training has caused humanity an untold amount of suffering. If you think about it, virtually every human death that has ever occurred at the hands of another and that wasn't accidental, from witch-hunts to political revolutions to international wars to genocidal massacres, was grounded in the belief that one group's *ideas* were right and the others' were wrong.

To perceive ourselves as *ideologically* correct means we're not required to change the way we *behave*. To acknowledge we're wrong means we must reconsider the way we're choosing to live, and perhaps even explore a new way of being, which can be terrifyingly uncomfortable. Change, even when we're desperately unhappy with our own lives, requires a scary step into the unknown. That's why evolution tends to work its magic through nearly imperceptible baby steps, urging us to inch our way incrementally forward to ever-higher states of being. Even so, the longer we avoid beginning the journey, the faster and more radically we're going to have to move if we hope to survive.

One thing that continues to hold us back is the fact that all our religions were established to define the ideological rightness or wrongness of our beliefs about life, so as to help us give life meaning. For millennia our major religions have told us stories about who we are, why we're here and what's likely to happen to us when we die. Many of us embrace those stories unquestioningly; in fact, to have blind faith in the stories is considered virtuous in most religious traditions. To harbor doubts or ask questions is considered dangerous or heretical. Some faiths even go so far as to shun those who challenge the status quo of religious beliefs, based on the presumption that our ancestors received divine revelations from God and therefore possessed greater wisdom than modern humans can possibly divine from the here and now.

Virtually every culture developed its own worldview around life and death, based on the wisdom and experiences of the people who guided the establishment of each culture's standing rulebook for beliefs and behaviors. Ironically, the behaviors we revere in our own religious stories are often the same behaviors we hate when we see them in other cultures. For example, American Christians despise the men who perceived themselves as Islamic martyrs for Allah on 9/11. Yet they revere Joan of Arc, who thought nothing of killing or dying for her own deep belief in Jesus as the Son of God. Jews may despise the Holocaust, but they honor Joshua's destruction of Jericho and his subsequent murder of every man, woman, child and animal within that innocent city's ill-fated walls. Muslims despise the Christian Crusaders who invaded their holy cities, but revere their own suicide bombers. It seems we're all so enamored with our own stories we've become willfully blind to our hypocrisy. Until we collectively open our eyes to the truth and denounce our *own* inhumanity, living beings will continue to suffer our ignorance all around this planet. Our collective inhumanity reveals itself in the way we economically and militarily oppress and destroy our global brothers and sisters because they happen to hold a different set of beliefs.

It can be eye opening to have deep conversations with those who hold different beliefs—or none at all. When we cease trying to "convert" others to our way of thinking in order to protect our cherished beliefs from external assault, we open ourselves to the possibility that our perspective may have been limited by our refusal to fully examine reality. I had one such experience recently when I participated in a group rendition of a play that modified the Genesis story of Adam and Eve being evicted from the Garden of Eden. Next to me sat a woman who had been raised in Communist

Lithuania, where religious training had been prohibited by the state. The shock and horror she expressed when she heard the Genesis story for the first time spoke volumes. I'd been raised in the Catholic faith, and had grown up absorbing the story's lessons from early childhood. My friend turned to me with profound compassion and said, "I had no idea what a terrible story that was. How awful for you all to have grown up believing such horrible things about yourselves." For a moment I envied her her freedom from belief in the tale. Hearing her words dredged up deeply painful feelings in my own heart; memories of my own childhood sense of unworthiness, my fears about my innate human brokenness, my horror in hearing that the feminine half of our species (my half!) had been declared the "cause" of all mankind's modern woes. At the same time, releasing my unconscious attachment to the story has helped me embrace my own wholeness and innate spiritual perfection, so I'm grateful for having been gifted the opportunity to consciously reject that negative story.

I now recognize and fully honor the beauty of my own femininity and the divine presence of life inside each of us. That journey, in its own right, has been a beautiful process of self-discovery I'm grateful to have taken. Still, the experience reminds me of the terrible weight of responsibility we adults have to be mindful of the beliefs we instill in our children. If we haven't personally challenged or fully explored the ideas *we* were taught as children with critically thinking minds and open hearts, using our prodigious powers of reason and intuition to discern if what we've been taught was accurate, how can we possibly presume that what we're teaching our children is right? If we're just blindly passing on old beliefs from one generation to the next, how will we ever develop the power to grow and evolve? And as protective as we are of our religious beliefs, we're equally protective of our social, political and economic beliefs—unexamined as they too may be.

Fighting to protect our beliefs from attack feels comfortable, like an old worn shoe. Conversely, responding by actively listening to another's point of view can sometimes be painful, because it forces us to set aside our own beliefs and allow the information to enter our minds unfiltered. Only after we've *truly* listened can we consider trying on new ideas, which may or may not prove valuable to us. The entire process therefore involves risks: the risk that comes from acknowledging that we *may* have been wrong about something, the risk that comes from experimenting with our own lives and modes of behavior, and the challenge of embracing the unknown that arises when we expose ourselves to new ideas or experiences.

We can begin to reclaim our power to grow by acknowledging that no idea or belief is ever completely wrong or right. New ideas emerge all the time as humanity's life experiences accumulate. Some ideas may prove to be somewhat more correct than the old beliefs we've held, while others may not pan out. In any case, science teaches us we can't ever prove the absolute "rightness" of anything. At best we can only demonstrate what doesn't work or isn't true through the process of trial and error. Ideas that do work may only work for a while; that is, they may work until the world around us changes and the idea no longer suffices. Human history is replete with examples of ideas that worked just fine until the world changed and demanded new approaches. In relatively short order we've gone from horses and buggies to airplanes and automobiles, from coal and wood to electricity, from corsets and hoop skirts to blue jeans, tee tops and flip flops. What haven't yet changed are our old, outmoded beliefs about what we are. We've yet to embrace ideas grounded in an evolving sense of our shared humanity.

What comes first—the individual realization that we're each part of a shared humanity, or a collective belief system proposing that humanity is one living organism occupying a shared reality? Perhaps, like the chicken and the egg, they're emerging right now, together. What draws us individually is what we try to manifest collectively. All any of us can do, then, is honor what's new and arising within *ourselves* about who and what we believe ourselves to be. Ultimately we must each be true to that.

We've been taught that to determine the right way to behave is to use our minds to sift through information. Meanwhile, we've been using our hearts to decide what's true, as with love. If we change that—by allowing our *hearts* to direct us toward the right thing to do and our *minds* to sense what's true about the world—we open up a whole new vista. In short, if it doesn't *feel* good for all parties concerned, it's probably wrong to do it. And if it doesn't make sense, it probably isn't true.

THE MEANS IS EVERYTHING;
THE END IS ILLUSION

For better or for worse, humanity finds itself imbedded in an ever-changing universe. This universe appears to be a living, self-evolving, consciously self-designing and fully creative matrix. It seems to be energetically exploring its own values and expressing its infinitely creative ideas *through* its eternal occupation of matter.

In practice, it seems the underlying consciousness that pervades and powers the entire universe inches closer and closer to the truth of its highest nature all the time, but perhaps its aim isn't to reach any final destination or draw any absolute conclusions about itself. Perhaps its true goal is the continuous perfection of the *means* by which it explores its inner visions and expresses itself in matter, instead of the arrival at some mythical end. That makes sense when viewed through the lens of the infinite and the eternal. After all, when something is both infinite and eternal, what point would there be in it reaching some final, frozen state of beingness? What would life then do with itself for the rest of all eternity? Sit there and smile?

Change, it seems, is what gives life its meaning and purpose. Change opens up life to the element of surprise and empowers it to find joy in its own existence. We already know that evolution mainly moves with a forward thrust, and that over time evolutionary changes lean toward ever-higher consciousness, greater structural complexity, expanding diversity, more specialized interrelationships, greater freedom and a continually higher order. Those facts alone make a strong case for the existence of a guiding universal intelligence that is both infinite and eternal. Why would it revert to lower states of being when it has already explored and experienced those to their fullest across the entire universe, especially when it has an eternity to thrust forward with new ideas? Why not create a seemingly infinite cosmic playground for itself on which to express a vast array of life forms, creatures that vary as widely as do the external conditions that promote their ongoing emergence?

What little we humans can grasp about such concepts provides us a window onto the essential nature of that which we sometimes call "God." Metaphorically, I sometimes like to visualize all of us as tiny aspects of awareness (God's eternal consciousness or presence) sailing on the wings of love (God's energy) through an infinite sea of life (God's ever-changing playground of matter). If matter is the infinite play-dough in which eternal consciousness rises to take form, love is the primordial energy that fuels their endless mating ritual. In that vision, everything around us is alive and, in some fashion, conscious.

Man's longstanding scientific perspective has been that so-called inanimate objects are dead while animate objects are living. That view, when first proposed, was severely hindered by our inability to see with our naked eyes the energetic goings-on and ordered behaviors inside a table, a rock or even a glass of water. Telescopes and microscopes have since shown us the error of our ways, but we haven't adjusted our thinking to match what we observe. We still draw false lines of separation between animate and inanimate and still imagine ourselves to be separate from all other things. If we let go of that worldview and embrace the realization that it's all one giant spectrum of energy endlessly creating and recreating itself like a living rainbow, the world becomes instantly friendlier, more peaceful and more joyful than before.

If everything is alive, then life itself must be indestructible. Matter just changes form from time to time to stimulate life. Birth and death are just doorways that enable the eternal field of life to enter and exit the field of matter and try on its various forms, the same way we humans wear costumes or different clothing for different occasions. Humanity thus becomes one type of costume while a lion, a tree or a star becomes another. None is better or worse than the other; all are equally crucial to the collective universal experience we're all sharing. When we at last realize everything is alive and nothing can truly be killed, what we do becomes less important than how we do it—how we relate to each other, how we express ourselves and how we choose to escort each other (and by extension all things) through that unavoidable doorway of death that awaits so we can someday become something new.

Assuming we're willing to open our hearts and minds wide enough to define God as the consciousness that creates, contains and informs our universe, we can't help but feel reverential toward all things. What has been created, what has emerged to become part of our shared reality, is here because the totality wished to experience those things as itself. It therefore falls upon us to approach everything we do in a sacred manner, knowing that anything we consume is a living entity we are depriving of its continued self-existence. Consumption then takes on a whole new meaning, as something that must be done purposefully and thoughtfully, that must be done with gratitude and viewed as beneficial for all life if we're to consider it right for us to do.

ENDINGS VS. INFINITIES

Understandably it's hard for us to avoid noticing boundaries and trying to reach conclusions when thinking about infinity and eternity. The material world we occupy is filled with borders and endings. We not only observe the end of each day, we eventually arrive at the end of every road, life and geological age. From our human perspective, then, which leans toward separation as a way of experiencing the world, it's difficult *not* to notice borders because our very eyesight informs us that "edges" exist. Electron microscopes and advanced telescopes are informing us all the time that we're not seeing life's entire picture, but it's hard to embrace that truth when we can't observe it with the naked eye. While modern scientists tell us all things appear to be interconnected, we look around and notice the spaces between material objects. We don't observe the invisible energy waves passing between those objects, or the silent communication occurring between each and every atom in existence. We therefore tend to believe that differentiation and separation are one and the same, although they're not.

Differentiation is a form of specialization *within* an integrated system, whereby all the parts, while independently functional and whole, remain fully interdependent. Separation, on the other hand, requires at least two distinct wholes, with each functioning entirely independent of one another. When we look around at our universe—*really* look—what we discover are wholes within wholes *within* wholes, which can only be defined as differentiation taking place within a single, fully integrated system.

Genuine *separation* doesn't appear to exist anywhere within our universe. While our universe does *differentiate* very creatively between its myriad self-contained parts, so far as we know it doesn't separate anything from itself. Only *we* do that, through our fictional beliefs about our place in the universe.

The only way we can really begin to appreciate the vastness of the infinite is through the exploration of our own minds, because it's only there we have the ability to discover a world without boundaries, a world beyond the limitations of time. The ground of our conscious being is vast; it doesn't restrict us the way our bodies do or the way time seems to do. And while our experiences change and our knowledge expands over time, the underlying awareness that observes those experiences and learns from them doesn't change, any more than the "you" that occupies your aging body seems older than it did in your childhood. Your body may change and your wisdom may expand with your experience, but the one who is having those experiences of change—the conscious, observing presence that is you—is still the same. That awareness, it seems, marks the point(s) in the universe where the infinite penetrates eternal matter and becomes *conscious* of the experiences it is creating. We humans are just one of many such windows the infinite has opened up in this world of form to enable it to experience itself—both through *being* and as *a being*. We currently live in a world where the infinite appears to be eternally redefining itself by playing with what appears finite and discovering what that means, or if matter *matters*. Energized by the life force, atoms everywhere coalesce into discrete forms following exquisite patterns and a higher cosmic order. They expand on those forms and evolve them over time, then dissolve the forms to make way for brand new creations. Underneath it all is the life force itself, having a wonderful time manipulating the field of matter to serve its intentions. In a sense, then, our primary role may be to uncover the truth about life's deep intentions by experiencing ourselves as something both finite and temporary, *and* as something magnificently eternal.

One important point to note here is that if there's any truth at all to the above it means no end can *ever* justify the means, so it's time we stopped justifying behavior that harms others for the sake of a hoped-for outcome for ourselves. Anything we do in the short run to advance our personal agendas that violates the truth of our complete connectivity to the whole—things like torture, diasporas, wars, polluting and the willful destruction of our environment—will become realities that the eternal totality (in which we are inextricably imbedded) will have to deal with as this infinite life goes on. In an infinite and interconnected eternal reality, the means *must* become the end unto themselves, because it's only through enhancing the means we use that the evolutionary process of creation self-enhances.

In other words, the cosmos endlessly creates a better world by continuously improving the process of creating, using all of life's creations to help it advance. Within this infinite universal feedback loop, our cosmos (universal consciousness) doesn't really change— it's simply that life's wisdom and dexterity, as applied through the field of matter, mature over time. With loving, patient practice, the play dough that is cosmic matter becomes self-rising, better acting, more self-aware and more capable of becoming self-directing. Experience is therefore life's teacher, while matter becomes the proving ground for life's most imaginative ideas.

COMPETITION FOR SOCIAL INFLUENCE

To believe we're right and others are wrong is to presume we personally know more about what should or shouldn't be than anyone else—including the larger universe, which created alternative viewpoints for a reason. When we fight to prove our point, to "make" others see the world our way, we may be able to force our opinions on them for a time, but at what price? Ultimately, we don't have the power to crawl inside another person's head and make him believe anything he doesn't want to believe. Killing a person if we can't make him believe as we do doesn't help either; it just reduces the amount of human energy available to help advance our world. Who knows how much talent, genius and capacity to better our shared reality has been sacrificed on the altars of war and human destruction? While killing others may eliminate some of the opposition (as with the unfortunate victims of the Spanish Inquisition or the imagined modern day "enemies" of Al Qaeda on 9/11), unless we murder every person who believes differently than do we, such behavior just creates new enemies of those whose loved ones we've destroyed. Ultimately, since no two people think exactly alike, to annihilate those who hold different ideas leads to total isolation. That, as we know, means species extinction, so it's not the path down which life intends us to head. The love of life is too deeply engrained in our psyches for us to want to cause our annihilation. We love life because we're *supposed* to love it enough to want to continue to live it, even though truly living it may feel difficult at times.

Some of you may find yourselves having serious mental arguments with me as you read these words, because my language doesn't mirror your understanding of the truth. That's fine. All interactions in which our ideas are challenged encourage us to explore the alternatives and seek ways to resolve our differences. That's how progress happens and where the energy for us to create something new will eventually arise.

So, if murder isn't the answer to our disagreements, what is? Again we can look to our personal nature for insight. We already know the universe has pre-programmed us to be attracted to certain things and repulsed by others. To pay attention then to those experiences our feelings encourage us to desire—love, connectivity, beauty, sharing, creative exploration, etc.—and to *avoid* those experiences our feelings cause us to dislike—pain, suffering, fear, isolation, etc.—would be a welcome start.

This doesn't mean that because some of us have begun to realize we're all connected the entire world population is suddenly going to stop competing, hold hands and sing "Kumbaya" together; far from it. Many people alive today have been deeply wounded by feelings of separation and the sense that they're not "good enough." We'll therefore need to design compassionate ways of dealing with the most deeply destructive among us, which may mean preventing them from acting out of rage while at the same time encouraging them to feel loved by us and recover their own wholeness.

As any parent of a young baby knows, there's a time in its early development when that child doesn't yet know its own fingers are connected to its hands, and it accidentally scratches and injures itself. We don't, however, punish the baby for failing to recognize its true nature. Instead we put mittens on its hands, swaddle it and lovingly treat its injuries until the baby develops an awareness of its body and ceases accidentally harming itself. For the Ted Bundys, Adolph Hitlers and Charlie Mansons of the world, the same process holds true. No man is *inherently* evil if all men are of and from the unified field of life. A man who does an evil deed is acting out of ignorance of life's connectedness. Unfortunately, most of our religions have labeled evil a thing unto itself, often with disastrous consequences. Letting go of the belief that certain people are inherently evil, trusting that *all* of life contains the seeds of good, and establishing proper protective boundaries around those who have not yet learned to cultivate those seeds is paramount to our social evolution.

CHANGING OUR APPROACH TO COMPETITION

Human competition over ideas can be far more insidious and socially destructive than our competition for food, water or a comfortable place to live. The people who control the channels of ideas that flow into the social collective have the power to set the overall tone for humanity, and thus the power to steer our destiny. That's why maintaining a free and independent news media is so important. When our media primarily serves the interests of capitalism, whether for profit or power, it puts out the information that our businesses want us to hear. TV advertising bombards us *not* because we enjoy it, but because it serves the interests of corporations that financially support our media. For example, the news stories we watch and the advertisements we see often make us afraid for our own health. Every "disease" becomes a potential problem that demands a medical cure—which comes at a price. Our fears produce stress that then becomes its own disease, and those symptoms are also treated for a price.

While I don't advocate restricting the first amendment rights of the media, we *do* have the power to investigate what they're telling us and demand that at least they be honest and held to account for their deceptions. One troubling consequence of the recent Supreme Court ruling (Citizens United v. Federal Election Commission) that effectively granted corporations the rights of personhood is that we've seen a huge influx of corporate money into media-run political campaigns designed to influence public opinion around the capitalist agenda, and away from the best interests of the public. Granting corporations the financial power to control the national dialogue and dictate the political course of a nation is detrimental to humanity because it places the for-profit agenda ahead of the needs of living beings. As individuals, we must reclaim our personal power and demand absolute honesty from the media sources we turn to for information.

We know the Internet has become a vast repository of information, some of it excellent and some of it conceptually suspect. Both types help us get a better handle on what feels right and what doesn't. Additionally, as social change continues, the media may take greater responsibility for the information it delivers to the public. Releasing the chokehold our businesses have on us as individuals can't help but impact the way we manage public information. We must always remember, however, that ultimately, we *are* our media.

We're presently fed news that makes us afraid because fear encourages us to place our trust in institutions instead of each other. (Since our institutions are paying the media's bills, this arrangement works quite well.) We buy auto insurance because we can't trust the "other guy" to take responsibility for the accident. We buy medical and homeowners insurance because we can't count on our neighbors to be there for us in a time of personal crisis. We hire attorneys because we need to make sure the other guy pays for the damage he caused, even if what happened was an honest mistake. We put money into financial institutions because the other guy might rob us if we don't tuck away our savings somewhere "safe."

When we observe how these institutions work in *practice*, we see that our insurance companies deny our claims, cancel our policies or raise our rates the moment we actually need them to help us out. They're happy to accept our premiums, but our claims cut into their profitability. We discover our legal system will represent us only so long as our case earns money for the lawyers who defend us. We find that our financial institutions are more interested in separating us from our hard-earned dollars than they are in helping us save them. Fees, charges, questionable investments, predatory mortgages, higher interest rates—all are the means by which banks make their profits off our need to store our cash in their vaults.

We've become so suspicious of each other that we don't even allow our children to play outside without supervision anymore. The media makes it sound like pedophiles and rapists are hovering on every street corner, just waiting to pounce on our innocent boys and girls. The truth, however, is that of the many thousands of children under the age of five who were murdered between 1976 and 2005, strangers killed fewer than three percent of them.[57] Ninety-seven percent of those children were actually murdered by family members, legal guardians or family friends. Even so, the media frenzy surrounding every single abduction and murder of a child by a stranger far exceeds our awareness of all the other deaths combined.

Our modern media outlets, particularly since the advent of 24-hour cable news channels, bury us in almost all *bad* news, almost all the time. Our news encourages us to fear each other, as well as to take sides in disagreements about which we receive very little information and have no real depth of understanding. Cable news delights in pitting two people against each other and allowing them to personally attack each other for the sake of high drama and ratings, instead of promoting rational and in-depth (i.e. boring) discussions around our most serious challenges. We're encouraged to choose sides based on emotionally manipulative sound bites. Our egos become inflated; "our" guy is right, so those others must be wrong. How all this trash talk enhances society's ability to examine itself and draw insightful conclusions about how to address its problems is an open question; in all likelihood it harms us more than it helps. When we accept a news system that quarrels in a moral and intellectual vacuum because that stimulates revenue streams, we wind up with conspiracy theorists and anarchists on the left and fundamentalist protestors and anti-government

---

57   "Homicide Trends in the US: Infanticide," Bureau of Justice Statistics, last revised January 31, 2011.

militias on the right. The higher interests of the silent majority go unserved in the quest for ratings and corporate profits. We've been programmed practically since birth to accept that "if it bleeds, it leads," so death and mayhem is the news we collectively tend to gravitate toward. How much better off we'd be as a society if we shifted our attention toward watching "if it *succeeds*, it leads."

To surrender control over our thoughts to the power elite (via the corporate media that has been bought and paid for) is to set ourselves up for a constant competition between those in power and those whose ideas are currently out of favor. We see such struggles all the time between nations, political parties and religions competing for spiritual adherents. If we decided that no channel holds a monopoly on truth and sourced our information from a variety of outlets we'd be better informed and better off as a species.

Unfortunately, it's easy to let others do our thinking for us, and we've been rewarded for doing so by our religious institutions (have faith in what we tell you), our schools (spit back without alteration what you've been taught), our governments (we know what's best for the people), and our judicial systems (we'll decide *for* you what's right or wrong). Thinking for ourselves can be hard work, because it requires us to buck virtually *every* system into which we've been indoctrinated. However, as Thomas Jefferson himself once said, the core of any democracy is an informed citizenry. He recognized that without full and accurate data to inform their decisions, people become as easily led as sheep.

Of late we've allowed ourselves to be seduced into becoming a highly *entertained* citizenry instead of an informed one. Entertainment distracts us from the quest for meaningful information. The ancient Romans spent their days in the coliseum, watching gladiators fight and kill each other for fun, while their entire civilization collapsed around them. It's high time we realize history is threatening to repeat itself; the fall of the United States, should it happen in the near future, will likely be directly traced to the unwillingness of the citizenry to set aside our love of entertainment in time to manage the problems that are overwhelming our country. Studying the science of climate change may not be nearly as exciting as watching the Steelers play the Giants, but if the icebergs melt we'll regret we lost sight of what mattered.

To cease competing with each other in destructive ways, and to trust people more than we trust our institutions is to hold life itself in higher esteem than capitalism or monetary profits. To encourage our politicians to *test* the truth or falseness of our ideas is to value life experience over abstract beliefs. If something doesn't work once we've tested it, we can always move on without suffering guilt or blame, knowing we've learned something of value from having tried and failed. What *does* work we can expand upon to see if it might somehow be improved.

For example, we know through trial and error that people tend to be happier when they're given the freedom to believe whatever they choose. That's why totalitarian regimes often fence their people in, as opposed to fencing out their neighbors as free nations sometimes do. Consider North Korea, which shoots its citizens for trying to flee, versus the European Union, which encourages its people to travel across any number of national borders. That's also true for religions that box in the faithful through the use of fear. People who believe in a loving, engaging and benevolent God (or cosmos) are generally happier and more compassionate toward others than those who've been taught to fear the hellfire and damnation of a punishing, paternal and highly judgmental God.

The more fear and judgment a given religion preaches, the more dysfunctional its followers are. Binding people to any system out of fear rather than lovingly drawing them to it is a much less effective way to forge lasting connections. And as we all know, loving connections feel far better than fearful ones when it comes to the mental and emotional health of the participants. Again we can look to nature for confirmation. If, for example, a particular species of flower tried to use the fear of starvation to entrap bees rather than entice them using the pleasant aroma of nectar, those flowers would go extinct. The bees, disliking the sensation of entrapment, would turn elsewhere for nourishment the moment they realized they could dip happily into other, more enticingly fragrant flowers that allowed them their freedom. The old saying, "you catch more flies with honey than you do with vinegar" is indeed a homespun truth.

Fear is constricting; love is expansive. Humanity self-actualizes when we grow and create, then give lovingly to others from our own abundance. Buddha, Krishna, Jesus and Mohammed all exemplified this truth, but many of the religious organizations that have institutionalized their teachings have turned their spiritual practices into businesses by preaching fear instead. While instilling fear may have benefited them in the short run, in the long run they too may go extinct once their adherents, exhausted from living beneath the yoke of fear, smell the sweet fragrance of a higher spirituality and move toward that wonderful scent to find a new heaven, this time with no hell attached.

To live richly is to grow and evolve through *healthy* competition. Healthy competition pushes us all to be the best we can become. It doesn't destroy us for daring to try something different. When practiced through ritual physical challenges and vigorous debates, healthy competition encourages us *all* to be better by inspiring us to discover what we're capable of achieving. Conversely, unhealthy competition generates hostility and fear between opposing sides and leads to policies of personal (or group) destruction. When our politicians stoop to name calling, hyperbolic labeling and accusing each other of bad behavior instead of remaining maturely centered on discussing their differing ideas, nothing of consequence gets done. Witnessing that level of incivility in turn causes the public to lose all respect for their political representatives. So disrespectful behavior, which some politicians might imagine elevates them at the expense of their opponents, ultimately comes back around on those who are practicing it.

How to push one another to heights of passion without shoving each other into the abyss of fear becomes our modern challenge. With healthy competition there is no such thing as failure, so long as we live to pick ourselves up to try again another day. If we can graciously accept and honor the success of the victor we can move past our egocentric need to be the one who achieved success. We can learn to revel in the success of each other, knowing that in our own way we contributed what we could to the total effort. It helps to remember that we all are embedded in the same universe, and that any one person's success enhances us all.

PROPERLY MOTIVATED COOPERATION

As a child I enjoyed playing in the sandbox with other children my age. If a fight broke out, our parents were quick to rush in and snatch the Tonka truck or plastic shovel from whichever child was banging it over the head of a sobbing target. Never, however, do I remember a parent interrupting our efforts if we came together to build ourselves a castle. Usually what we managed to create together (at least when the battles over who owned which toys weren't distracting us from our mission) turned out grander and far more beautiful than what we managed to build whenever we worked alone.

The same, we can assume, holds true for adults today. Our highest collaborative efforts have the power to advance society beyond what we can accomplish when we work alone. And still we pass laws that prevent corporations from working together, or from merging to become too monolithic. The question we must ask ourselves is, why? Why must we discourage corporations from behaving in ways we've found are helpful? Might it have something to do with the fact that their quest for profits inspires them to *collude* against the interests of the public? If so, it means our companies have an inherent motive to work *against* their customers, whether or not they choose to work together. That's a realization we'd do well to reflect upon as a society.

COOPERATING TO SATISFY PERSONAL GREED

Cooperation between businesses has been problematic in the past because capitalism has chartered companies to place greater value on profits than they place on human or environmental welfare. The very term "anti-trust law" explicitly spells out the problem we have with corporations that get too cozy with each other. We simply can't *trust* them. If we can't trust our corporations collectively, why should we trust them individually? One rabid dog is no less dangerous than a pack of them running wild in the streets. The only advantage of encountering the lone animal is we're only bumping into one set of fangs. That doesn't make the bite we receive less deadly.

Why would we willingly choose to work for an organization we can't trust to do right by us or by our planet? The problem is that our pressing need to earn a living means we're rarely given the option to choose who we work for or what they decide to produce.

That may explain why so many of us find our jobs unfulfilling, unsatisfying and damaging to our dignity. It's why whistleblowers have been coming forward more and more of late; so many that we've had to pass laws to protect them from the vengeance of companies whose misbehavior they're trying to tell us about.

While profit motives encourage companies to collude against the best interests of humanity, properly motivated cooperation has long been recognized as valuable to the whole of society. For example, let's say Pharmaceutical Company One has a research team that discovers a new way to time-release one of its products, making their medicine easier for patients to tolerate. That means patients need to take less and will have fewer side effects. Company One patents its new method, which means all other pharmaceutical companies are forbidden to use that technology despite the benefits the new method offers patients. Pharmaceutical Company Two may offer Company One a licensing fee in exchange for the right to use the new time-release system. That fee then gets tacked onto the price tag Company Two's patients must pay when they buy their medicine.

This amounts to a windfall profit for Company One, because it doesn't cost Company One anything to share the new technology with Company Two. They don't even manufacture the same medicines, so there's little chance that Company Two will steal Company One's customers. Now, Company One may make the case it deserves to be rewarded for work done by its in-house researchers, whose salaries and benefits it paid while they invented the delivery system, but the truth is Company One has already been rewarded because its employees did the job they were paid to do: they invented a brand new time-release system that helps Company One improve its products for the benefit of its own customers.

The notion that Company One deserves to earn profits indefinitely from whatever advancements it creates for society means social advancement is often slowed through a lack of cooperation between organizations. Instead of encouraging corporate sharing for social advancement, we reward companies for hoarding their best ideas.

In the above example, Company One is rewarded for its invention. Overall, though, society winds up paying Companies Two, Three and Four much higher prices for their newly improved medications than was warranted, due to the licensing fees that each must pay Company One to use its system. But let's take this argument even further: if Two, Three and Four's patients are entitled to Medicare, the government will pay those higher prices, which in turn come out of our collective taxpayer dollars. If those patients are covered by private insurance, their insurance companies will pass those costs along to consumers in the way of higher premiums and co-pays. (Which partly explains why insurance premiums have risen one hundred thirty-one percent since 1999, while wages have risen just thirty-four percent.[58]) It's important to note that the added licensing fees being charged will cost society much more over time than the wages earned by Company One's researchers, although they *do* pour straight to the bottom line of Company One's profit statement.

---

58   Victoria Colliver, "Health Care Insurance Premiums Outpacing Wages, Inflation," *The Seattle Times*, September 16, 2009.

If you're wondering who benefits when Company One's profits rise, you should know it isn't really their stockholders. Years ago, companies used to raise their annual dividends whenever profits rose, which distributed those profits to their stockholders. Or they may have paid off their outstanding debts early, which meant retiring their bonds or preferred stocks through lump sum cash payments and increasing shareholder value. Over the past thirty or so years, however, the trend has increasingly been to count solely on inflating stock prices to provide financial returns for corporate stockholders while diverting excess profits to a handful of company executives in the form of annual bonuses and huge grants of company stock.

The trouble with that strategy is that stock prices can't be counted on to rise forever and benefit stockholders, particularly during periods of recession, even if a company's profits are sound. Expecting stock prices to reward owners also means the shareholder must sell his stake to *realize* his profit. Many stockholders feel reluctant to do that, since every stock sale incurs a commission cost and triggers a taxable event. Besides, if people genuinely like owning a particular company they don't want to have to sever their relationship to the company in order to realize a capital gain on the stock. That means they're inclined to hold onto their investments for many years. It's quite possible, then, for a company to reap enormous profits for decades, while its individual stockholders never see a single dime of the company's annual gains.

Corporate executives don't get to the top of the ladder because they're dumb. They set their own salaries and determine their own bonuses through boardroom deals and powerful backroom relationships. Since business executives commonly serve on each other's boards of directors, they have a vested interest in being as generous as possible with each other when it comes to voting for wages and bonuses.

The average chief executive of a Fortune 500 company in 2009 earned five hundred fifty times the salary of the average corporate employee.[59] Let's think about that for a moment. We know that the minimum wage in 2009 was set at $7.25 per hour, and that the average wage hovered around $18.50 an hour.[60] Meanwhile a highly compensated executive was earning approximately $10,175 per hour. Given a forty-hour workweek for a fifty-two-week work year with two weeks of paid vacation, that executive earned $20,350,000 as compared to the $37,000 income earned by the average employee and the $14,500 earned by the minimum-wage employee. I don't know about you, but I can't imagine any individual so brilliant as to be worth over ten thousand dollars per hour, *every* hour. Just think—those executives earned more before *lunch* on January first than their typical employees earned the entire year! For heaven's sake, the President of the United States earns only two hundred dollars an hour, and I'd say that's one of the toughest jobs in the world.

Is it any wonder so many ego-driven, ruthless and greedy individuals have scampered across each other's backs to make it into those high-test corner offices? Dennis Koslowski of Tyco, Ken Lay

59   Professor G. William Donhoff, "Who Rules America?" Sociology Department, UC Santa Cruz, 2011. http://sociology.ucsc.edu/whorulesamerica/

60   Laura Conaway, "Average Hourly Wages Rise Again," National Public Radio: Planet Money, January 31, 2011.

of Enron and Bernie Ebbers of WorldCom are just a few examples of formerly successful corporate executives who wound up publicly disgraced when their selfish, self-serving behaviors were exposed. Unfortunately for us, it seems that in a "trickle down" reality the qualities that have the greatest tendency to trickle down from our corporate executives might be considered humanity's least attractive traits and attributes.

As gratifying as it might be to label such people intrinsically evil, they're not. They love their spouses and parents, contribute money to charities and protect and nurture their children as best they can. What they *are* is socially entrained to behave in Pavlovian ways around money and the promise of success—just like the rest of us have been trained to behave. Neither is Pharmaceutical Company One evil for doing what it's been chartered by us to do—earn more money through every means at its disposal. The fact that we *encourage* Company One to make money with little or no consideration for the public or planetary welfare is the part we need to evaluate. What makes reconsideration difficult is that to shift corporate focus away from profit for its own sake and point it instead toward creating a better society for all would mean we'd have to restructure our entire business culture. While that may not be easy it *can* be done by changing the way we choose to reward our companies. Currently, our only options are to reward them through greater sales and higher stock prices, or to punish them by boycotting their products. Neither of those choices gives the public real power, though, particularly if what those companies sell is something we need in order to function, like gasoline, water or electricity. However, if we were to remove the temptation for businesses to profit through greed by eliminating patents and intellectual property rights, and in addition if we honored and patronized companies for acts of public altruism, we would be taking a step toward building a better world for everyone.

Rewards might consist of public acknowledgment of corporate generosity, which would provide good public relations feedback and encourage the public to support (and its employees to work harder for) those companies. Under the current system we sometimes offer tax breaks to companies for behaving in ways that benefit society, but tax breaks are purely financial incentives that serve to reinforce our dependence on financial motivations rather than decrease our attachment to the overarching profit motive.

Another benefit for engaging in more altruistic behavior is that cooperative companies would likely begin to receive reciprocal acts of generosity that would improve their own products and practices. If Company One offers helpful information to Two for free and Two returns the favor by freely offering new information to One, *both* companies and *all* their customers are certain to benefit.

The longstanding argument against corporate altruism's working is based on the false belief that companies will be far less likely to innovate if they can't earn a profit for their efforts. The truth is that companies are comprised of human beings, so if human beings can learn to behave in altruistic ways then surely the institutions they create can mirror that behavior. While it's true that freely sharing information and ideas may in the short run reduce a company's profitability, who can say how much they stand to profit in the long run through altruistic and reciprocal sharing arrangements? If more customers can afford to buy a company's products, and if the products work better for its consumers, isn't that what we're trying to accomplish?

Once again, the argument against business cooperation relies on our modern definition of what constitutes a profit. As long as we feel compelled to view money as the sole definition of profit, the argument against cooperation has merit. If, however, we shift the *definition*—should we decide to value the social profits earned and the environmental profits gained from corporate behavior *higher* than we value monetary profits—companies *will* perform for social benefit and *will* care for the environment instead of focusing strictly on the bottom line. Our businesses will do whatever we reward them to do...because we *are* them. No business can exist without at least a few living workers to run the basic equipment. And they all need human managers to make decisions on their behalf, as well as consumers to purchase their goods and services.

One business that hasn't waited to change its own definition of profit is Café Gratitude, a multi-location eatery based in San Francisco, California. Early on, the owners of Café Gratitude made a conscious decision to run their organization around a specific set of spiritual and deeply moral guidelines. They chose to focus on providing organic and healthy food to the public, through employees who enjoy being friendly and connecting with customers more intimately than simply playing the roles of servers and patrons. Employees play games with the customers and encourage them to talk about themselves. For them, creating a sense of family within their community, sharing their ideas and joys with each other, constantly looking for ways to improve their business, and honoring life as a sacred experience takes *precedence* over monetary profits. That they manage to "do well by doing good" proves the public values what they've achieved.

Of course, to design a complete turnabout of any company's purpose may seem like a radical notion, but—as Café Gratitude demonstrates—it can be done. And while it's always easier to have top-down support for major changes, history is filled with examples of bottom-up changes as well. The formation of American labor unions was just such a bottom-up shift. Too often, though, the people in control, who fear they have much to lose and little to gain from supporting change, meet bottom-up efforts with powerful top-down resistance. For decades corporate executives have fought unionization and tried to bust the unions, using lockouts, mass firings and other punishments—including police-supported physical violence—to exert control over their workers. Even so, while union membership has been on the decline in the past forty years, the collective bargaining power of the unions remains strong.[61] However, that too is coming into question, particularly with regards to public employee unions. Politicians have recently begun to pit the wages and pensions of workers in the public sector against those in the private sector in an attempt to reduce budget deficits, and are creating new laws to restrict the ability of public employees to collectively bargain and strike. That may, in the future, enable corporations to take bolder steps to limit the power of private enterprise unions as well.

To transform our companies peacefully into collaborative social partners instead of continuing to allow them to dictate their

---

61   Barry T. Hirsch, David A. McPherson and Wayne G. Vroman, "Estimates of Union Density by State," Monthly Labor Review, July 2001.

own terms from on high may be the greatest challenge we face when it comes to saving ourselves from extinction. In life, the real power *always* comes from the people. The public has the capacity to close down all organizations whose products and missions don't serve it by refusing to support them anymore. The difficulty, though, lies with releasing the belief that we're subservient to the pyramidal power structure we've lived beneath for such a very long time. If we don't *believe* we hold the power to restructure the very system that's killing us with its desperate search for profits at our expense, we won't even try. Like the fabled frog sitting placidly in the pot of heating water, we'll boil to death before we realize we should have jumped.

Those who benefit most from the current top-down power structure may continue to resist any populist attempts to change it. Some people were born into wealth and feel an innate sense of entitlement. Others have struggled hard to move beyond their birth circumstances, so feel they've earned the privileges that come with higher status and monetary power. In either case, the belief that "I clawed my way to the top of the heap, so why should I have to *share* my privilege and wealth?" is born of separation consciousness. It's grounded in the illusion that a person can benefit at the expense of others and never suffer any consequences of the pain he or she is inflicting. Wealthy people rationalize their behavior, refusing to believe that when they use more than a reasonable share of the planetary resources that means someone else, somewhere else, is being forced to make due with less. When poor and oppressed people react angrily toward Western civilization, we often accuse them of being savages instead of looking in the mirror at how our consumptive ways have negatively impacted others.

Raising awareness of the interconnectedness of all things is as difficult as changing the way we reward our businesses, so that they serve *our* needs instead of abusing us to serve *their* profit-making agendas. Like the chicken and the egg, I suspect businesses and individuals must evolve hand in hand, each encouraging the other to tiptoe forward experimentally, until our shared experience is one we can *all* enjoy.

ANTITRUST COLLUSION AND MONOPOLISTIC PREDATION

Competition, we're often told, creates fair prices and inspires ongoing technological advances. It's therefore unhealthy to encourage companies to collaborate, since competition is the only thing that protects consumers from monopolistic aggression. Indeed, consumers have often been the victims of price fixing when competitive companies have "cooperated" in the past. Antitrust laws have been designed over the years to protect us from predatory behind-the-scenes arrangements. Once again, if we consider the word "antitrust" we must ask ourselves this: who isn't able to trust whom in that equation? The fact that antitrust laws were put into place because society can't trust its businesses to behave morally while operating under the profit motive is a powerful enough insight to encourage us to reconsider the way we motivate them.

Illustrating the point is a highly publicized case from 2008 involving LCD manufacturers Sharp of Japan, LG of China and Chunghwa of Taiwan. Prosecuted for price fixing, the three companies ultimately agreed to pay five hundred eighty-five million dollars in fines for having illegally fixed prices for more than five years on their LCD panel displays, which were used to make cell phones, televisions and computers.[62] Since the LCD market generated over seventy billion dollars in revenues annually, that fine amounted to a minute percentage of the profits those companies gained from their illegal price collusion. On top of that, consumers aren't likely to see a penny of the penalty money; it goes straight to the United States Justice Department to cover the cost of prosecuting the case on behalf of the American people. It's important to note here that the laws we have in place against collusion don't seem to stop it, because the opportunities to earn enormous profits from price fixing far outweigh the judicial risks of being caught and slapped with comparatively tiny fines.

Corporate collusion against the public interest isn't the sort of business cooperation we want to encourage. What we *ought* to promote is greater transparency, with social benefit and a reverence for all of life becoming our new yardstick for determining what constitutes a profit. One new aim might be to create win/win situations. What we have now is a system that works fine for corporations and a few high-level individuals, but comes at the expense of most other people almost all the time.

---

62   Steve Lohr, "LCD Makers Fined $585 Million for Price Fixing," *The New York Times*, November 13, 2008.

If this seems like an unattainable goal, it isn't. In *The Translu-cent Revolution,* Arjuna Ardagh provides numerous examples of business owners who have already shifted (and continue to shift) their workplace behavior based on spiritual insights and realiza-tions they've had. Ardagh tells the story of George Zimmer, the founder and CEO of Men's Warehouse, who promotes a policy of "reciprocal altruism" among his salespeople. Zimmer encourages his commissioned staff to assist each other with customers, with the understanding that when they need help in the future some-one else will step up and help them. Then there's the tale of Ray Anderson, who founded Interface Carpet in Atlanta, Georgia in 1973. Although he'd never given much thought to his company's environmental impact, in 1994 Anderson created a task force to study the question. Less than three years later, by making care of the environment a top priority in the way they conducted business, Interface Carpet had managed to eliminate over six daily tons of landfill waste and lower their carbon emissions to almost nothing.

The best way to reshape corporate behavior, then, is to change human motivation and promote into positions of authority those individuals who aspire toward a higher vision for humanity and who honor the interconnectedness of all things. When our com-panies and their executives feel called to serve the public trust and to care about the long-term welfare of this planet because they realize what they do impacts us all (including themselves, their families and future generations), public service will at last be woven into the public job market, where it rightfully belongs. This ridiculous notion of a "private sector" whose motives aren't fully aligned with humanity's values and future survivability can be mercifully retired as a bad idea we experimented with and decided not to continue.

COOPERATION BETWEEN BUSINESSES, GOVERNMENT AND THE GENERAL PUBLIC

Virtually every day the news media reports a story from one research agency or another that declares some product or another is bad for us. For years now we've been warned about problems stemming from the use of antibiotics and growth hormones in livestock, about the negative effects of tobacco, and about the questionable safety of drugs like Vioxx and Phen-Fen. Not surprisingly, when the news first broke about those products, denials were quick to come from the businesses that profited from them. Though on June 12, 1957, Surgeon General Leroy E. Burney made it official that the United States Public Health Service believed there was a causal link between smoking and cancer, it then took forty years of legal wrangling to force Big Tobacco to admit smoking was a health risk, even though their own internal medical studies had proved so beyond any reasonable doubt.[63] In a similar situation, Merck suppressed its own in-house research showing Vioxx doubled the risk of heart attacks and strokes, and as a result it faced billions of dollars worth of

---

63 "The Reports of the Surgeon General: The 1964 Report on Smoking and Health," Profiles in Science, National Library of Medicine, National Institutes of Health; Jon Weiner, "Big Tobacco and the Historians," History News Network, George Mason University, February 26, 2010.

personal injury lawsuits from people whose health was negatively impacted by that callous corporate disregard for the truth for the sake of continued sales.[64]

As for the sub-therapeutic use of antibiotics to foster weight gain in factory-farmed animals: just one of the negative results seems to be the new, high levels of drug-resistant bacteria now appearing in our meat products.[65] Still, the meat industry declared as recently as 2008 that there wasn't enough evidence to support a proposed ban on the use of such drugs in our livestock.[66] Could the reason for their denial be that discontinuing the use of harmful antimicrobial drugs would decrease feeding efficiency, raising their food costs and reducing their meat production—and thus their profits?

When the choice comes down to profits or public safety, a little consumer illness—say salmonella or e-coli—dispersed through a wide swath of the population may seem like a small price to pay in exchange for greater industrial productivity and efficiency. That's particularly true if the company involved conceals its involvement in the spread of an illness so its profit margins can grow for many more years. It's not true, though, if *your* husband, mother or child happens to be one of those few whose organs failed or who died from a corporate-caused illness.

---

64   Mike Adams, "Merck Caught in Scandal to Bury Vioxx Heart Attack Risks, Intimidate Scientists and Keep Pushing Dangerous Drugs," *Natural News*, November 6, 2004.

65   Andrew Gunther, "USDA Admits Link Between Antibiotic Use by Big Ag and Human Health," *The Huffington Post*, July 20, 2010.

66   Christopher Doering, "Antibiotic Ban May Hurt Food Safety," Reuters News, March 24, 2009.

Some of the production pressure being placed on food companies comes from an increase in population and a concurrent rise in demand for additional food. When we logically consider the fact that our planet can support only so many people sustainably, and that our very success has made us resemble the wildly overpopulating family of squirrels in the field, it becomes clear that collectively we need to consider how best to manage our reproductive behavior, or else our planet is going to do some herd thinning for us.

Unfortunately, human population control is a subject too many people remain unwilling to entertain—either because of ancient religious proscriptions against practicing birth control or out of concern that our governments might begin to interfere in our personal choices. How foolish it is, however, to avoid having the discussion because it makes us feel uncomfortable, when by refusing to deal with the problem we may trigger the very results we hope to avoid. If we ignore the opportunity to practice voluntary control, we may reach a population crisis point where our governments have no choice but to insist we apply for permits to reproduce, or even force birth control on the population to keep us all safe. When we insist on thinking like children, plugging our ears and refusing to hear the things we don't want to hear, we shouldn't be surprised when we're treated like children.

Social pioneer and conscious evolutionary Barbara Marx Hubbard, who has unflinchingly addressed the question of human overpopulation for many years, recently came to the conclusion that perhaps the answer is for us to reach higher as a species, to discover how to join our *geniuses* joyfully rather than continue to focus on joining our *genes* for personal fulfillment. She refers to the joining of human geniuses as "suprasex," because the act of co-creating something of value has the ability to provide us with the same kind of shared excitement, energy outlay and deep satisfaction we experience during a sexual encounter.

How, we need to ask ourselves, did it come to pass that our businesses, even those so attached to the public welfare as are our food corporations, found it in their best interests to lie to the government, and to us, about critical safety issues? Is *that* the sort of behavior we want to encourage in our children? Do we really want to promote a system that allows our companies to do lasting damage to our health and our environment in exchange for higher short-term profits? What about the excessive carbon emissions that lead to climate change, or the continual pollution of our lakes and rivers with industrial chemical waste? How might we change our corporate culture so that greater cooperation with the public—and with governmental agencies whose job it is to protect the public interest—is deemed to be in *their* best interests as well? Is it possible for us to restructure our society so we don't have to rely so heavily on external rewards and punishments to make other people behave the way they should?

To bring business interests into alignment with humanity's long-term interests won't be easy without a major shift in human consciousness. Initially, we might have to consider attaching harsher punishments to corporate crimes as a method of last resort. Some states have placed 'three strikes' laws on their books so they can lock away repeat felons for life. While I don't necessarily approve of those laws because they discount an individual's unique circumstances for the sake of "scalable" justice, let's assume for the moment we created a 'one strike' policy for our corporations. A one-strike law would punish any company that betrayed the public trust by knowingly marketing a harmful product. The penalty would be that the government would shut the company down. What about a one-strike law for illegal corporate polluters, price fixers, aggressive monopolizers and so forth? Threatening federal revocation of a corporation's charter has a much bigger bite than the sting of a paltry fine. To date we've been gradually granting businesses more and more benefits and privileges of personhood without demanding they concurrently take full responsibility for their misdeeds. That's just plain crazy policy, since *somebody's* got to pay for the social costs of corporate crimes.

Unfortunately for the people, the United States Congress, which is funded by and answers to corporate America, has displayed a distressing tendency to overlook harmful corporate behavior until it becomes so egregious that many citizens suffer irreversible harm. At that point Congress has, in the past, passed a tepid law or two to curb the worst behaviors. Over time, though, even those laws are watered down or get eliminated once the public has forgotten about the problems those practices caused.

One such example that nearly crashed the entire global financing system pertains to the repeal of the Glass-Steagall Act, which was enacted in 1933 after hundreds of banks collapsed during the Great Depression. Glass-Steagall, in part, prohibited banks and investment underwriting firms from merging, fearing that they would become too powerful and that the opportunities for financial self-dealing would be too tempting if banks and investment firms were allowed to join forces. While the Reagan administration started chipping away at the act in 1980, the Clinton administration repealed the whole thing in 1999. At that point, however, Republicans controlled both houses of Congress, so blame for the flawed decision flows across both party lines. Republicans, it's interesting to note, often express a determination to allow the "free market system" to operate with as little government regulation or intervention as possible, based on fears of government corruptibility and concerns about excessive governmental power. Strangely enough they seem to admire the way corporations conduct themselves more than they trust the capacity of the government they're being paid to serve. This holds true despite the fact that corporate motivations are all about profits, while the government's purported motivation is to serve the people.

The repeal of the Glass-Steagall Act, which was triggered by Citigroup's successful bid to merge with Traveler's Group in 1998 and was wholly supported by the banking industry lobby, enabled mergers between banks and investment houses to occur without requiring banks to divest themselves of the investment houses' underwriting interests. That led directly to the 2008 banking collapse, which was caused by a global collapse of derivative securities that had been underwritten and sold by mega financial institutions for the benefit of their owner/parent banks. The banks, which by that time were classified as "too big to fail," then demanded taxpayer bailouts to rescue them from the consequences of their own greed and stupidity, which added insult to the massive financial injuries already inflicted on an unsuspecting public.

The repeal of corporate regulatory laws are encouraged— and the bills to deregulate are sometimes even written—by the special-interest lobbyists who work for companies that stand to benefit from the repeal. These lobby groups, it should be noted, are the same folks who channel enormous sums of corporate money into our political campaigns, and who entertain our senators and congressmen with international golfing junkets on private chartered jets and luxurious visits to foreign countries to "tour" their facilities. Speaker of the House John Boehner has been reported to play in excess of one hundred rounds of golf every year, mainly with congressional lobbyists.[67] It seems, then, that Republican fears about our government being corruptible may indeed be accurate. What Republicans fail to note about their preferred approach, however, is that it cedes control over our economic policies to our corporations, the organizations that are doing the corrupting! When the fox runs into the henhouse, the solution isn't to feed the hens to the wolf outside the door.

Our judicial system has the power to impose fines on corporations to punish them for committing harmful acts. Those fines, however, as noted before, typically represent a small financial risk to a corporation compared to the enormous profits it gains by breaking the law. Fines don't deter corporate misbehavior any more than fining a thief a fraction of what he made by pawning stolen goods will deter him from committing future thefts.

So how do we deter bad behavior in corporations? Punitive measures like fines and penalties always spring from an "us vs. them" mentality, which is why they should only be methods of last resort. They are tools of separation consciousness, tools we reach for when we can't reach collective accord about how else to

---

67   Joan Walsh, "Let Them Play Golf," Salon.com, August 10, 2010.

be. The better approach to long-term corporate management is to bring business intentions deliberately and thoughtfully into full alignment with what benefits society, both by changing the way we reward corporations *and* by changing the mentality that runs our corporate cultures—one person at a time. We can, of course, do so by financially rewarding businesses for doing the right thing, using standard methods like cap and trade credits for companies that successfully control their carbon emissions. Still, depending on financial rewards to improve our business culture when the desire for financial reward is what creates the problems in the first place is hardly the long-term answer.

The real solution lies in changing our individual beliefs about the importance of the corporate profit motive for business success. Harder, yes. But ultimately, it's the only way we'll ever be sure we can trust our companies to serve humanity's best interests, as well as protect and preserve our planet's resources and environment.

The current corporate system, where we must exercise constant vigilance over what is an inherently untrustworthy structure, has been a recipe for disaster. The financial scandals that have cost taxpayers trillions of dollars proved that. We can keep on doing more of the same (which is the classic definition of insanity) by addressing merely the symptoms of our social disease. We can build larger and more unwieldy governmental oversight bureaucracies and continue to tweak our ineffective laws—at least until some smart MBA finds another new way around them. (We should never underestimate the power of human creativity, or the intellectual ingenuity of America's MBA's.) *Or* we can cure our disease once and for all by eliminating the for-profit motive as the primary driver for corporate success. *That* is the fundamental root of our problem, the one we'd rather not face because of what it means for our desire to succeed at the expense of our neighbors and friends.

Every time we purchase a first-class airline ticket, buy a fast-pass at an amusement park so we can cut in front of the lines, or make an expensive political donation so we can gain front row seats to some high-profile political event, we're confirming our support of a system that encourages people to win at any cost, because it rewards the wealthy by allowing them to live better than most other people. Why, we must ask ourselves, do we believe it's OK for someone who has more money to be treated more humanely, more graciously and respectfully, than someone who isn't so rich? We must remember the values we embrace as individuals will be reflected and magnified in our larger systems. Perhaps it's time we each decide which values we wish to perpetuate and which we'd like to surrender.

INSTITUTIONS OR PEOPLE?

It may surprise you to learn that almost fifty percent of the companies listed on the New York Stock Exchange are incorporated in Delaware, although most are headquartered and operate out of the other forty-nine states.[68] Companies choose Delaware because its laws grant enormous day-to-day powers to management. They

---

68 "What Area of Law Interests You Most?" LexusNexus Summer Associates Community, 2011.

do so at the expense of stockholders, who are in fact the *real* business owners—not, though it may sometimes appear otherwise, the CEOs or the members of the board. Managers like to incorporate in states where they can maximize their financial benefits, under laws that grant CEOs more power and greater financial control of the revenue stream. They're far less concerned with maximizing stockholder value or creating genuine benefits for their customers.

Most banks are incorporated in either Delaware or South Dakota because those states allows banks to charge customers much higher interest rates than are typically permitted by the states where their headquarters are located. If you've ever wondered why your bank can charge you thirty percent interest on your credit card balance, which is often a violation of your own state's usury laws, it's because the laws of incorporation in Delaware and South Dakota supersede the laws your state created to protect you from such predatory lending practices.

Delaware also allows corporate management to define its own compensation plans, as well as to nominate its internal board of directors. Directors are often management's business peers, not stockholders or employees who work in the field and understand the moving parts of the business, including its problems. CEOs often serve on each other's boards in a very close "old boy network" arrangement, which explains why a CEO can get "fired" by his board for poor performance and still receive a golden parachute containing fifty million dollars in stock and severance on his way out the door. The unspoken agreement is that if ever the other board members get caught in the same situation, the disgraced CEO, who sits on *their* board, will gladly return the favor.

Stockholders may complain about these arrangements from time to time, but what power do they have to do anything about it? Not much, according to current Delaware law.

Delaware has also set up special business courts (Courts of Chancery) designed to meet the "special" needs of corporate enterprises. The state requires no initial capital outlay in order for a business to incorporate there. So, for the cost of a filing fee, literally anybody can establish a Delaware corporation. Delaware doesn't even make the names and addresses of company management public, which hinders business transparency but protects management's privacy from public investigation. Additionally, it doesn't charge any taxes on income a company earns outside the state. Would that we "regular people" had a similar right to choose the state in which we wished to declare our residency, regardless of where we actually lived and worked.

Just imagine if residents of highly taxed states like California or Massachusetts could, without physically relocating, suddenly declare themselves residents of a no-tax state like Nevada, Wyoming or Texas, simply because they preferred that state's tax laws. Likely we'd see brand new competitive tax advertisements popping up all over the country. Can you picture what might follow? "Declare residency in South Dakota and get two free acres of land with your two percent tax rate!" "Pay one percent to reside in Alaska, where you don't have to actually *live* to experience freedom from state regulation!"

Not only do companies have the right to incorporate in states where they aren't even headquartered, they were also seemingly granted the rights of legal personhood under an initial 1886

Supreme Court decision (Santa Clara County vs. Southern Pacific Railroad) that predated by over a century the Citizens United decision. It's important to note, however, that the original lawsuit in question was filed by a county intent on pursuing a railroad for having broken a county law. In the case, the Southern Pacific Railroad tried to shield itself from being sued by Santa Clara County, claiming that only "persons" could be sued for breaking the law. The court ruled against the railroad, declaring that corporations could not successfully shield themselves from lawsuits by declaring they weren't persons. It did not, however, ever declare that corporations were *indeed* persons. Clearly, the original intent of the ruling was merely to legally bind corporations to their debts and enable them to be sued like any other entity. The ruling has since been woefully misinterpreted in favor of corporations possessing all the privileges and rights of personhood, and is badly in need of judicial and/or congressional review.

What the 1886 ruling did was inadvertently grant to these newly declared corporate "persons" the right against self-incrimination, the right to privacy and the right to lobby the government on behalf of its shareholders. The nightmarish spectacle of lies and distortions surrounding President Obama's attempts to initiate medical insurance reform in 2009 was in large part created by business interests acting as corporate persons. Medical businesses, insurance companies and the pharmaceutical industry lobbied, funded and gained access to our politicians as well as to the news media in order to instill fear and undermine the determination of the public to address the issue. That sixty-five percent of the population supported a public medical insurance option, yet congress felt constrained from passing a law that included that option, is a direct consequence of that misinterpretation of the 1886 ruling and the special interest lobbying that has resulted.[69]

Another fine example of how corporate lobbying, under the protected designation of personhood, works against the interest of the general public becomes apparent when we examine the changes made to our bankruptcy laws in late 2005. Thanks to fierce lobbying efforts by the banks and financial institutions, Congress passed a law making it far more difficult for ordinary people to discharge their debts through bankruptcy. Was it coincidence that the bankruptcy laws were made stricter shortly before the collapse of the mortgage industry and the onset of a bank-triggered recession—a collapse that supposedly "shocked" the banks, and which has generated the highest levels of personal bankruptcy we've seen since the Great Depression? How suspiciously convenient it seems for banks that the people suddenly found it more difficult than ever to get out from under their credit card debt and restart their shattered lives.

I was still employed in the financial services industry in 2005 and will attest that I was fully aware of the looming mortgage crisis and the potential pain the new bankruptcy laws would soon inflict on an unsuspecting public. I observed those problems expanding from my home in California, three thousand miles away from either Washington or Wall Street. If *I* could spot the catastrophe coming from my quiet suburban location, why didn't the geniuses at the center of the maelstrom, the folks who were earning millions of dollars a year to pay attention, notice it coming? Perhaps it

69   Rachael Weiner, "Poll: Public Option Favored by 65% of Americans," *The Huffington Post*, September 25, 2009.

was easier for them to collect their huge paychecks, accept bonuses for advising management on how to reduce company losses, and look the other way when the public got hit by the tsunami. Once again, we must acknowledge that the behavior we reward is behavior we get more of. When we make it more lucrative for people to look away from a problem than we do for them to face it and find a solution, we're creating a world where we're less likely to meet our challenges because our system has been designed to discourage us from doing what's best for life.

Speaking of life, another major problem with classifying corporations as "persons" is that corporations, unlike people, don't die. Neither are they subject to inheritance taxes like the rest of us mere mortals. They also don't have to put their kids through college or worry about an illness destroying their livelihood. They can pay off their thirty-year mortgages and be earning a robust income many years later, and they never have to save for their own retirement. That means corporations have the ability to accumulate wealth and concentrate power for decades, perhaps centuries. It was exactly that sort of wealth and power concentration, exacerbated by their ability to self-deal, that led the U.S. Government to proclaim in the fall of 2008 that some institutions, like AIG, General Motors and Citigroup, had become "too big to fail." It's interesting to note that General Motors was founded in 1908[70], Citi's roots trace back to 1812 [71] and AIG was incorporated in 1900.[72] That

70   William Berg, "The History of GM: General Motors," EZine Articles.com.

71   Derek Lenehan, "Citibank: Large, Established and Still Accommodating," ArticleSnatch.com.

72   American General Life and Accident Insurance Company, www.AIG.com.

means the youngest of these corporate "persons" is over one hundred years old, while the oldest is pushing two hundred, and none give any sign of being ready to die just yet. So how do we human beings stack up against the power and might of these long-lived institutions? Perhaps we should ask ourselves this question: how many *people* do we consider "too big to fail?"

Let me state for the record that I'm not advocating the wholesale massacre of public corporations. The beautiful thing about reality is that it always trumps false concepts, and since corporate personhood doesn't work it will eventually disappear in history's dustbin of bad ideas. What's necessary for that to happen is for enough of us to notice that it doesn't serve humanity's interests to allow our corporations to become so powerful we can no longer control them, and make some noise.

THE DEATH OF CORPORATE PERSONHOOD

If you ever played cops and robbers as a child, you may recall that the kid who acted the part of the robber often used a particular line to great effect: "Your money or your life!" The challenge usually worked. The victim would hand over his pretend wallet because, given a stark choice between two options, most reasonable people surrender their money before they choose to die.

That challenge is the *exact* choice reality is currently pushing upon us all. We're being pressed by nature itself to give up our unhealthy attachment to money, or else go extinct. Whether through global warming, toxic levels of pollution, the deforestation and de-struction of natural habitats we depend upon for our survival, the growing lack of fresh water to sustain our agriculture, or some other as-yet-unknown problem that may result from the capital-istic pillaging of our planet, human beings will surely die by the billions in the very near future—*unless* we agree to surrender our love for the dollar, and replace it instead with love for each other and respect for our Mother Earth.

We need do nothing radical to change the system at this point; our corporate culture is already dying of the symptoms of its own disease. It's true that certain special interest groups may manage to prop it up for a while longer by throwing additional dollars at the problem. That isn't necessarily a bad thing, assuming we wisely use the additional time to rebuild our infrastructure, explore re-newable energy alternatives and develop more sustainable ways of living. Sooner or later, though, it needs to end.

The most important thing we can do for our world right now is invest time in better understanding the problems we're facing as a species, and adjust our own thinking away from a belief in our separateness toward a deeper awareness of the interconnect-edness of all living things. When we cooperate with others because our need for cooperation is overcoming our decaying competitive paradigm, we're more likely to be part of the solution than to per-petuate the problem.

BY THE PEOPLE AND FOR THE PEOPLE

The best way for us to support and encourage change is to honor the words of America's Founding Fathers: "A government of the people, by the people and for the people shall not perish from the Earth." Supporting changes in governance that encourage greater populist involvement and discourage corporate control over Congress would be a great start. Electing only politicians who refuse to accept lobbyist's money and corporate funding and who pay honor to the will of their constituents would be another. Ignoring party platforms and instead taking the time to be better informed about the *individuals* who are running for political office would do much to break the stranglehold our political parties have on us, as well as end the gridlock that's been infecting Washington.

We have much to do as a species and little time to argue over which group was right in the past and which was wrong. We must each begin to practice the fine art of social cooperation that we wish our corporations to embrace. As we go, so go they. If we personally support policies and practice behaviors that revere life and encourage it to thrive, while letting go of our capitalistic ideologies and ceasing behaviors that are dehumanizing, disrespectful and detrimental to all forms life, we will help advance the interests of humankind.

CREATING A WISDOM CULTURE AS OUR NEW GROWTH MODEL

WE'VE ALL HEARD THE PHRASE, "KEEPING UP WITH THE JONE-ses." The Joneses, we know, are a mythical family who consume whatever they want and possess the best that capitalism offers. They own a big house and fancy cars, take tropical vacations, buy the finest designer clothes, wear lots of expensive jewelry and play with amazing toys. The Joneses never go broke or find themselves unable to pay their bills; they're a shining beacon of success in an otherwise struggling world.

Who would we be without the Joneses to spur us onward? What would our lives be like if we opted to be satisfied with what we have, rather than feel afraid we're being left behind by families like the Joneses? Perhaps the recent success of the "Left Behind" novels, which detailed a mythical rapture of all the good people and the horrors that befell the rest of humanity, tapped into our longstanding fears about not being good enough or having enough to "make it." Both historically and religiously speaking, we've all longed to be part of some special group of chosen ones, even if it meant all the others would become the rejects.

All modern systems—from our religions to our political structures to our judicial systems to our economies—are founded on the premise that we somehow need to *get* more from this world (or the next), whatever it takes to achieve that. We've therefore handed the reins of power over to those who promise to give us more than we currently have, only to belatedly discover they're often more interested in getting more for themselves than they are in providing more for the rest of us.

That level of consciousness—the need to accumulate more for ourselves even if it comes at the expense of other people—is the same consciousness that constructed our civilization. While that attitude provided us with some benefits during humanity's rapid growth and expansion phase, we're beginning to recognize that to continue along that path is a species dead end. Our planet can't sustain our continuous, unfettered growth any more than an adult human body can grow beyond a certain height and weight without becoming morbidly obese. We've grown up as a species, and we now encircle and occupy all of Earth. It's time we acknowledged the truth: with great freedoms and abilities come concurrently greater responsibilities to our environment and to each other.

As adults we know that freedom and responsibility go hand in hand, which is why we parcel out freedoms to our children as they demonstrate they can be responsible. The same philosophy is true for society, only we've been so caught up in our individual issues that we've lost sight of the need to claim our share of responsibility for the success of our human family. The clamoring we're hearing today from certain special-interest groups to preserve our individual freedoms "at any cost" is a childlike, rebellious reaction to the sobering fact that we *must* begin to take responsibility for our actions, and that those actions have consequences we can't ignore. Freedom is only as beneficial as the concurrent self-restraint we develop to keep our egos and destructive behaviors in check.

Our judicial system was founded on the realization that *my* freedom to fully experience *my* life ends where *your* right to life and happiness begins. In that same vein, my freedom to consume whatever I desire and to reproduce without restraint ends where your family's need to survive begins. My behavior must therefore not only be sensitive to the individual rights of others at this moment, but must also be tempered by a sense of personal stewardship for our shared planetary resources, such that *my* behavior doesn't impinge on *your* ability to survive.

Any changes we make in our social structures must come from a higher level of consciousness than the thinking that created our current problems. The old way of thinking valued unfettered growth and the accumulation of more stuff as a measure of individual success. Our new, more modern understanding must be based on the recognition that we're all in this same life together, come what may. The fear that we'll personally be left behind must be released in favor of the realization that it's all of us or none of us when it comes to human survival on this planet.

Unfettered growth, especially growth based on continuous material consumption, wastes excessive amounts of natural resources and threatens the long-term survival of our species. It also reduces the survivability of other sovereign species. A more intelligent measure for the success of a society would be its ability to understand, live and work successfully within its natural environment while advancing the standard of living for all its members through sustainable and regenerative consumption. That requires us to design and implement new holistic systems of production and consumption grounded in wise stewardship, rather than to wantonly destroy the limited natural resources we've been gifted.

Everything in the known universe is busy consuming something. Humanity, for many millennia now, has been consuming material resources in its unremitting quest for security. Clearly, humans are *designed* to consume a certain amount of natural resources; that's evidenced by the fact we have mouths, skin, lungs and stomachs to bring in external resources, and sweat glands, urethras and bowels to eliminate waste. But is material consumption the reason we're all here?

When we explore our own capacities, especially when we note the depth of our own emotions and our ability to reason, our higher purpose may be more apparent. Perhaps our higher purpose, which so far as we know is as yet unmatched in this universe, is to thrive in order to consume *experiences* and convert them into *wisdom* for the benefit of the higher creative process. Whatever we need to consume by way of material resources has been given to us to support us in that mission.

If as a species we mapped our place in the cosmos through recognition of our higher purpose (greater wisdom) *and* contextualized ourselves by noting our rightful place in the chain of life (inextricably interconnected to all that is), we might discover we already have the power to create the experiences we wish to have. We could direct the flow of human exploration and research toward the insights we collectively wish to accumulate. Were we to do so, society would change dramatically. Each person's focus would shift from accumulating more things to contributing whatever unique gifts he or she has to offer toward humanity's becoming a genuine wisdom culture. Such a shift could create a joyful, peaceful and exiting worldview for many generations to follow.

NOTHING WE KNOW GROWS OR LIVES FOREVER

Our belief that constant growth is the goal of a healthy society has no foundation in reality. Everything we see—be it a tiger, a tree, a mountain or a star—follows the same universal life cycle. Everything is born, grows, reaches maturity and experiences the world through its interconnectedness with all other things; it then offers up something of value to the cosmos and eventually decays, to be efficiently recycled by the world. So far as we know this creative feedback loop has been going on for as long as our universe has been in existence. Humanity's place in that feedback loop may well be to contribute our unique form of human wisdom to the over-arching cosmic life experience. Human wisdom is a richly textured blend of shared physical, emotional and intellectual experiences. It constantly flowers and expands as we move through our physical reality, hand in hand.

Certain forms have longer life spans than others, along with much greater growth capacities. For example, a mountain might grow and last for many millennia before time and weather even-tually erode it to dust, while a flower might bloom for only a day or two. Still, not even the largest mountain grows forever. If it did our entire planet would eventually become a single enormous mountain, at the expense of biodiversity everywhere else. Unfettered material growth obviously goes against the practice and principles of nature, which seems to delight in constant change and expanding diversity.

We humans reach physical maturity in our late teens or early twenties, at which point we stop growing taller. We may grow a bit rounder or denser with time, but our body mass has a defi-nite upper limit. Sail past it by becoming too obese and death will claim you far more swiftly than if you lived in a healthy and sus-tainable way.

No living body can sustain itself for long outside its own rela-tively narrow band of mass parameters. If its mass grows too high (or falls too low), the organism collapses. This is also true of spe-cies masses. If a single animal population grows too large for its ecosystem, a predator must step in and reduce its numbers or their overconsumption will decimate the system. The animals would then starve themselves down to a smaller, more balanced popula-tion, or they might disappear.

Whenever a species disappears, its ecosystem is thrown out of balance because the role once played by that species is no longer filled. Whatever that species consumed for energy—be it minerals, plant life or animals—will be left to accumulate unchecked, until something new steps in to consume *its* growing population. It's important for us to remember, then, that every time we cause the extinction of another species, we're upsetting the delicate life scaffolding that nature has painstakingly constructed over billions of years—the very same scaffolding that holds and nourishes *us*.

When it comes to age, trees may live for many thousands of years. Some of the giant sequoias and olive trees living today sprouted long before Buddha and Jesus walked the Earth. The human lifespan, however, seems to cap at around one hundred years of age. Doctors believe we may someday be able to extend that to a hundred and fifty years through advanced technologies and a greater understanding of the aging process. Still, many reputable scientists have proposed that a hundred and fifty years may be an absolute upper limit for a human lifespan.

It seems that a desire to be immortal while bounded by the physical limitations of a body flies in the face of everything the universe has taught us about itself and about creation, balanced consumption and recirculation. But in a society where "left behind" fears have become the norm and we've been programmed to despise both aging and death, the craving to cling to our physical bodies at any cost has hindered our ability to embrace the beauty of the wondrous living systems that contain us.

We've lost touch with the beauty of our own material transformation, and have come to believe that these puny mortal human bodies, despite their many limitations, are the best this universe has to offer us. We've lost sight of the fact that everything dissolves in order to become something fresh and new, and that the evolutionary trajectory for the totality (of which we're an inextricable part) is thrusting us inexorably toward higher consciousness, greater specialization, more complexity and continually more love, joy, peace and personal freedom.

We might *want* to live forever inside these particular bodies and on this specific planet, at this specific time, alongside the specific people we love, because we've been programmed since birth to fear the alternative. None of us want to be left behind as this majestic universe unfolds without us. However, when we realize that for the universe to unfold without us is impossible, since we're not separate from either the eternal universe or its infinite process of unfolding, we begin to release that longstanding, culturally and religiously instilled fear. The fact is whatever happens we'll be a part of it, embedded in whatever form our universe chooses to take. Once we embrace the idea that everything is indeed one living field of energy (which is supported by modern science based on the theories of quantum physics[73]), the notion of any aspect of reality—including ourselves—being left behind can be seen as a ridiculous assumption. We must realize that we've believed in a myth, one told by those who've used it through the ages to control our collective behavior with the weapon of fear. Control and fear go hand in hand. It's love that sets us free. As soon as we let go of our fears about life, we surrender our need to control the world around us. The moment we choose to love and support each other instead of

73   David Bohm, *Wholeness and the Implicate Order*, Routledge, 1995.

fearing each other and competing against each other for survival, we become free to give our love to all other beings. We then make this world a better place by being here, and simply by being ourselves, for as long as we are in these material bodies—and beyond that into the infinite realm of eternity.

IN DEFENSE OF NATURAL LIFECYCLES

What *is* the reason for life to exist, at least as we presently understand it? What do we currently grasp about this universal birth/growth/death cycle in which we all participate that we can translate into a more meaningful embrace of our own place in creation's magnificent system?

For starters, science teaches us that nothing in our universe seems ever to be lost, nor is anything ever truly wasted. Einstein's equations proved matter and energy aren't lost or destroyed; they just constantly change form. According to Einstein's most famous equation $E=mc^2$, matter is simply a very highly condensed form of energy. This equation set the foundation for the original atomic bomb. By splitting an atom in just the right way, the astounding force of the energy contained inside it was released, triggering an explosion of energy that cascaded throughout the surrounding atoms. The atoms weren't destroyed then, so much as the condensed energy that comprised them was released into the cosmos.

Do you know that stars originally forged the atoms that make up your body? Stars cast your atoms into space by way of massive supernovas, where they then flowed throughout the cosmos on un-seen currents of plasma until they coalesced into the person you know as yourself.[74] It's also been said that every human being is made up of millions of atoms that once comprised dinosaurs, an-cient redwoods, woolly mammoths and even Mars. Because we walk around shedding our atoms everywhere we go, within you today you have atoms that once belonged to Catherine the Great, Attila the Hun and, yes, even Jesus Christ.[75]

The universe, then, *is* the ultimate recycler. Everything we've ever created and that we imagine is nearly indestructible, from plastics to airplanes to skyscrapers, will in time return to nature's womb to be reborn as something else. Even if it takes millions or billions of years for that to happen, everything we know and observe takes form, passes through this world for a time and then moves on.

We've also learned from quantum physics that what we assume are discrete objects, the material things we perceive as separate through the limitations of our five senses, are all actually integral-ly interconnected by the invisible field of energy that surrounds us. We can't actually *see* energy flowing around us (although we can *feel* it in the sun's heat and as the wind brushing softly against our skin). We get to observe energy only when we can watch it mov-ing and changing the objects we *can* see. Objects thus *appear* to exist in isolation, until the invisible energy that envelops us moves or visibly changes an object—sometimes dramatically, as in a

74   "Physicists Find Out Why We Are Stardust," *Science Daily*, June 25, 1999.

75   Bill Bryson, A Short History of Nearly Everything, Broadway Books, 2003.

tornado, hurricane or earthquake—and disabuses us of our erroneous notion.

As was mentioned earlier, Einstein's equations demonstrate that matter and energy are made of the same essential stuff. They're just operating in different states, much like ice and water. Ice appears solid to us, though if we study it through an electron microscope we'll quickly notice that what appears frozen to our naked eyes is actually bustling with energy in motion. Water, on the other hand, appears to us to be in perpetual motion, flowing so fast that when we try to grasp it we aren't able to confine it. Unalike as they may appear to our senses when they're in these different states, ice and water, like matter and energy, are—at the ground of their being—both the same.

There exists a third state of water: steam. When we compare steam with consciousness, we might consider them to be quite alike. Both have a diffuse, lighter-than-air quality that can't be localized or pinned down through observation. Metaphorically speaking, then, if matter is life's first state and energy is its second state, consciousness may well be life's third state, the way steam represents the third state of water and ice.

If consciousness is indeed just a lighter manifestation of the same substance that comprises matter and energy, it would then seem likely consciousness doesn't disappear when we die any more than steam disappears when it evaporates, to rain down again somewhere else in the form of water. Like steam, perhaps consciousness is merely transformed and relentlessly recycled by our universe. Perhaps humanity's longstanding fear of death relates to our fear of "losing" consciousness. If, however, we acknowledge that we *are* consciousness, that we don't *have* a consciousness that is separate from ourselves, and that nothing in the universe is ever lost—not even consciousness—then our fear of death dissolves. Wherever your consciousness travels, there you'll be!

The only constant we humans can actually observe in our reality is the constancy of continuous transformation. Death itself appears to be a transformative, ultimately regenerative process. Take a walk in any forest and you'll see life bursting forth in profusion from the remains of whatever has died. Even rabbits and squirrels that have been eaten by coyotes become transformed. Their bodies and energies are converted to food for—and ultimately become an integral part of—the living cells of the organism that ate them. It's only our limited capacity to appreciate the transformative nature of death that has turned it into a fear of decay rather than an adventure in rebirth.

Human anxiety and depression, which can be statistically measured by the amount of medication being prescribed to the general population, seems steadily on the rise.[76] Perhaps our growing unhappiness is a measure of how far removed we've become from the very beautiful natural cycles of life. When we fail to understand what we're part of or to appreciate why we're here, anxiety swells.

Many of us mistakenly believe that life and death are opposites. In reality, it is birth and death that are opposites. Birth is the doorway through which consciousness energizes the material realm; death is the doorway through which it eventually departs. The part that comes in and goes out—manifesting as human

---

76   Charles Barber, "The Medicated Americans: Antidepressant Prescriptions on the Rise," *Scientific American*, February 27, 2008.

consciousness—*is* life. That part has no opposite. It seems as ethereal as the wind: indestructible, formless, timeless and ageless. Why, then, would we want to box it forever inside a restricted and limited physical body, or (even worse!) a computer or manmade machine? What if the universe has much greater things in store for consciousness as this world continues to evolve? What makes us imagine these puny mortal bodies we presently occupy mark the apex of creation's constructive capacities?

Nature limits the growth and life span of everything it creates in order to ensure the ongoing diversity and advancement of its own creation. That's a crucial part of life's ability to survive. Nature demands the wasteless, relentless recycling of all her raw materials so she can continue to create inspired systems that meet the continual challenges of an ever-changing universe.

Human consciousness does seem at present to have an upper limit on what it is capable of learning, retaining and putting into effect in one physical lifetime. As people age they grow more calcified in their thinking and often find it harder to adapt to the rapid pace of change in the world. I know from my own experiences that the way younger people embrace technology is very different from the way I relate to it. While to them responding instantly to a ringing cell phone may feel as natural as breathing, to me it's an intrusion into my privacy to be ever at the mercy of a ringing phone. That's all the more reason for us to recognize and honor the natural life spans of our individual bodies, our social systems, our religions and our corporations. Our role isn't to judge *any* system—either individual or collective—as evil or failed once it grows old and its ideas become outmoded. Our role is to lovingly hospice those systems out of existence, the same as we do with our dying elders, and concurrently to provide adequate space and nurturing for the new ideas being birthed by our growing wisdom.

Many elderly people today have trouble using computers, PDAs or even ATM's, yet young people take them for granted and are proficient with what seems to their elders like a dizzying array of features and applications. Perhaps death, then, actually *prevents* consciousness from becoming trapped inside the rigid limitations of whatever finite form it has briefly taken. Perhaps death empowers consciousness to try on new life forms that are more capable of housing our ever-expanding wisdom than the forms we've previously occupied. Like a hermit crab in a too-tight shell, perhaps consciousness discards our aging bodies in order to seek a new shell that is more pliable, offers more room and provides greater capacities for new life experiences so our wisdom can continue to grow and evolve over time.

WISDOM CAN GROW WHERE THINGS CAN'T GO

Our strange belief that a society grows successfully through continuous material consumption is an abstract concept based on the demand our system places on our companies to turn a profit. Companies are forced to sell new products (or sell more of their existing ones) all the time if they hope to remain in business. We've already told them we'll consider them successful only if they earn more money each day, so increasing their annual revenues with an eye toward generating money has become the Holy Grail for every corporation, including most non-profit organizations.

The problem with that way of thinking is that when companies sell hard goods, the raw materials used to produce them must be constantly harvested from nature. Some of those raw materials can be replenished while others cannot. Producing some products (palm oil, cattle and lumber) requires massive destruction of sensitive ecological systems such as rainforests, plains and natural waterways; to acquire others (steel, oil and coal) we must strip-mine nature, drill dangerously into Earth's bowels and pollute the surrounding environment. Our insatiable need to consume material goods has already had a huge environmental impact on this planet. We've unthinkingly done things that have degraded the biodiversity of Earth and have rendered nature less useful to itself. The price life has paid for humanity's quest for monetary profit has yet to be determined, but the numbers so far don't look good.

Somewhere along the line, humanity came to the faulty conclusion that the continual replacement of material goods and the constant upgrading of perfectly serviceable items (TV's, computers, cars, etc.) is desirable behavior. We reached that shortsighted conclusion long before we realized our material resources were finite, so it's nobody's fault we've accepted that myth as truth. It was only fairly recently in the course of human history, after we developed our first urban centers perhaps nine to ten thousand years ago, that we lost touch with the limited resources at our disposal. City dwellers began collectively dumping waste and destroying their surroundings without regard for the environmental degradation they caused. Historically, those large collectives amassed enough political and military might to extend their control to surrounding ecosystems. That gave them the ability to plunder the resources of distant lands and enslave the conquered peoples to serve their growing consumption needs.

Only recently in the scheme of things have we circumnavigated the globe and settled most of our remaining wilderness areas. We've just now reached the stage where we're realizing we have nowhere left to go to find virgin resources, short of outer space. Since we haven't yet developed the art of space travel well enough to solve our immediate problems, whatever needs we have today must be met with resources we already have. In fact, the likelihood of us being able to develop highly complex forms of space travel that might enable us to colonize other planets or visit other star systems when we're not working together on a species-wide level to accomplish those objectives seems rather low. The immense amount of creative energy, intelligence, skill and talent it would take for us to design such complex processes practically demands we invite input from people all around the world if we want to succeed. Perhaps it's also a good idea that we learn how to get along on a planetary level, as well as figure out how to live sustainably here on Earth before we venture toward the stars, so we don't carry our greed, fear and environmental destructiveness into space and cause inadvertent harm to other worlds.

The challenges we face when it comes to the distribution and replenishment of limited natural resources are fairly recent realizations. Years ago our hunter/gatherer forefathers figured out how to denude an area of its resources in part and then move on, allowing the local resources to gradually regenerate. The trouble arose when we began to construct more permanent urban sites, because we never really made allowances for their ongoing impact on the surrounding environment. What we've learned from our own history is that when a city's resources become so overtaxed that its population can no longer sustain itself, people flee the urban setting and surrender it back to nature, which in time reclaims the city and replenishes itself. Ancient Rome, which once housed over a million people, was abandoned in just that way, as were many of the great Mayan, Greek and Egyptian cities of old. Only recently have we dug their ruins from the sands of time and the jungles that overran them, testaments all to the risks of ignoring the ecosystems that house us. It's time, then, for us to reexamine modern civilization from the vantage point of what we know today about cities and natural resources, versus what we understood about them a few thousand years ago when we first began settling and trading with each other.

If the world was flat and extended forever, social growth could conceivably go forever. A species could emerge near the world plane's "center" and gradually move toward the plane's infinite edges, continually claiming virgin natural resources. We, however, live on a spherical planet, in a cosmos made of ever enlarging spheres. What goes around in our world must eventually come back around, albeit permanently changed from making the trip. We therefore don't have the luxury of assuming we can continue to find new resources to plunder. We must acknowledge that what we have may be all we're ever going to have—at least in our brief lifetimes—and act accordingly.

For a while, particularly during the first few thousand years of human expansion and social development, unfettered growth enriched our world, the way rapid physical growth is helpful for children. By the late twentieth century, however, human population growth, exploration and social migration had already taxed the boundaries of our planet's upper limits on resources. Now, having reached our present level of physical maturity, it's time for us to shift our attention away from physical growth so we can focus on cultural growth and sustainability. Just like a child stops getting bigger and eventually heads off to college to expand his understanding of the world, so too must our entire species cease growing in size and instead shift our attention to gathering wisdom.

The two growth paths *are* different, with different purposes and very different results. Physical growth will always be strictly limited by the carrying capacity of the resources that support it. Wisdom, on the other hand, expands through experience. It involves the application of new knowledge to meet some new challenge, which in turn enhances our collective wisdom and creative capacities. So far as we yet know, no upper boundaries exist to limit a culture's potential wisdom or creative capacity.

If we truly wish to become a wisdom culture, we must shift the way we measure corporate success by bringing our economic values into greater alignment with the principles of creation. What we might wish to encourage our businesses to produce is ever-greater amounts of *wisdom* to enhance our culture and improve our capacity for planetary regeneration, rather than ever more *products* for financial profit. We could do so through an enhanced focus on research and by freely bringing forth new ideas that support sustainability and encourage creativity for everyone's benefit. Any new ideas we embrace for the future *must* be environmentally friendly because all our living systems are interconnected, so the damage we do to one, we do to all.

Using that approach, the development of solar, wind and geo-thermal energy would no longer be constrained by how much money it might cost in the short run to undertake the necessary research and development to produce those technologies. Nor would it be based on how much money companies could earn by selling people the energy they need to sustain their lives. Companies would instead be measured for success based on how much they enhanced humanity's ability to survive (and thrive) *freely* over the long haul. Food growers who learned to produce organic, healthy products that aided human health would be encouraged and supported. In fact, we might need more of them producing less food per acre to provide for our dietary needs in a healthier way. New construction projects would be undertaken to build zero carbon footprint houses that would recycle and reuse as many items as possible. (For a wonderful video on modern "eco-tecture" check out "Earthship Living:" http://www.youtube.com/watch?v=3ENIhmDskmY.) Repairing, restoring and creatively reusing old goods would become celebrated behaviors in our new society.

Businesses that today create affordable products designed to serve humanity's needs for a long time (as opposed to businesses that encourage hasty obsolescence and frequent product replacement to generate more business and higher profits) should be *rewarded* for the good they are doing for our planet, not *penalized* because they're costing the public less money and using fewer resources. Companies that self-design to mimic nature by recycling and remanufacturing new goods from old goods—what's been termed "cradle to cradle" technology—should also be rewarded. Businesses whose innovations enable us to redesign our energy systems, our agricultural systems, our transportation systems and our health systems should not be dependent upon short-term profitability for their existence. Neither should they be subjected to economic and political pressure from existing companies that want to suppress new ideas to protect their old technologies. The fresh ideas innovative companies bring to the social table in terms of *genuine* benefits to humanity far outweigh the importance we've been placing on annual financial profit margins that get recorded on some corporate balance sheet.

Are humans mature enough yet—let alone courageous enough—to consider radically reconstructing our business systems so they truly respond to our needs? Instead of continually making new toys to entertain and distract our Prozac population, can we rise to the challenge of building affordable and energy-efficient housing, while at the same time providing healthful food, potable water and basic daily comforts for people everywhere? Will we someday embrace the need to educate every child so as to tap into the limitless wellspring of potential that is our human ingenuity? Can we honor the needs of all people to receive decent medical attention and to live in a world where life isn't about suffering, but is something to be appreciated and enjoyed? If indeed humanity is here to consume experiences and transform them into wisdom, can we at last begin to—consciously and collectively—create new experiences from love and kindness, instead of from greed and fear?

Perhaps not. Then again, reality has always had a way of pushing us into being whatever it needs us to become for our own survival. Otherwise we'd still be dinosaurs.

THE POWER OF FEWER CHOICES, USING HIGHER VALUES

NEAR MY HOME IS A RESTAURANT CALLED THAI PERU THAT boasts a menu of over one hundred and fifty entrees. I've eaten there a few times, mainly for their very tasty Pad Thai. Whenever I've taken friends there for the first time, though, I've witnessed them struggle mightily to make a dinner decision. Quite often we're on our second beverage before everyone's orders are placed. Not surprisingly, most new patrons tend to gravitate toward the Pad Thai option as well. It's a name that sounds comfortingly familiar to the average American diner, so it stands out like a beacon of safety in a sea of too many options.

Considering the restaurant is only a simple neighborhood kitchen, we can't help wondering how proficient their chef can possibly be at preparing such a dizzying array of entrees.

At some point, it becomes clear that too many choices paralyze consumers and hinder our ability to decide what's good for us, or figure out what we want. That makes it harder to choose what we need. It's likely we've all experienced a mental freeze similar to what my friends experience in our local restaurant. Think back to the first time you ever entered a Starbucks. Intimidating, wasn't it? Without someone to guide you through the confusing haze of options, you might have settled for a tall house blend and been happy to make your escape from all those frappes, lattes, cappuccinos and mochas.

The experience is what's known as "information overload." Certain manufacturers factor it into their marketing strategies as part of their effort to sway our decision-making. Offer us so many options we can't begin to understand the ramifications of all our choices and we're likely to reach for the first thing that sounds familiar—perhaps the soothing comfort of a company's brand name.

The more options we're given between products that do the same thing, the more likely it is their differences are mostly surface distinctions, such as brand name choices or packages with slightly different appearances. When differences are superficial, the costs and labor expended to promote different brands are wasteful, because they set up a choice that doesn't benefit consumers or enhance society. Setting up a false consumer choice benefits only those manufacturers who manage to draw profits to their bottom line and away from those of another corporation.

Walk down the detergent aisle in any grocery store and you'll catch a glimpse of false choice marketing madness. You'll encounter floor to ceiling stacks of brightly colored boxes trumpeting All, Tide, Bold, Cheer, Gain, Oxy-Clean, Purex, Ecos, Seventh Generation, Method and Essentials, to name but a few. These soaps come in powdered form, liquid form, gel-paks and super concentrates, and in packages that range from travel size to industrial-sized containers. They come lemon-scented, spring fresh and unscented for sensitive skin types. They come made for different water temperatures and different water types. They come at you in such a wild array of sensory overload it's a wonder any human being can make an informed choice about which to buy. My *nose* hurts when I leave the detergent aisle!

How do we actually choose products like laundry detergent, crackers or light bulbs? Do we conduct experiments where we launder our dirty socks, washing them first with Tide and then with Bold to discover which one gets whites whiter? Do we test them to find out which one turns whites yellow over time? Do we observe how our colors degrade or remain bright though multiple washings? Not hardly. Who has time to notice if their reds have become slightly duller after twenty-seven washings with Bold, while their blues have retained their brightness after similar washings with Tide? Who has the excess energy to perform that kind of experiment?

Either we buy the brands our mothers used because we're familiar with the packaging, or we buy a brand because we watch TV commercials where people who look just like us swear (on the box they're getting paid to promote) that their brand works better than all of its competitors.

Sometimes we'll buy what's on sale if we're pinching pennies; other times we redeem manufacturer's coupons. But mostly we're creatures of habit. We distrust the unknown, so all things being nearly equal we tend to buy the product with which we're most familiar. That kind of inertia works to the advantage of the manufacturer whose brand has "earned" our loyalty, but it works against companies with whose brands we are less familiar.

What makes it even harder for competitors to win our business is that women no longer—if they truly ever did—hang out in the park on Saturday mornings and discuss the trouble they're having getting stains out of Johnny's tee-shirts. They're busy with their own careers, around which they must coordinate Johnny's soccer practices, piano lessons and play dates, and between which they sandwich grocery shopping and the construction of little Suzie's dance recital costume. In some houses it's actually Dad doing most of the laundry and housework in our modern world. And *he* certainly isn't folding clothes with the guy next door, pondering aloud whether it's better to use Tide or Bold.

We've definitely made some beneficial changes in the way we select our products, in that lately we've become more sensitive to their impact on our environment and on general human health. As a result many products are now being labeled heart healthy, organic, environmentally friendly, made from biodegradable ingredients, having a low carbon footprint and so on. Unfortunately, all that labeling has created yet a new information overload problem: what does each term really mean, and how do we know what we're getting? For example, is a cage-free chicken the same as a free-range bird? (Hint: it's not. Cage-free still means cooped up inside immense chicken farm warehouses, with access to the outdoors often limited to a tiny, two-foot square opening in an immense building that houses many thousands of chickens. Outdoor access, for all intents and purposes, might as well be nonexistent. Free range is exactly that—birds that roam around outdoors, the way chickens are supposed to live.) What about non-toxic as compared to eco-friendly? Heart healthy as opposed to low cholesterol? Pesticide-free as opposed to organically-grown? The list goes on and on.

Given inconsistent labeling and rapidly expanding choices, we're left to guess exactly what we're buying, which works to the advantage of manufacturers. When we're confused, price and brand name automatically rise to the top of our list when deciding what to select. Since those are the main areas where manufacturers can influence our decisions through promotions and advertising, they remain in control of what we choose to buy.

THE ADVERTISING MINDFUCK

A majority of targeted advertising is mindfucking, pure and simple. Advertising's primary purpose is to attempt—by hook or crook—to worm its way into our brains in order to affect our decision-making processes. When it comes to altering our minds, we should recognize that advertisements are far more dangerous to us than illegal drugs. At least we know when we've ingested a drug and can determine both when and how we use it, or if we should stay away from it in the future. Ads, on the other hand, bombard us from every direction without our informed consent. A 1997 study determined that the average American was exposed to over three thousand ads every day.[77] Yet contrary to the mind-altering drug business, the advertising business is a perfectly legal, multi-billion-dollar, profit-making industry.

Ads primarily alter our thoughts in two ways: they either make us fearful and insecure (manufactured need) or they inspire lust and desire (manufactured want). They do it so we'll buy their products, either to make ourselves *feel* more secure or briefly to satisfy the cravings that they've successfully aroused in us.

If you're female, have you ever watched an ad for diet pills and begun to worry if perhaps you're getting a bit overweight? If you're male, have you seen an ad for Viagra and wondered if maybe you're starting to fade and perhaps should try it? What about those pills that purport to make your penis look longer? Or if you're a woman, those ads for wrinkle creams and hair coloring? Perhaps it's time we asked ourselves this: does it make us feel *good* to have our attention continually drawn to the fact that, yes, we are indeed aging?

Manufacturers create ads that turn aging into a problem simply so they can build a business around it and offer us handy solutions—for a price. Aging, however, isn't a problem. It's a natural part of living. That we're being systematically trained to believe it's a problem exposes the absurdity behind these corporate marketing machines.

---

77   David Shenk, *Data Smog: Surviving the Information Glut*, HarperEdge, 1997.

An unfortunate byproduct of the corporate desire to turn aging into a profitable problem is the way it's degraded our natural appreciation for our elders and their accumulated wisdom. What a shame it is we no longer venerate aging as a badge of life and experiential success. Instead we relegate our elderly to assisted living facilities, where we don't have to observe the process of their dying. How much of life we miss out on when we lose touch with its natural rhythms, and how disconnected we become from our personal life trajectory due to that ignorance. No wonder Westerners have gotten so uncomfortable around death. We're so anxious about death these days that we've turned the sanitization of human death into yet another industry, with embalming, caskets and funerals generating over twenty billion dollars in revenue each year.[78]

Aging isn't the only natural process that's been converted into a business. The diet industry annually generates fifty billion dollars in revenue in the U.S.[79] It hawks diet books, fad diets, exercise programs, exercise equipment, gym memberships and dietary food products all in the name of creating solutions for our myriad weight problems—although none of these so-called solutions have proved successful over the long term for most consumers. Obesity rates have escalated even as diet and weight loss systems have proliferated throughout society. According to the World Heath Organization, globally there are nearly two billion overweight adults, of whom more than three hundred million are classified

---

78   http://us-funerals.com/funeral-articles/usa-funeral-market.html

79   Mike Adams, "U.S. Weight Loss Market Worth 46.3 Billion in 2004—Forecast to Reach 61 Billion by 2008," NaturalNews.com, March 30, 2005.

as clinically obese.[80] Obesity rates have risen more than three-fold since 1980 in some areas of North America, the United Kingdom, Eastern Europe, the Middle East, the Pacific Islands, Australasia and China.[81] Childhood obesity is also on the rise, and medically we know that fat children will tend to struggle with weight and health issues for the rest of their lives.[82]

If we really *do* have a globally growing weight problem, it's because we're eating more calories than we burn each day, every day... for a very, very long time. Certainly a few of us have metabolic issues, but for the vast majority of obese individuals it's a mental issue and not a physiological one. We're eating large quantities of cheap, unhealthy, processed and fattening foods to fill up the inner voids that our vapid world has created. We're racing mindlessly through our meals, often in front of television or other entertainment distractions, downing empty calories without taking the time to savor and fully appreciate the sources and quality of the energy we're taking into our bodies to nourish and sustain ourselves. Take a few extended nature walks each week, eat a little less food at every meal (but do it consciously and appreciatively and *savor* it more), and the "weight problem" will clear itself up without much fuss in most human beings. It takes a lot of time to take off weight, of course, but not much more than it takes for weight to accumulate in the first place. One thing we humans hate to do, however, is

---

80   "Obesity: In Statistics," BBC News, January 2, 2008.

81   http://www.worldometers.info/obesity

82   "Childhood Obesity," Centers for Disease Control, National Center For Chronic Disease Prevention and Health Promotion, last modified June 3, 2010. http://www.cdc.gov/obesity/childhood/index.html

be patient to get what we want. We've been trained to believe we can and should have it *all*; right here, right now.

The shortcuts we're encouraged to purchase are aimed at our juvenile egos, not our adult selves. Companies pander short term "solutions" that allow us to avoid taking responsibility for having created our own weight problem, which is why so often the weight piles right back on as soon as our diet or exercise program is over. Nothing makes the diet industry happier than being able to sell its concepts and products to the same suffering people all over again. They know their products don't *cure* obesity problems; they only temporarily treat its symptoms. The question nobody wants to explore is why we feel so *compelled* to stuff ourselves into fatness in the first place. Could it be we're so dissatisfied with the stressful states of our lives that food becomes a weak but acceptable substitute for human intimacy and connectivity? When our deepest needs aren't being met, our subconscious invites us to meet those needs we *can* meet—and to do so to excess—as a kind of sensory pacifier.

If you're female, the stress imposed on you through marketing may seem particularly acute. Ad agencies know women do most of the household shopping, so they specifically target female audiences. (If it's true that eons of evolution have genetically hardwired men to be hunters, women seem to have been equally hardwired to be the primary gatherers and nurturers of our species.) Are you *still* wearing last year's fashions, the magazine advertisements ask? Quick, better race to the mall and pick up the latest styles before your friends and associates notice you're way out of date.

Not only does the fashion industry target women, so too do the plastic surgery industries, hair product industries and the fragrance and cosmetics companies. Believe it or not, *Newsweek* reported in 2009 that in the United States, girls between the ages of eight and twelve were spending forty million dollars a *month* on beauty products.[83] *Forty million dollars!* How much more beauty does a ten-year-old girl need beyond the natural beauty she's already been gifted? And for what? What kinds of messages are we sending to our young girls when we imply they need to do more with and to themselves to be seen as attractive? Who are we encouraging them to become attractive *for*? Could it be our own insecure, adolescent egos that are being satisfied when we look to our youngsters and smugly think, "My daughter's better-looking than my neighbor's little girl!" After all, most ten-year-old boys aren't worried about the way girls look or dress. So who's pushing this style competition amongst our girls, and why?

CONSUME AND BE BETTER

The shared mantra of most advertising is this: consume, consume, consume…and you too can become a better person. The hidden subtext, of course, is that there's something generally wrong with you to begin with and you'd better consume our product if you hope to repair it. Most advertisers are out to convince us we need or want something we didn't even *know* we needed or wanted.

83   Jessica Bennett, "Generation Diva," *Newsweek*, March 30, 2009.

Others will try to convince us to buy their version of some product we're already buying from their competitor. That's primarily what ad agencies do to earn money. Set a pretty girl on the hood of a car and suddenly that car appeals to a targeted demographic—say males between the ages of eighteen and fifty—because the not-so-subtle message of the ad is this: if you can *afford* this car, you'll get to have sex with beautiful women.

Advertisers often dodge the truth about what they're selling, spinning their sales pitches and information, and misdirecting our attention through the use of subliminal cues. One of the most insidious ways they mislead us is by wrapping their clients' brands in feel-good ads that purport to provide us with helpful information about all the great things their client is doing for the world. Sometimes that information *is* helpful, but don't be fooled that it's being offered in the public interest; it's highly one-sided and the truth is often skewed. When we hear on TV about how environmentally caring BP (the old British Petroleum, which changed its name in 2001 to draw our attention away from their involvement in oil drilling) feels toward our planet, and how its focus is on promoting clean energy solutions for the future, it's important we remember that their *aim* is to make us feel kindly toward their brand so we'll forget about their long history of safety violations, their exploding rig in the Gulf of Mexico and the horrific environmental destruction they've caused.

When companies gather information about their own products that might depress their sales, you'll rarely see them advertising *that* for the sake of keeping society well informed about their kindly feelings toward the planet and humankind. Most often they'll fight tooth and nail to keep any bad news out of the media. Some companies even pay enormous sums to public relations firms to "repackage and rebrand" products that have been tainted by bad news, or whose sales are declining due to a changing tide of public opinion. Kentucky Fried Chicken, for example, changed its corporate name to KFC so its food *sounded* less fatty and greasy, but do you think for a moment it ceased deep-frying chicken? As for Altria Group, if your stockbroker touts its profitability without explaining its core business, it may *sound* like an innocuous investment worth adding to your portfolio, but it's still RJ Reynolds tobacco in a brand new wrapper.

Marketing and sales are the in-house versions of corporate advertising and promotions. Most companies invest enormous sums in training their internal sales forces, and sales people are often the highest paid group of workers in any company. I worked in sales for most of my life, and can attest to its cutthroat nature. Where money flows as freely as blood is where you'll find the most financial sharks. In 1988 Harvey Makay even wrote a bestseller called *How to Swim With the Sharks* as a primer to instruct salespeople how to outmaneuver their competition. Being morally virtuous in corporate sales is a lot like being a nun who lives in a brothel. It can get pretty lonely at times, and it doesn't pay well.

Corporate sales training often consists of inventing multiple ways to tell a potential customer things that make him unhappy, in order to sell him something that makes him feel better. A difficulty I encountered during my brief career as a copier salesperson in the early 1980s was that I wasn't supposed to tell a customer he needed a feature he didn't yet have if I wasn't then able to offer a valid

solution. Yet occasionally while I was researching a target operation I'd notice a printing need my products couldn't meet, though I
knew somebody else's products could. Did I mention those findings
to my potential customer? A few times I did. But I'll also admit that
more often than not I'd leave it up to the customer to figure out he
still hadn't solved all his problems after signing my copier contract
on the dotted line. That's how sales works. Sales people typically
are paid on commission. If they don't sell enough products their
families don't get to eat and they lose their jobs. That doesn't exactly inspire moral action or full disclosure on the part of the person
whose future is at risk.

While many salespeople walk a fine line between outright dis-
honesty and disclosing details that might hinder their chance to
make a sale, occasionally there are those who cross the line. I observed plenty of criminal behavior while I worked in the financial
services business because there the monetary stakes were a whole
lot higher than they were in copier sales. The Bernie Madoffs of
the world (and the financial industry is *full* of them) possess enormous egos that won't allow them to admit they aren't as terrific at
what they do as they imagine themselves to be. So they lie to people, or perhaps they cheat or steal money from their most trusting
clients, hoping to somehow make good on their deception before
they're exposed.

I once knew a fellow who pilfered huge sums of money from
his own in-laws' accounts to cover the losses on his personal trades.
He then pilfered even more money to keep his wife in the style
to which she'd grown accustomed since childhood. When it all
came tumbling down I felt deep compassion for *all* the parties—the

in-laws, whose trust was shattered; the wife who left her husband in the aftermath of the scandal but who'd never worked outside the home so didn't know how to manage on her own; the wonderful kids who got caught in the painful crossfire; and even the broker who lost his job, his family and future, when all he'd wanted was to be viewed as successful in the eyes of his wife and family.

I knew another gentleman who frequently made risky trades for his own account. Turned out he was profiting by journaling his losing transactions into the accounts of clients he believed wouldn't notice the unsolicited trades. (They eventually did.) I even encountered a fellow who had illegally named himself as the *beneficiary* of several life insurance policies he'd underwritten for some elderly clients, explaining to them that it would enable him to ensure the cash was appropriately disseminated to their heirs after they died! The instant they became my clients we changed those policies, but it shook them to realize how close they'd come to being taken by an unscrupulous advisor. Eventually most of the worst offenders do get fined and/or drummed out of the business, but not before they cause a lot of suffering to innocent people.

The temptations to subvert one's moral values while working in sales are almost constant. Most salespeople are clever and think fast on their feet, which is why they make good salespeople to begin with. It also makes them harder to catch when they're doing something illegal. It's important to note here that in corporate sales, rewards for doing the *right* thing are much harder to come by than rewards for doing the *wrong* thing. Nobody gets paid for pointing out the flaw in his own company's product and encouraging a potential client not to buy it, but to buy a superior product instead—or at least one that will better meet the client's needs. The only reward a salesperson receives in that situation comes from inside himself, for following his conscience and maintaining his integrity.

When a client's trust is earned and deserved, the relationship between salesperson and client can be gratifying for both. When trust is misplaced, however, tragedy sometimes results. Consider the families who handed over their life savings to Madoff Investment Securities, based on recommendations of their friends as well as on Madoff's reputation. An estimated fifty billion dollars in client money evaporated, taking down with it the lives, futures and dreams of many thousands of innocent people.

Countless professional techniques give a salesperson an advantage over an untrained layperson, but *every* salesperson relies on a single basic principle: "Buy what I'm selling and you'll be better off tomorrow than you are today." If you remember that when you watch commercials or sit through a high-pressure sales pitch, you'll recognize it when a clever marketer attempts to seduce you.

Sales people may try to seduce their clients, but they're often being seduced themselves by the firms they represent. After the financial services crash in 2009, the media attacked the perks, bonuses and corporate junkets still being offered by the likes of AIG, Citigroup and Bank of America, but those things have been standard rewards for salespeople for decades. The publicized explanations behind such company trips label them as continuing education to help companies retain quality sales people, since sales are what drive a company's bottom line. The *unpublicized* reason I observed during my many years in sales was to pit the company's salespeople against each other in a race to be known as "the best."

If the company was offering an all expenses paid trip to Hawaii at year end for employees whose sales exceeded a designated target, *and* the results of the contest were to be publicized throughout the entire company, every single employee would know who was—or wasn't—"good enough" to qualify for the trip. It also wasn't unheard of for a company's competitors to acquire copies of those trip lists and use them to recruit the most successful salespeople.

Accolades and shame are the carrots and sticks of sales. They fan the fears, self-doubts and egos of the people who do the selling. Walk into any auto dealership and you'll likely see a prominently displayed plaque celebrating the "Salesperson of the Month." What is that but a tribute to the person who's sold the most cars? How do you imagine seeing that plaque staring out at them every day makes the losers feel? What might they be willing to do to get their face on that plaque next month, so they can feel better? Might they be willing to lie to make a sale and be seen as "good?" And what does any of that have to do with selling a potential customer the car she really needs and can afford? Is the person who sells the most cars even the person we want to deal with when we walk into a showroom to look at cars?

Sales careers are highly paid because it is a profession with one of the highest stress and burnout rates in business. When you begin each month with your paycheck meter at zero, *and* you know you'll have regular bills to pay that will total way beyond zero by month's end no matter how many hours you intend to invest in your job, how can heading for work *not* trigger emotional stress? In the 1980s, New York City was the world's cocaine-snorting capital because cocaine helped the kings of finance feel indestructible.

It also enabled them to work outrageously exhausting hours. Last but not least, snorting coke became a status symbol because it was *expensive*, which implied success. If you could place a big bowl of free cocaine on a table at your party, it fairly screamed to your associates you had arrived.

In the world of commissioned sales, money and success are inseparable. It's also true that the best clients tend to gravitate to the most successful sales people. They assume that a successful salesperson has earned the respect and trust of others, so he or she must be good. That means the more a salesperson hopes to earn the more important it is to show the rest of the world how successful he *already* is. Ironic as it may seem, then, some of the world's biggest, flashiest consumers happen to be the men and women who work in commissioned sales.

THE PURSUIT OF SALES AT THE COST OF RESOURCES

None of this chasing after bottom line profits is healthy or genuinely improves society. When people are competing in cutthroat ways to push unnecessary products onto consumers, the amount of capital and human labor we squander trying to convince potential buyers to purchase those goods is incalculable. Worse, when companies compete to push *inferior* products onto customers because they're cheaper, society becomes the loser for the benefit of some company's bottom line.

The good news is that the expanding flow of information has been improving with the growth of the Internet, enabling consumers to become more thoughtful shoppers. Where once *Consumer Reports* was the primary source of information about product ranking and safety considerations, the Internet has opened up a vast new array of options from which we can choose. The challenge is finding the time to do the kind of in-depth analysis necessary to make the best choice possible when making a buying decision.

For example, growing public awareness about the environmental damage caused by phosphates (and other non-biodegradable chemicals) has triggered the introduction of new products like environmentally friendly dish soaps. Originally these soaps may not have been as good as the competition at getting things clean, but over time the quality has improved. Still, does the realization they're selling harmful products deter soap manufacturers from continuing to produce non-biodegradables now that safer environmental alternatives exist? It doesn't, because to acknowledge their products are harmful and that consumers would be better served buying a competitor's products would reduce their short-term profitability. Their best bet is to challenge the cleaning power of biodegradables through negative ad campaigns, and if that doesn't work to undercut them in price. Price cutting allows companies to market their harmful or dangerous products in quantity to the working poor (of whom there are many) and to concede the narrow wealthy upscale market (which is relatively small) to higher priced quality products.

It would be vastly preferable for us to encourage the billions of *poorer* people around the planet to use biodegradables instead of only the wealthy few who can afford them, particularly if our aim is to protect our drinking water. But capitalism just doesn't work that way. Better products tend to cost more to produce, so buying based on quality, service and craftsmanship remains the domain of the wealthy. The poor will buy only what they can afford, no matter how inferior—or even dangerous—those products may be. What's unwittingly been left out of that equation is the external, unfactored cost to society of the added pollution and environmental degradation caused by harmful products, as well as the waste of resources being used in marketing products that don't last.

We also fail to take into account the negative impact of the massive financial subsidies our governments grant to protect the profits of established industries. As mentioned earlier, enormous federal subsidies presently go to big agribusiness concerns, large oil companies and the like, which enable those businesses to successfully suppress new companies by selling their products at artificially low prices. Business lobbyists have been bending congressional ears for decades to ensure subsidies are included in every federal budget, even though subsidies make it harder for companies with better approaches (like permaculture farming) or new technologies (like solar and geothermal energy) to succeed against the established industrial forces. Government subsidies flow to those with the power to make significant campaign contributions, which *don't* come from the coffers of struggling startup companies.

This issue is brought into sharp focus when we consider the limited availability of organic produce. Ask a few people on the street if they'd prefer their fruits and vegetables laden with pesticides or without, and you'll find most would prefer their food to be grown organically. The problem is organic foods, while they promote better health and are safer for our environment, almost always cost more to grow than do commercially farmed and pesticide-treated foods. If you can afford to eat healthy, then by all means you may do so. If not, you'll have to take your chances with all the chemicals. Unfortunately, most small organic farmers aren't eligible for the agricultural subsidies that help keep prices low for industrialized agribusinesses.

Why the majority of us blithely accept these stratified social benefits is an open question. Perhaps it's because we've been taught to imagine that we too—if we work hard enough—can become one of the few whose earnings will grant us access to the best this world has to offer. Just as soon as we've "made it" we'll be able to afford to be more charitable toward the less fortunate, to care about our health and our environment, to be resource-conscious for future generations. Until then, we've got to hang on with all we have to what little we've managed to accumulate so far.

The trouble is that by its very nature exclusivity will *always* be limited to a few. For every person who realizes his or her dreams, the needs of a million others go unfulfilled. Not only is exclusivity restricted, the mark of success moves farther out of reach the faster we run toward it. A few decades ago a person with a million dollars was considered rich. In 2011, a million dollars would barely buy a middle-class home in suburban Los Angeles County. Penthouse apartments in New York City used to sell for a million dollars. Now they go for forty-five or fifty million a pop. Only mega-millionaires or billionaires can afford those sorts of prices. And fewer live at that rarefied level than ever before in our history.

Ordinary millionaires may own expensive cars, live in a nice home with quality furnishings and put their kids through exclusive private schools, but they don't belong to the rarefied clubs of the rich. They aren't flying around in private jets, renting private islands for their family vacations or toting around eight-thousand-dollar handbags. Inflation and continued wealth concentration have seen to it that today's millionaire is yesterday's "thousandaire."

You would never know how few people are seriously wealthy from our magazine ads, however. Pick up a copy of *People* and you'll be treated to a breathless recounting of the activities of the rich and famous as if those lifestyles were within reach of most ordinary people. They'll even show you where, for a mere four hundred dollars, you can purchase a knock-off pair of Manolo Blahnik shoes that would cost you three thousand if you'd bought the real thing. As if most of us could or would or even should! Still, when compared to the designer brand, the magazine makes four hundred dollars for shoes sound almost average. Readers can't help but wonder what's wrong with themselves if four hundred dollars still seems like too much to pay for some strappy footwear.

TAXES MITIGATE (BUT DON'T SOLVE) THE CONCENTRATED WEALTH PROBLEM

A common conservative maxim we hear these days is that the top wage earners have been forced to pay an unfair percentage of U.S. income taxes. Conservatives prefer to promote "trickle down" economics, where the wealthy get to keep more of their money after taxes and are then encouraged to spend and invest it in ways that stimulate the larger economy and eventually provide new benefits for the poor. The theory presumes that if the wealthy are permitted to spend and invest more of their disposable dollars, the middle class will eventually receive promotions and raises as the businesses owned by the wealthy expand, and the poor will receive cost of living increases at their lower paying jobs. After all, the theory proposes, the wealthy are responsible for most of the job creation in this country, so to reduce their ability to spend their wealth eliminates new jobs.

Of course wealthy people create new jobs! Not too many impoverished people are looking for loans to start up brand new businesses. Even if they were, no self-respecting banker would take them seriously *unless* they had already created an amazing new product with some history of success and had a solidly written business plan to back up their idea. That argument on behalf of jobs creation, then, is nothing more than a parlor trick meant to distract us from more important concerns surrounding leaving more wealth in the hands of the already wealthy.

Jobs in a capitalistic economy will always be created around *money*, wherever that money happens to wind up. If it winds up in the hands of the wealthy few, the wealthy will create some new jobs. If it winds up in the hands of the middle class, the middle class will create new jobs. If it winds up in the hands of the government, the government will create new jobs. Is, as some people imply, one institution or group more honest and efficient than another at creating those jobs? Take a look at your newspaper headlines for the past ten years. Note how many companies have been sued, fined or forced to admit wrongdoing for the sake of profits, how many wealthy individuals have been accused of embezzlement and other financial crimes, how many government officials and agencies have been charged with accepting bribes or otherwise being derelict in their duties for financial gain. Perhaps, then, it's not about whether wealthy individuals, corporations or governments are better at creating new jobs and aiding society. Perhaps the real issue is that the way society is presently constructed we encourage and reward everyone for doing *wrong* by society—just so long as they don't get caught.

The question that seems to be coming up more and more lately is: why aren't there enough jobs to go around? We've been doing the trickle-down thing for years now, yet we're still way short of the number of jobs necessary to employ everyone who wants to earn a living. The answer to that question, at least in part, is that a primary goal of industry for the past one hundred years has been to increase productivity. But what does that word *mean* exactly, and how has increased productivity negatively impacted the job market?

When a business increases its productivity, it's making more goods with fewer man-hours, due to increased mechanization and enhancements in modern technology. Translation: fewer jobs, while creating many more products. The fact is we can't possibly create enough jobs in our newer, highly mechanized factories to replace the human jobs we're systematically eliminating—let alone provide for the job needs of a growing population—no matter how many new companies form. Too many of the so-called "new jobs" we're creating are trickling down to machines and computers, not people.

We don't have to go far to notice the effects of increased mechanization. Walk into any major grocery store or home improvement store these days and you'll encounter automated barcode checkout scanners that require you to scan and bag your own purchases. One clerk now monitors perhaps five or six checkout lines that used to be manned by individuals. Good for the company's bottom line? Indeed. Fun for you or the harried person who has to help everyone figure out how to use those scanners? Not so much. And when was the last time another human being pumped your gas, washed your car windows, or answered the telephone when you called a business for assistance?

Some economists will point to the rise of the service industry as a potential cure for the decline in industrial jobs. The service sector has indeed grown because many people stopped working in industry when production jobs dried up; they reeducated themselves and/or applied their own ingenuity to invent service businesses designed to help others become happier, healthier and more time efficient. Still, it's growing clearer that the so-called "services sector" is fast becoming the purview of the wealthy few. Masseuses, dieticians, personal chefs, new age healers, investment advisors, business consultants, tax preparation specialists, private pilots, adventure guides, travel specialists, gardeners, maids, housekeepers, personal shoppers, hair stylists, manicurists, motivational speakers and spiritual advisors—all are people whose job it is to cater to the needs, desires and whims of the wealthiest few, for a price. Those without jobs or who find themselves underemployed and/or stuck in low paying jobs can't afford to pay such people for services they can perform themselves or do without.

Certain service jobs created by aspiring middle-class members once paid quite well, but they have lost pricing power after being co-opted by immigrants. And while we often complain about immigrants taking jobs away from our citizens, we usually don't think twice about transferring our patronage from the local manicurist who charged forty dollars for a set of acrylic nails to the Vietnamese shop down the street where the workers charge twenty dollars for that same service. While it may be better for our pocketbooks to make the switch, we ignore the fact that the local woman who has a home and is raising a couple of kids can't survive on the income the immigrants are willing to accept just to get their feet inside the American door.

Additionally, many service jobs that were once the restricted milieu of licensed providers who were able to charge high fees for their offering—services like stock market investing and personal travel arrangements—have become freely available to the public over the Internet. It seems, then, that even our service jobs are lower-paying, becoming more computerized and utilizing less human labor than before.

Clearly, as we keep striving to improve productivity, we must also acknowledge that we are moving toward eliminating the need to put people to work in exchange for cash and benefits. No one has yet successfully addressed the impact that shift will ultimately have on humanity, but perhaps it's time we all gave it some thought.

The entire capitalistic infrastructure was *designed* to encourage people to work to produce goods and services in exchange for money, which they were then expected to spend to purchase other goods and services. On the surface it seems like a simple enough feedback loop. What was never considered, however, was what would happen to the entire process if one side or the other became permanently unbalanced. As we looked around in 2010, we noted that in the United States alone over six million jobs were *shed* from the national economy in the previous two years.[84] Meanwhile the nation's steady population growth and immigration inflow demand the economy must *add* at least a hundred and twenty-five thousand new jobs each month just to keep the overall employment rate from declining.[85]

Europe has also been experiencing a high level of job stagnation, and for an even longer period of time, because Europe long ago reached the end of its physical ability to spread into new territory through manufacturing expansion. It has few new resources to exploit and little free space remaining for the development of new business infrastructure. Some countries have attempted to address the problem of declining jobs by reducing the length of their average workweek and by expanding the amount of personal vacation time in order to support *fuller* employment. They've also imposed higher taxes on wages and spending so governments can subsidize the more essential services: things like health care, education, food, energy and housing. While that helps alleviate the *symptoms* of chronic underemployment and unemployment, it isn't the long-term solution to the problem. The only way to solve the problem is

---

84   Mike Shedlock, "Six Million Benefit Paying Jobs Vanish in One Year," The Market Oracle, November 17, 2010. http://www.marketoracle.co.uk/

85   Chad Stone, Chief Economist, on the December Employment Report, Center on Budget and Policy Priorities, January 7, 2011. http://www.cbpp.org/staff/chad-stone.htm

to eliminate the need to sell our time in exchange for money. That will, however, require a massive restructuring of our global economic system.

THE NEGATIVE IMPACT OF TAXING ALL THE WRONG THINGS

Rising unemployment has been causing massive social problems that require government spending to successfully address. Unfortunately, the damage taxation does to our paychecks—and by extension our ability to purchase the goods we need from our highly productive and mechanized corporations—has never been satisfactorily addressed. What we're really taxing today isn't the accumulated wealth of our nation that could be used to address the problems and needs of the poor, rather it's an ever-shrinking pool of labor *wages*. Unfortunately, increased productivity has allowed the real wealth of the nation to flow to a very small pool of corporate executives and affluent investors who have the ability to shelter their income and defer or avoid taxation, not to the shrinking pool of regular workers whose paychecks are being automatically taxed. Thus it is that responsibility for the care and nurturing of the poor in the United States has, by default, fallen onto the shrinking middle class. If we want to understand the hostility and anger that inspired the Tea Party movement we need look no further than that for our answer. The Tea Party members aren't the most affluent or highly educated Americans; they're average folks, blue collar and mid-level white collar workers who are sick and tired of being asked to provide for the poor, when they view themselves as (at best) a couple of paychecks away from becoming poor themselves.

While all those corporate executives who've been reaping massive stock grants and bonuses may think they're making out by funding political action committees that encourage tax cuts for the wealthy, in the long run they'll see their incomes shrink because fewer and fewer customers (who are really only day laborers in drag) will be able to afford to buy their company's products. That's because the more the federal tax burden gets shifted onto the middle class, the less money the middle class will have left to spend. The problem with their strategy, in a nutshell, is that the affluent can already afford to satisfy their every whim, so more cash in their bank accounts doesn't translate into more spending the way it does when more income flows to the people who have rents to pay, who need groceries and auto repairs, and whose kids need clothing, books and medical care.

When the middle class loses purchasing power and fewer products get purchased, corporations begin to compete for those limited dollars. Product and price competition ultimately leads to price deflation and a decline in manufacturing, because too many goods wind up sitting unsold on shelves and in warehouses. If economic stagnation continues, it eventually triggers business collapses and bankruptcies.

The questions thus become: Can we continue to pretend that increased productivity, mechanization and job outsourcing to foreign nations with cheaper labor forces doesn't negatively impact the worker/consumer feedback loop that drives our modern domestic economies? Can we continue to ignore the excessive tax burden being placed on the middle class by the affluent, and the way that exacerbates our economic problems? Can we continue to claim this is somehow all a "political failing" and that the appropriate public policy will magically turn our job market around? Since we're moving inexorably toward eliminating the need to draw upon human labor to staff as many businesses, places and positions as we can, is it fair to continue to cling to an outdated economic system that demands human labor be expended in exchange for the right to survive?

Wouldn't the best thing we could do for ourselves be to embrace a new economic reality where we're meeting our needs without individually having to work so hard, so we can devote more time to doing what we enjoy? Creativity, the arts, intellectual pursuits, quality family time, the exploration of personal passions and so forth would be the fruits humanity would reap from such a system. The only trouble is, under the current paradigm we can't afford to "waste" our time with such "trivial" pursuits, because our present system demands that we continue to scrabble to earn our daily bread.

OUR MOST TAXING LIES ABOUT INCOME TAXES AND THE REDISTRIBUTION OF WEALTH

One fascinating thing about statistics is the way they can be twisted to prove just about anything a person wishes to prove. While the people quoting statistics don't usually lie outright, they often spin the data the way they want it to appear. That strategy seems effective because as a population we're not exactly trained (nor do we have the free time) to be the most informed consumers of statistics. Many of us turn on the Nightly News and hear one-sided sound bites, depending on which cause is being promoted or attacked. It's like the old joke about a car race between the Soviet Union and the United States, where the Soviet commentator calling the race announced that the Soviet car came in second while the United States car finished next to last. Such sound bites, which grab our attention, then become the data points we use to help us make *our* case whenever we're arguing issues with other people—for or against. Rarely do most of us dig further to seek the underlying truth behind the sound bite.

Let's look at some raw income tax numbers for the United States, *without* redacting information that doesn't reinforce a given position. By doing that perhaps we can uncover the truth about who's really paying what in taxes.

For fiscal year 1999—the most recent year for which we have an in-depth study that breaks down taxation in the United States not just by the percentage of federal *taxes* paid by each group of workers, but also by the percentage of national *wages* each group earned—the record is as follows:[86]

% Of Taxpayers	# of Families	% taxes paid	% US Wages earned	Avg. income
Top 1%	1.2 million	29%	15%	$719,000
Top 5%	5.9 million	50%	30%	$276,000
All	116.8 million	100%	100%	$49,500
Bottom 50%	58.4 million	0%	13%	$30,000

---

86   Sugi Sorensen and Stephen Cobb, "The U.S. Income Tax Burden: An Analysis of the CBO Numbers," April 17, 2000. http://www.allegromedia.com/sugi/taxes/

What this chart informs us is that yes, the wealthy *do* pay a disproportionate amount of the income tax revenue collected by the US Treasury. The top one percent of taxpayers paid twenty-nine percent of all federal income taxes collected, while the top five percent paid fifty percent of all income taxes collected. What it also shows us, though, is that the burden probably doesn't mean that the top five percent of taxpayers sent their children to bed hungry or made due without heating oil during the winter. While it may cramp the *lifestyle* of a top wage earner to pay a thirty percent federal tax bill on an average income of seven hundred nineteen thousand dollars, his net take home pay will still be north of five hundred thousand dollars, which doesn't tax his *ability to thrive.*

Take a look at the third column in the chart and you'll note that the top one percent of families in the United States collect fifteen percent of the nation's total paid wages. That means the other ninety-nine percent are battling it out over the remaining eighty-five percent of available national wages. In turn, the top five percent of wage earners are taking home a combined thirty percent of the nation's total wages, which means the other ninety-five percent are left to duke it out for the remaining seventy percent of available wage dollars. This inequity in the distribution of national earnings continues to scale down to the point where the bottom fifty percent of wage earners find themselves fighting over a paltry thirteen percent of all available wages paid in the country.

That means less than thirteen percent of all wages being paid nationally are not subject to federal taxation, since many of those bottom fifty percent earners pay at least something in federal taxes. All wages—even those of the poorest workers—are subject to social security, Medicare and disability insurance taxation. For low-income earners, every dollar they're required to pay in federal and payroll taxes means a decision that could make the difference between whether or not they can afford to treat their child's illness or have necessary dental work done. It means sometimes making a choice between putting food on the table or gas in the car so Mom or Dad can get to work in the morning. It means driving on dangerously bald tires or else forgoing that new computer so their children can compete successfully in school. When was the last time someone netting a half-million dollars a year had to make those kinds of choices?

Note too that these figures date back to the Clinton administration. In 2002, under the second Bush administration, taxes paid by the rich were lowered to promote trickle-down economics. The enormous inequity in the distribution of national wages, however, was not addressed at all in that tax cut plan. As things turned out, the Bush tax cuts didn't increase the wages being paid to the bottom earners; they increased the concentration of wealth at the top.[87]

INCOME ISN'T THE SAME AS WEALTH

One last point about taxes: what gets taxed in this country isn't wealth; it's ordinary income. For the most part, income means the wages we earn in exchange for our daily labor. Taxing income is

---

87   G. William Domhoff, "Who Rules America?" UC Santa Cruz, September 2005 (updated September 2010). http://sociology.ucsc.edu/whorulesamerica/

in many ways like stripping a tree of its leaves before the tree has borne any fruit. Those leaves (like income) are vital for providing the tree (the worker) with the necessary energy to thrive and grow. They also help the tree protect and provide for its fruits (the children) as they slowly mature. When we rob a tree of its ability to feed itself and care for its unripe fruit, we wind up with a stunted, dying tree.

Real wealth in a capitalistic society isn't measured by our annual income; it's measured by the amount of cash we're able to accumulate *after* we've covered the costs of our daily survival and provided for our children until they're old enough to take care of themselves. We use *that* wealth the way a tree uses the leaves it no longer needs. It becomes the fertilizer we spread around to create more wealth for ourselves and for society (i.e., our children) in the future. Unfortunately, in our economically stratified society, the social fertilizer piles up in enormous heaps beneath a very few large trees. The wealthy control its distribution and hoard it for their future use, leaving the rest of our global topsoil impoverished. And we wonder why so many of us are struggling!

Why is it so important for us to differentiate between ordinary income and wealth? Let's consider the plights of the nearly three million families that in 2009 lost one partner's salary or experienced dramatic cuts in their work week hours due to the deepening global recession[88]. Those families then lost homes because they were carrying mortgages they could no longer afford to pay[89]. Those

---

88   Lynn Adler, "2009 Foreclosures Shatter Record Despite Aid," *Reuters*, January 14, 2010

89   Ibid.

same people, however, were still expected to pay their income taxes. That's one way to differentiate the necessary leaves from the fertilizing kind. If you need your hard-earned cash to keep your lights on, the heat flowing, food on your table and a roof over your head so you can live to contribute to this world for another day, it ought not to be going toward taxes of any kind. That's just plain stupid. It's like stripping the bark off a tree, denying it water, and then getting angry because it won't produce good fruit. We capitalists call them the "lazy" trees, and we try to make them feel bad that they're not contributing something of value to society, even though we've made it nearly impossible for them to produce anything.

In 2008 CNBC produced a documentary called "Untold Wealth, The Rise of the Super Rich." Some interesting information came to light in the course of that show. For starters, over the next fifty years in the United States alone, twenty-seven *trillion* dollars' worth of inheritance money (those accumulated, spare leaves) will pass from American parents to their children. That's not income; it's hoarded wealth designed to provide the children and grandchildren of the über-rich with unearned, unfair advantages over the far more numerous kids of the working poor. Whose child, do you suppose, will be more likely to succeed and grow even wealthier in the future?

According to the CNBC documentary, a mere one percent of the population controls over fifty percent of total U.S. wealth. Historically, very high levels of wealth concentration have triggered economic disaster, like the Great Depression of the 1930s. The present global recession is a reflection of the expanding problem of wealth concentration, which cripples most people by forcing them to scrabble over crumbs for their survival. We wind up fighting each other for the little bit of cash that's been left behind by the wealthy, but which they don't seem to have given up trying to collect.

According to numbers from the U.S. Census Bureau, of the one hundred fifteen million households in the nation, the United States has so far given rise to one thousand billionaires. Another forty-nine thousand families have accumulated a net worth of between fifty and five hundred million dollars, while one hundred twenty-five thousand additional families have a net worth that falls somewhere between twenty-five and fifty million dollars. Add up all those wealthy households and you'll find they represent considerably less than one percent of American families. Meanwhile the nation's median income in 2005 was twenty-six thousand dollars. That same year, the nation's top four hundred wage earners averaged two hundred fourteen million dollars—apiece.[90] That tiny slice at the pinnacle of society is where the real wealth of this nation goes home to roost, not in the already too-lean pockets of the other ninety-nine-plus percent of the general public.

If we started taxing *real* (accumulated) wealth in this country instead of the ordinary wages we need to survive, I'd venture to guess the wealthiest two hundred thousand or so families might wind up paying a whopping ninety percent of this nation's taxes. Perhaps they should, since they account for ninety percent of its accumulated wealth. In fact, from 1944 through 1963, the top marginal tax rates in the United States exceeded ninety percent.[91] That

90   http://www.census.gov/hhes/www/wealth/wealth.html

91   Top US Marginal Income Tax Rates. 1913-2003, Truth and Politics.org

policy discouraged executives from paying themselves exorbitant salaries, because if they did they'd have to give the federal government more than ninety cents out of every dollar over a certain amount. Even more to the point, when executives aren't claiming large salaries for themselves it means there's more money in the corporate coffers to pay higher wages and provide better benefits to the company's regular workers.

It's important to note as well that many individuals who have inherited or otherwise accumulated wealth no longer need to earn a daily wage. They don't work, so they pay no income taxes. They invest their *accumulated* wealth in tax shelters, tax-free bonds and other creative investments designed by highly paid professionals to help the rich get around the national tax code.

That we don't tax wealth—that we actually provide the wealthy with tax *shelters* so they can further protect the passive income they earn off accumulated wealth—is due to the fact that the wealthy have both the cash and the clout to successfully lobby Congress, which writes our tax codes. Remember too that payroll income is easy for the government to monitor, therefore to tax. Companies are required by law to withhold payroll taxes from their employees every month. That forces workers to *prepay* their annual income taxes by making an interest-free loan to the government. Companies must also provide their annual payroll information to the government, which makes it nearly impossible for the average person to dodge paying income taxes.

While individual workers may have difficulty dodging taxes, small business owners often shelter their income beneath a mountain of so-called business expenses, so that (on paper at least) their companies barely break even. The IRS is aware of that tactic but lacks enough resources to audit the millions of small business owners; so many get away with dodging the tax burden suffered by W-2 earners. Politically at least, the problem seems difficult to fix. Again it boils down to which group wields the power of the checkbook over the politicians. As long as we allow the wealthy, corporations, lobbies and professional business interests to provide the bulk of the funding for political campaigns we'll have politicians who cater to those interests *before* serving the public good. That means the middle class and the poor aren't likely to get a political break anytime soon.

Yet another challenge faced by workers is that many small business owners don't provide retirement or medical benefits to their employees, because doing so would drive up their costs of doing business or perhaps even put them out of business. They're already operating at a competitive disadvantage because larger companies have the ability to purchase in bulk, negotiate prices, block ship, pool their risks and self-insure to lower their overall costs. However, if *all* businesses were required to provide medical insurance and offer retirement benefits to all employees, wouldn't that make for a level playing field? Political rhetoric aside about the potential damage that would do to small businesses, surely some entrepreneurial person would figure out a way to pool small business risk successfully and package employee insurance costs so they remained competitive with larger companies and still provided decent healthcare for employees. Here again, the powerful lobbying forces paid for by small businesses, in particular the Chamber of Commerce, have overridden the needs of real people when it comes to getting the attention of members of Congress.

POVERTY RESTRICTS CHOICES

People whose incomes fall below thirty thousand dollars a year don't have the luxury of thinking about whether or not to buy organic produce or if they should worry about whether their dish soap contains harmful phosphates. They're grateful to have a few dishes still worthy of washing. Labeling important health choices "privileges" and conceding them to the rich comes at a cost to society. On the other hand, advocates for capitalism tout the benefits of empowering the poor to work hard and eventually become the middle class, and for the middle class to strive to become the rich. Where else, they'll insist, will you find a country where a Bill Gates can emerge from middle-class obscurity to become a mover and shaker of global industry?

What they don't mention is that for every Bill Gates there exist a million Bill Smiths, ordinary people struggling every day to put food on their tables and clothes on their children's backs. But at least the Bill Smiths *have* a table, which is more than we can say for the peasants of old. If nothing else, we've certainly gotten cleverer about providing just enough for the poor so they don't rise up and massacre the rich. In fact, we've gotten so clever in our defense of a continued upper class that we've actually convinced the poor they too can become rich if they just put in enough effort. If they don't succeed, well…it must have been *their* fault. But thanks for playing.

Unfortunately for the poor, however, life isn't just a game where someone wins and we all go to bed. It's a matter of life and death.

Restrict their choices too much, and the poor and disenfranchised will resort to crime as the easiest way to get around a system that refuses to let them go through it. That explains why American prison populations are the highest in the world, holding 2.3 million people behind bars in 2007.[92] In the same year China imprisoned only 1.5 million people while managing a population four times the size and while incarcerating its political dissidents on top of that.[93] Why does the so-called wealthiest nation in the world feel compelled to lock up so many of its own citizens? Could it be that our ongoing inequitable distribution of wealth has led to a massive crime spree targeting the wealthy?

There's no disputing the fact that the overall standard of living for all Americans has risen over time; if it hadn't, we'd have experienced a peasant uprising long ago and we'd have already jettisoned capitalism as a failed economic system. In practice, though, what we've observed recently has been a shrinking middle class, a rising tide of working poor and a shrinking wealthy class. The insidiousness of capitalism, then, seems to be that it elevates the collective standard of living just enough to convince most people it's working, but not enough to *truly* benefit society. The bulk of the benefits attained through capitalism go directly to the elite members of the plutocracy—the business über-wealthy—while the rest of the people bear the brunt of capitalism's very real (but mainly hidden) costs.

Humanity at large bears the high costs of crime in the form of personal suffering and the expense of running our prisons, along

---

92   http://www.scribd.com/doc/328143/World-Prison-Population-List-2007

93   Ibid.

with the costs of drug abuse, poverty, publicly supported healthcare for the uninsured, stress-related diseases and mental illness, slums and city overcrowding, homelessness, environmental pollution, the degradation of our food and water supplies, species extinction and excessive natural resource depletion. All those problems are mostly being borne by those who benefit the *least* from capitalism. The businesses and individuals whose policies and behaviors *create* these social problems are all earning enough money to buy their way out of having to face the consequences of those messes—at least in the short run.

The true costs to society for industrial pollution, environmental damage, the squandering of scarce natural resources and the emotional depletion that comes from our stressful, pay-before-you-go way of life aren't priced into the products we buy every day in our stores. If they were, none of us could afford them. That doesn't make the costs to us any less real; it just conveniently shifts the accounting "off the books." Why would the economic system allow those very real costs to interfere with their illusory corporate paper profits in our consumer-driven economy?

The truly important question to ask ourselves is this: is it *reasonable* for the rest of us to continue to pretend such costs are nonexistent? If so, why? Are we too afraid to deal with the changes we'll need to implement the moment we acknowledge that the continuation of capitalism, at least as it's been practiced historically, is costing humanity more than we'll ever be able to pay in real life capital? How long can we continue to measure our so-called "successes" in terms of paper dollars, while ignoring our failures in terms of their real life costs?

ACCOUNTING FOR ACTUAL COSTS—
WHAT PRICE CAPITALISM?

In 1981 Buckminster Fuller's book, *Critical Path*, was published. In it he argued that the growing energy crisis was coming to a head and we'd better address it soon, before it destroyed our civilization. He offered some fine ideas for doing so, many of which involved enhanced cooperation between nations rather than pursuing continued warfare and competitiveness. Over thirty years later much of what Fuller predicted has come to pass; and sadly, we're not much closer to solving our energy crisis than we were when the book first appeared in bookstores.

One of the points Fuller made had to do with the *actual* price of oil versus the price we pay at the pump. In an effort to understand resource pricing under a capitalistic system as opposed to the actual cost of natural resources, Fuller spoke with the leading scientists of his time and asked them to calculate what it would hypothetically cost for humans to manufacture a barrel of oil, presuming we were able to acquire all the necessary raw materials and expend the amount of time and energy Mother Nature originally spent to produce it. The answer he received came back in excess of one million dollars per barrel, in 1980 dollars. Yet in 2009 we could purchase that same barrel of oil for less than the cost of an equivalent barrel of milk![94] Believe it or not, a barrel of oil costs hundreds fewer dollars than a barrel of Starbucks coffee.[95] Yet milk and coffee are *renewable* resources and can be replenished within a reasonable human time frame. Oil cannot.

What are we *thinking*? We must ask ourselves why we're allowing our energy companies to extract irreplaceable natural resources out of our planet just because they've purchased the dirt that sits above those stockpiles. Why do we then permit them to sell those resources back to the rest of us on the cheap, driving up our dependency without any of us considering—let alone *paying* for—the long-term costs of replenishing that oil. According to Fuller's calculations, society today would be much better served if we paid people to stay at home, instead of requiring them to drive their cars and use precious oil to get to and from low-wage jobs. Yet we mindlessly burn oil to drive to jobs we don't enjoy—jobs that deplete and degrade the quality of our society—in exchange for minimum wages and a slew of household bills we need to pay. Ponder *that* truth the next time you insert a nozzle into your gas tank.

---

94   A barrel of oil equals 42 gallons. In 2010 a barrel of oil averaged $89.00, according to the U.S. Energy Administration. Meanwhile, in 2010 the average gallon of milk in the U.S. was priced at $2.65 per gallon, according to The People History table of average prices. Thus a barrel of milk would cost at least $111.30, as compared to $89.00 for a comparable barrel of oil.

95   According to the Starbucks official website, the average cost of a tall regular coffee in 2010 was $1.50 for 12 ounces. Since a gallon contains 128 ounces, each gallon of coffee contains 10.66 tall cups. That means a gallon of Starbucks regular coffee sells for $15.99, which in turn means a 42-gallon barrel of Starbucks coffee would sell for a whopping $671.58!

WHY TRUE COST MATTERS

Just for a moment, imagine what life might be like if we didn't have to waste our time listening to advertisements or promotions that bombard us with pitches to buy all the unnecessary things that are being mass-produced and that must be sold to support our economic need for increasing profits. Imagine what it would be like if fewer products were available to us, but those we did produce were the absolute best in their class. Imagine a world where innovation meant exactly that—not, say, the gimmicky addition of some new scent to a standard laundry detergent—but a *genuine* improvement in quality or of benefit to society or the environment. Imagine businesses that didn't cannibalize or try to destroy each other, but instead collaborated to ensure all people had free access to all the best ideas and corporate research. Imagine what it would be like to have companies publish information sheets on their products that detailed both the positives and negatives, so we could compare items and make wiser selections. Imagine how it might feel to work fewer hours—perhaps *far* fewer hours per week—but take pride in the products and services your organization offered? Imagine, if you can, an economy where the only items produced were products and services, not profits? Imagine an economy where people didn't work for wages, but worked for the sheer satisfaction of contributing something of value to the whole, which in turn provided them with everything they needed. Imagine all that without the constant stress over bills that needed to be paid or an ever-present fear of not having enough. Might that be a world that you'd enjoy?

There would almost certainly be tradeoffs in creating such a world. Not everyone could dine on lobster every night of the week unless we figured out how to sustainably and humanely farm-raise lobsters. The top one percent of the population would certainly have to surrender their status as privileged and entitled, along with some of the accompanying benefits. In exchange, the bottom ninety-nine percent would no longer need to worry about meeting their next mortgage payment, nor would they experience sleepless nights wondering how to educate their children and not go bankrupt. Additionally, someone would still be needed to mop floors and clean the toilets. Still, with most people working far fewer hours it would be possible for us to share the burden of our least desirable tasks, so that no single person would be forced to bear the brunt of distasteful labor. Parenting our own children would likely come back into vogue in a really big way, as would the fine art of instructing them in ways that fostered greater creativity and higher wisdom, instead of teaching them to squeeze themselves into the economic system.

Under that scenario, the organism that is humanity would function much like every individual human body does, with each cell (person) specializing in and doing what it is best at, and most loves. We would then share relatively equally in all the advantages that arise from being full participants in a body (our society) whose sum is greater than all its myriad parts. The more we each willingly contributed to society's overall success, the more collective bounty would be available for all to share—including ourselves. Likewise, the more selfishly or greedily we consumed what was available and the less we gave of ourselves to support the whole system, the less would be available for all of us in the future. Such a system is, in fact, the way organic systems *always* function. It's the way of life because it places responsibility for success or failure precisely where it belongs—not in the hands of a powerful few to serve their personal needs, but in the powerful hands of *every* individual it serves.

Not surprisingly, much of that utopian ideal is already available and has proved successful in the society we're living in today. We already know we're at our best when we're creating from our hearts. We can tell we're at our worst when we're over-consuming scarce resources and leaving nothing for future generations. It's why we sometimes cringe when we leave food on a restaurant plate, and why we smile whenever we give a gift to another. Our minds may work overtime to justify and rationalize why we "deserve" more than our fair share of what planet Earth has to offer, but our hearts already know and accept the truth of the fairness doctrine.

Whether we like it or not, humanity is a single organic system, interconnected and alive with nearly infinite possibilities that remain as-yet-untapped. We just haven't all admitted our abilities yet. To accept that we're indeed more capable than we've previously imagined—and then to realign and redesign our systems consciously so they reflect the *best* of what we're capable of rather than focus on protecting us from our worst human inclinations—is the challenge we presently face. The creativity and energetic potential we might unleash in ourselves when we fully come together as a species is as yet still unimaginable, but we can be certain it will far outpace the creative genius humanity has so far gifted itself.

RECOVERING TIME TO LIVE

"TIME IS MONEY." I REMEMBER THE FIRST TIME I EVER HEARD somebody say that. I thought to myself, "Wow...is it possible some people don't understand how different those two things are?" It stunned me to realize people actually equated time and money, as if they were interchangeable parts in a machine. Plug in some time; pull out some money. Everything runs smoothly and everyone's happy. But are we happy if we make that deal? Is it really a fair and reasonable trade for human beings to offer?

Money is something we can get in lots of ways. We can earn it, print it, steal it, borrow it or grow it. Time, however, is the irreplaceable gift of life itself. It's the very essence of life, and as such it carries a preciousness for which no amount of money can compensate. Dying rich is not at all the same as dying, having richly lived.

Somewhere along the way we've been hoodwinked into believing a conceptual fiction.

Our time on this planet is finite. Selling our time in exchange for money will always place an upper boundary on humanity's ability to achieve, because our time on Earth is limited both individually and as a species. Over ninety-nine percent of all species that have ever lived have already gone extinct, and the probability is that we are no exception. At some point it's likely our external environment will change drastically enough that we'll have to evolve into something entirely different if we hope to continue, or else we'll disappear and some new species will arise that *can* survive. We shouldn't be counting on time, then, to deliver us or take us where we want to go.

That we've structured our entire economy around the selling of our precious time in exchange for money means we've designed a system for success that has an upper limitation imbedded in its design. With only so many hours in a day, those who are paid by the hour (the vast majority of human laborers) swiftly bump into the upper boundary of their ability to sell more time. Beyond a certain point, they'll find it increasingly difficult to accumulate wealth. Meanwhile, they're forfeiting the only thing that gives real meaning to life—the time to enjoy it!

The truth is that money is valuable because it's relatively hard to accumulate. However much of it we earn, we're always being pushed to spend a lot more than we have. If we could just pick it up off the ground, like leaves or pebbles, and hand it over in exchange for the items we need, how much worth do you honestly believe humanity would assign to money?

Spare time is also not terribly easy to come by. We get the life we're gifted at birth—be it long and healthy or short and problematic—and beyond our limited capacity to nurture ourselves into longer life or do bodily damage that eventually shortens our lives, that's pretty much the extent of our human existence. Although we're embedded in a universe that may be eternal in age and infinite in dimension, we've each been granted a short span of perhaps one hundred conscious years in which to experience life as a modern human being. When we swap our precious time for limited money, we wind up with an economy founded on dual scarcities. No collective experience of abundance can possibly emerge out of trading something precious for something scarce, particularly if that is our primary mode of exchange. What we've created through capitalism, then, is a manufactured sense of "never enough." That colors our feelings and attitudes about everything we do.

THE LIMITATIONS OF TIME

Each day contains twenty-four hours. Of those, most people need to sleep for at least eight hours a night to remain healthy. We also need to prepare meals, eat and clean up after ourselves for at least another two hours each day. The tasks of bathing, dressing, undressing and managing our basic bodily functions consume, on average, another daily hour. Granting ourselves an additional hour to commute two and from our job, and adding in the standard eight work hours per day we sell to a business in exchange for the cash to survive, we're left with four remaining hours each day into which we're expected to cram our personal lives.

Modern capitalism allots us about four hours a day of personal freedom in which to experience life! Four hours to interact with our family members and keep up with our many friendships; four hours in which to shop, do our laundry and complete our household chores; four hours to learn something new, to sit in quiet meditation, to exercise, make love, watch TV or play silly computer games; four hours in which to volunteer in our communities or take care of our personal health needs; four hours in which to commute to and from all the places (outside of work) we need to go.

The problem is, most of these items on our personal to-do list are difficult to perform in a quality fashion with only four hours a day in which to accomplish them. Not only that, but our employers demand the best and most productive of our waking hours. Many of us barely return home from work before darkness descends, only to find our children require feeding, bathing, assistance with homework and so on. Although we have an additional twenty-six free hours every weekend, many of us still find it hard to cope with the demands of our everyday lives in that small space of time.

Weekends have become the days we set aside to do yard work, maintain our homes, play with our children or perhaps watch sports or a movie on TV. They provide large enough blocks of time for us to start a new project and see it to completion. We can plant a garden, clean the garage or take our children to the beach for an excursion. Weekends are also the time during which we could, if we so chose, invest in keeping ourselves more fully informed about the state of the larger world in which we live. Unfortunately, the sheer bulk of information available to us in the form of books, magazines, newspapers, Internet websites and blogs can seem overwhelming, so we instead devote our precious free time to activities and hobbies we enjoy. Focusing on the world's many problems just makes us feel more anxious about our future than we already are. And who needs more stress in their lives than they already have?

When we expand our thinking beyond a single twenty-four hour day, we find that the average person works for somewhere between forty and sixty years. That leaves us each with some thirty to fifty *unpaid* years, depending on how long we live, during which we still require financial support. Before the age of twenty we're too uneducated and immature to sell our time to society, so we must count on our hard-working parents to pay for our needs. Later on, once we've reached sixty-five or seventy, our bodies have begun to wear down and our mental capacities may have grown too calcified to enable us to be fully productive any longer. Putting in forty years of hard labor also leaves most of us craving a little peace, relaxation and tranquility in our declining years. That means while we're working hard and providing for our children we must also plan well enough ahead to ensure we have enough money set aside to take care of ourselves for some unknown length of time beyond retirement.

What makes planning for retirement so difficult is that the expenses we'll be expected to cover in the future are unpredictable because of inflation and ongoing advances in technology. The future value of our savings is also unpredictable due to portfolio fluctuations, changing tax laws and changes in the interest rates paid on savings. None of us has a crystal ball that allows us to see the future, but society classifies us as failures and views us as a drain on the public if we're unsuccessful at preparing for the unknown.

The whole concept of retirement, of the need to cease working, is an interesting idea for us to unpack. Some of us choose to retire because we wish to explore the aspects of ourselves that got put on hold when we first entered the workforce. Others retire because our bodies and minds are physically broken or spent. Still others retire because we're told we're supposed to do so, and we're used to behaving according to societal norms. Most of us, though, look forward to retirement mainly because we perceive our jobs as work, not as the fulfillment of our life's purpose. I'd venture to bet that none of us, when asked as children what we wanted to be when we grew up, declared that we hoped to be pharmaceutical salesmen or clerks scanning goods by barcode in a checkout line. We aimed to be astronauts, firemen or dinosaur bone collectors. If we did wish to work in a store, we imagined ourselves serving our customers by connecting with them and offering genuine help. Some of us even dreamed of exploring the stars, inventing flying cars, or creating works of art that would stir peoples' souls.

How many of us were forced to surrender our dreams to the naked reality of an economy that didn't support our creative geniuses? Is it any wonder we all hope to "retire" so we can at last find the time to discover and explore the things we feel in our hearts we were put here to do?

The process of natural human development requires our family members to nurture us for our first twenty-plus years of life, during which time we make little or no financial contribution to our own upkeep. After that we need to become self-supporting for the next forty years, plus prepare successfully for our final twenty-plus retirement years. During our productive years, whatever extra money we earn after our basic expenses and taxes are covered must first go toward the upkeep of our own growing families. Whatever remains, if anything, must then be managed efficiently enough to ensure we're not left broke in our old age, no matter what the economy chooses to do or how our investments decide to perform for us. We must therefore squeeze our understanding of the nation's monetary situation and our exploration of various investment options into our limited four free hours of daily time. It's little wonder that most of us remain woefully uneducated around the complexities of successful saving and investing.

SHIFTING RETIREMENT'S BURDENS AND RISKS

For years, corporations have pulled back from offering their employees guaranteed pension plans and replaced them with 401k plans. That's no accident. Pension plans used to be funded with *company* profits. They promised retirees a guaranteed annual income until the death of the recipient (and usually involved the recipient's spouse as well). But 401k plans are funded mostly through *employee* payroll deductions and promise nothing except whatever value those private accounts achieve, based on their long-term investment performances. As executive pay increased over time, pension plan contributions vanished and 401k plans replaced them. Companies now claim they "can't afford" to pay for their workers' retirements. Of course not—they're too busy paying for the stock grants and bonuses earned by their top executives. What business wants to be burdened with caring for a bunch of elderly ex-workers when what we reward it for is generating wealth for a powerful few? When morality and business conflict, we rarely let our morality get in the way.

There was a time when some business owners, those whose small enterprises enabled them to get to know all their employees personally, felt a moral obligation to care for their people when they could no longer work. But at some point in our expanding and industrializing capitalistic system, someone in a larger, more impersonal corporate environment realized it was possible to shift the burden and financial risks associated with retiree care *away* from the company and *onto* the employees by creating a plan funded solely by employee contributions. Doing so meant companies would no longer have to worry about paying employee pensions in the future, which would leave their financial profits flowing freely to the bottom line, instead of out the door to useless retirees.

Although 401k plans were initially designed to enable employees to *supplement* their pensions through the accumulation of tax-deferred savings, over time they've become the only retirement program most companies offer. Pensions have gone the way of the dinosaur, and for many of us what's disappeared along with them is any hope for real financial security in our old age.

Not only does it create hardship in our daily lives for us to set aside income to fund our retirement plans, it's also hard for us to protect that wealth from forces beyond our control. When the stock market plunged in late 2008 and early 2009, bond values slid and real estate also collapsed. People then found themselves with literally nowhere to turn to find shelter for their dwindling 401k assets, and no one to trust for assistance. Wall Street and its companions, the major money center banks, had already plundered much of our 401k money by selling us overly aggressive investment products, as well as through greed, outright criminal behavior and general portfolio mismanagement.

Prior to 2008 we'd already experienced the painful collapse of high-flying stocks that had been touted by financial investment companies during the Internet heyday of the late 1990s. Dutifully, we listened to our brokers and bought those growth stock darlings for our retirement portfolios, only to watch the NASDAQ index that monitored their values plunge from a high on March 10, 2000 of 5132 to a low of 1114 on October 9, 2002—a whopping decline of seventy-nine percent.[96] We then learned investments we'd been told were rock solid—companies like Tyco, WorldCom, Global Crossing and Enron—had cooked their books and "fooled" the analysts whose job it was to know better. These were analysts whose professional opinions we relied upon when we put those shady investments in our portfolios. Their heartfelt apologies did nothing to repair the long-term damage to our portfolios caused by those losses. Combine the effects of all those collapsed investments with the fact that the Dow Jones Industrial Average then plunged from a high of 14,164 in October of 2007 to a low of 6443 on March 6, 2009, a fifty-four percent decline in value in a little more than

96   Andrew Beattie, "Market Crashes: The Dotcom Crash," Investopedia, 2010.

a year[97], and we understand why people, especially those getting close to retirement age, began to panic. For nearly ten years we'd consistently lost money by listening to the advisors we were paying to keep us solvent. What added insult to this grievous financial injury was that the banks we'd just bailed out to the tune of many trillions of dollars then offered to pay us only a fraction of a percent in interest on the cash we stashed in our 401k money market accounts, which seemed by far the safest place for nervous investors to put their money. When we lost our jobs, those same banks then lent our accumulated—but federally restricted—savings back to us (along with lots more cash they were able to create out of thin air under the Federal Reserve's reserve requirement rules), charging us between fourteen and twenty percent for the lines of credit and credit card purchases we needed to survive their bank-inspired recession. That thirteen to nineteen percent "spread" we're paying in interest to borrow our own money from the banks (and by extension from each other) represents pure profit for them. Yet had we tried to avoid the predatory policies of the banks by borrowing our own money from ourselves, we'd have had to pay taxes and penalties on our 401k withdrawals.

Banks are simply middlemen, transactors designed to bring together borrower and lender. The price they charge the borrower is always much higher than the interest rate they pay the lender for making good use of his money. How nice it would be for both borrower and lender if they could agree on, say, a standard six percent interest rate, and eliminate the bank from the arrangement.

---

97   Stock Market Crash, The Crash of 2008-2009, Wikipedia—for DJIA high/low statistics only.

Failing that, regular Americans unfortunately can't work enough hours in their lifetimes to overcome the greedy money seizure that banks are imposing on both borrowers *and* lenders. And heaven help those who both borrow and save, because they're paying banks on both sides of their transactions. It's far better to borrow money from yourself than from a bank, even if that means you must "surrender" your so-called savings. To save money and earn miniscule rates of interest on your savings, while borrowing money from a bank on credit at a much higher rate of interest is foolishness, but we're encouraged to do just that by professional bankers who make their living from investing our savings while collecting interest on all our long-term debts.

What makes this middleman positioning held by the banks more egregious is the fact that much of the cash they received by way of the federal bailout is being lent to the general population at regular (high) rates of interest. The banks borrowed it from the Fed at almost zero percent, then lent it to private debtors for anywhere from five percent for home loans to as much as thirty-five percent to finance credit card debts. That money is the same money we the people are *already* obligated to pay back to the government, *with* interest, in the form of higher taxes down the line. Thus the banking/government complex nailed the public with paying interest on the same debt from two different directions, with banks behaving like a giant sucking filter in the middle. Had we actually lent *ourselves* those same many trillions of dollars at the negligible interest rate we've gifted our banks, we'd have been a lot better off than we're going to be when the bill for all that lending finally comes due. For that matter, we could have gifted ourselves those trillions of dollars and simply let it go at that. Why should we bother to pay back money we've borrowed from ourselves, just so some company can earn a profit from the transaction?

By the summer of 2009, many financial pundits began touting the resurgence of the stock market and the potential end of the 2008 recession. Why wouldn't they? Their careers are based on the public making new investments. When public interest in investing falls off, their opinions no longer have value. That's also why stockbrokers remain biased toward continual investment. If they told you *not* to invest they'd be out of a job! What those same advisors fail to inform investors about is that the volatility that has become such a routine occurrence in the stock market is not a friend to the longer-term investor. Once the stock market plunges fifty percent it then needs to rise one hundred percent in order to eradicate its losses. A decline from 14,000 to 7,000 on the Dow represents a fifty percent decline in market value. For the market to then climb back to 14,000 from the 7,000 level requires the market to experience a full one hundred percent gain. That's why large losses are so disastrous to investors—it takes much more time and requires the taking of proportionally greater risks for an investor to recover from a statistically large loss than it does for him to shoot for slower but steadier financial growth. The following example exposes how market volatility can confuse our understanding of true performance:

> *Janine invested one thousand dollars in a fund that*
> *climbed fifteen percent in year one, fifteen percent in*
> *year two and fifteen percent again in year three. In*

*year four, her fund declined by twenty-seven percent
but in year five it rose again by twenty percent. Meanwhile, her friend April invested one thousand dollars in a fund that gained only seven percent per year
for those same five years. Which of them do you think
wound up with more money at the end of five years?*

The answer, which may surprise you, is risk-averse April. April would be sitting with fourteen hundred dollars in her portfolio after five years, while Janine's one-thousand-dollar investment would have risen to only thirteen hundred and thirty-two dollars. As we can now see, big performance numbers don't necessarily equate to big long-term gains.

TIME CONSTRAINTS AND THE HEALTHCARE BURDEN

Access to quality medical care has again became a huge concern for Americans, culminating in the hotly contested Health Care Reform Act of 2010. Hard working Americans have long clamored for consistent and reasonable universal access to health care. For years we've demanded the elimination of preexisting condition exclusions, lifetime caps and insurance company nullification of policies based on historical medical details unrelated to current health problems. We also wanted our coverage to be protected when we changed jobs, and most especially we wanted lower insurance rates to enable more of us to receive good medical care. Meanwhile the insurance and medical industries fought fiercely to protect their turf and keep the government out of the business of offering low-cost insurance to all Americans.

What we wound up with was a bill that accomplished *some* of what the people wanted, but not nearly enough to meet the needs of all. At the same time, the bill succeeded in irritating the corporate special interests and the wealthy who already have great coverage and aren't interested in paying higher taxes to ensure that the rest of the country receives quality medical services on par with the sort that they receive. They fear that more people flooding into the health care system will make it that much harder for them to continue to access the level of care they're privileged enough to purchase for themselves already. The thinking here is obviously that—beyond basic emergency services—medical care is a privilege and not a basic human right, and that only those who can afford it ought to be able to access the health care system.

What disproves that self-centered thinking when we take even a cursory look at the health of the general public is the fact that when even one of us gets sick and goes untreated, that illness has the potential to spread through the community and cause a ripple effect of disease that harms us all. We lose workdays that cost us money, our kids miss school and we spend our hard earned money on medicines and medical co-pays. Even highly paid workers who have excellent health insurance can't afford to get sick for very long. Most of us don't get paid to stay home for more than a few days each year, so we drag ourselves to work when we don't feel well, even if it means spreading our germs to our fellow employees.

The net costs to both businesses and our families from the constant spreading of infectious diseases—a practice called "presenteeism"— are estimated to range from between one hundred-fifty to two hundred-fifty billion dollars per year in the United States alone,[98] but most employers still insist on limiting our sick days. On average, companies grant only eight sick days each year.[99] Even if half their employees wind up working at half-strength for weeks on end, employers would rather run their operations that way than pay a sick employee his full salary to stay home until he's healthy. Their fear, of course, is that too many people would take advantage of every opportunity to stay home sick if they were paid for doing so, which would cost the company money and hinder production.

What, we must ask ourselves, does that fear say about how employers imagine their workers feel about the jobs they're expected to do? How happy can employees be with their jobs if they're that anxious to take advantage of the chance to stay home? Isn't that an issue our businesses might be well served to address? If more people viewed what we now call "work" as the fulfillment of their life's purpose, they might be less inclined to avoid doing it.

Not only are employee sick days discouraged, our illnesses are not supported by the companies that were designed to help us through them—insurance companies and healthcare providers. Contrary to the propaganda we sometimes hear, the primary cause of personal bankruptcies isn't greedy, immoral overspending by thoughtless people. What's really happening is that for many

---

98   Patricia Schaefer, *The Hidden Costs of Presenteeism: Causes and Solutions*, Attard Communications, Inc. 2007.

99   BLS Report on Paid Sick Leave, Bureau of Labor Statistics, May 26, 2010.

families, a sudden catastrophic illness depletes their savings and hinders their breadwinner's ability to work. In 2003 and 2004, for instance, families that possessed health insurance but incurred uncovered medical expenses accounted for over fifty percent of all American bankruptcies.[100] Long-term illnesses, whether suffered by the household's primary wage earner or by a child within the household, wreak havoc on the average family's finances. We all know our insurance companies do their best to avoid paying out on expensive claims—some even bonus claims adjusters based on the total dollars saved by denying claims—so that the families will have to bear the burden of paying those costs. The more claims their adjusters reject, the more profitable the insurance companies are, even though higher profits result in the catastrophic loss of life and the destruction of families.

Prior to the Health Care Reform Act of 2010, which some politicians are still angling to repeal as of this writing, if a person suffered a major illness they often became uninsurable if they subsequently lost their job or decided to change jobs. The insurance industry's blanket exclusion of "preexisting conditions" trapped people in place because they couldn't afford to jump to another company only to be turned down for insurance because of an illness they once suffered. Others couldn't retire because they couldn't afford to surrender their private insurance coverage until they became eligible for Medicare.

How many years we'll be able to work and how hearty we'll be while doing so is in part a function of how well we manage our health, and in part a whim of fate. Yet most companies do their

---

100   Bankruptcy and Medical Debt, BCS Alliance.Com, Medical and Debt Solutions.

best to shove the *entire* financial burden of healthcare (along with the burden of retirement care) onto the backs of individual workers by charging ever-higher premiums for insurance, assuming they even offer medical coverage. Meanwhile, insurance companies also do their best to *keep* that burden on individuals and off themselves by denying claims and making it hard to navigate the blizzard of paperwork required for reimbursement.

None of us knows when we'll have an accident or suffer an unexpected illness. To have our entire life, including our ability to provide for our family's future, be dependent upon our ability to stay healthy is a tremendous risk that capitalism insists we all take. Those who remain under- or uninsured, usually the poorest among us, are taking the biggest risk of all in this arena. Not only are the lives of the working poor shattered when their health takes a catastrophic turn, but the rest of us suffer the consequences too. The general public pays the cost of an indigent person's medical care, sometimes for an illness that could have been avoided had we offered free basic or preventative care instead. We also lose out on that person's potential future contributions to society, an immeasurable loss for humankind.

Where's the morality in allowing people to become ill or even die because they can't afford the care we know how to provide? Set aside the belief that we're all "supposed to" take responsibility for providing adequate coverage for ourselves. That notion is only as good as a person's capacity to earn enough money to pay the insurance bill, and we've already seen the inequity of modern wage distribution. In a nation that often prides itself on its Christian historic roots, I'd venture to guess that Jesus would shudder at the callous way Americans have been trained to treat each other. I can't help but wonder what Jesus would charge Lazarus to raise him from the dead if he hung around the medical profession today.

Because we all know our health isn't something we can always control, stress arises around that uncertainty. Certainly we can improve our chances for good health by taking care of ourselves, exercising and eating healthy foods, but that still doesn't mean we won't get cancer from environmental toxins or be hit by a car tomorrow. Some of us will win the health care lottery and manage to put in a full forty years of employment. Others will experience extreme medical hardships through no fault of our own and find our productive years cut painfully short. When our ability to care for ourselves in old age depends almost entirely on whether or not we happened to win a medical game of chance, something seems wrong with the system we've created. Will we be lucky enough to remain healthy for our productive working years, so we can earn enough money and invest it during a lucky period of national expansion, so we can provide adequately for ourselves in our old age? That's a question no one in a moral society should have to ask.

FINITE TIME OR INFINITE CREATIVITY?

Unlike time, which so far as we know remains finite for all living things, human creativity seems to be in infinite supply and can be sourced without any limitations. We don't need to be physically strong or healthy to be creative; we simply need to be able to use our imagination and apply our talents. Imagination is limited only by our ability to dream, which itself is limited only by our attachment to whatever has already been dreamed up and converted into reality. Consider cars, for example. Someone first imagined the internal combustion engine, and then some other people built it. Society gradually adopted the car as the favored mode of transportation, so now we're all attached to cars for getting around. They conveniently carry us to and from wherever we need to go, and have freed us up to travel amazing distances that in the past would have seemed impossible to cover in a single human lifetime.

Most of us can't imagine a world without cars, yet before they were dreamed up, we existed just fine without them. Sure, we traveled more slowly than we do now and had to deal with the care and feeding of horses, but had cars never been invented we wouldn't even know what we were missing. Likewise, when something more compelling than cars appears on the horizon—flying vehicles, for example—we'll eventually let go of our attachments to cars in exchange for a new way to travel. It may take time, though, to convince the hardcore car lovers to change, the same way it took decades for people to let go of their attachment to horse-drawn carriages.

One of the biggest difficulties in implementing imaginative new changes lies in persuading people who are afraid of changing that the change is at least worth testing to find out whether or not it's helpful. We're reluctant to let go of what we know in order to embrace what we don't yet know, even when what we know isn't working. We're terrified to surrender our dependence on cars, for instance, even though they contribute huge amounts of environmental pollution, run on a nonrenewable resource, lead to sedentary life-styles and obesity and cause many annual deaths and injuries. In 2006, forty-two thousand six hundred and forty-two people were killed in automobile accidents in the United States and another two and a half million were injured.[101] What other social tool do we approve of that carries with it such wide acceptance of catastrophic loss? We've already spent over a trillion dollars to fight a war on terrorism, which killed around thirty-five hundred innocent Americans and several thousand more soldiers who have been sent to fight that war.[102] Why are their deaths so much less acceptable to us than over forty thousand annual deaths from auto accidents? Is it because we consider the random risk of dying in our cars a basic cost of doing business in America, while random acts of terrorism have a huge negative impact on our sense of "business as usual?"

Thoughts of eliminating our monetary system and thereby transforming our economy through implementing imaginative new ideas triggers the same fear in people as does letting go of cars. We tend to forget that somewhere back in the lost pages of human history, some unknown person originally dreamed up the notion of us paying each other to facilitate the exchange of the things we create. Before that, we traded things or gave each other whatever we made for free. For whatever reason the idea of money caught on, and so it became our modern reality. Most of us now can't imagine a world without money, even though humans got by without it for many thousands of years. Still, it will take a collective imagining of

101   National Motor Vehicle Crash Statistics for 2006.

102   Amy Belasco, "The Cost of Iraq, Afghanistan and Other Global War On Terror Operations Since 9/11," Congressional Service Research, September 2, 2010.

something far more compelling than money for us to detach from our old way of being and jointly embrace a new method of creative exchange. Personally, the thought of nobody having to ever again stress about "making a living" in order to survive, as well as being able to witness humanity shifting to creating and giving out of joy and love for life, seems to me a compelling substitute for the need for us to work in exchange for money.

When it comes to imagination and human creativity, if we turn once again to nature's playbook, we discover nature doesn't set a standardized time limit for creative productivity on life's many diverse participants. An ocean may spend eons eroding a cliff into a white sand beach; a tree might grow several years before it bears fruit. The birth of a star out of interstellar gas and dust might take a million years or more to express, while the birth of a cell might take only a second or two. In nature, creativity (and the changes it inspires) takes as much time as is required in any situation. Nature seems content to allow every process that needs to occur to unfold in its own sweet time to ensure success.

Nature not only encourages diversity between different things, it also encourages it *within* a group of like things. If nature demanded that every star come into being at the same moment, burn only for a certain length of time and at a specific intensity, and then extinguish itself without fuss when its time had ended, our universe would be a very different place. It would not only lack diversity, it would lack the wonderful element of spontaneity that contributes to our endless surprise and wonder at the miracle that is our world. Instead, nature makes room for stars of all shapes and sizes: for brown dwarfs and supernovas, red super-giants, bright blue stars and everything in between.

Do we really wish to continue to do battle against the self-imposed limitations of time and money as we move toward our shared future? Do we want to become as automated as the machines we've been constructing? If not, we'd best realize that we've been deliberately encouraging whole generations of children to plug themselves into corporate jobs like so many duplicate cogs, only to be discarded like spent batteries once their productive years are behind them. Conformity, uniformity, productivity and scalability have become the buzzwords of modern day business. We humans add nothing much to that system but energy and time. What a waste of human potential that seems!

What if, instead of toiling in manual labor for forty years at minimum wage, everyone felt collectively empowered to learn, grow and self-train until each acquired the knowledge and skills necessary to fulfill his or her own life's purpose? Perhaps that purpose is something as helpful as figuring out how to make a toilet that doesn't require water with every flush. Perhaps it's as complex and esoteric as painting the Sistine Chapel. Perhaps, like Einstein's theory of relativity, it arrives as a single brilliant idea that bursts forth in a flash of awareness—like a new understanding of how we might travel through space without rocket propellants.

If we lived in that kind of world, individuals would no longer be measured or rewarded based on the time it took them to achieve their objective, on the energy spent achieving it or on the complexity of their achievement, because every person's objective—like every objective we already observe in nature—demands its own unique amount of time, imagination and energy to accomplish.

The human desire to achieve being what it is, some of us would complete our first objective and then strive to fulfill another, because we love to see how creative we can be. Conversely, some of us might never see our first objective realized, but we'd at least lay the groundwork in our lifetime for those who came after us to be able to see our project through to its completion. In either case, directing our unlimited human creativity into channels that would offer the highest benefit to society and would enable more of us to contribute something of lasting value to humanity seems far nobler than asking people to sell their precious, finite hours in exchange for wages.

DECOMMODITIZING LIFE

In a capitalistic world, everything gets classified as either an asset or a liability on our business balance sheets. A balance sheet has no other categories. Businesses list their marketable inventory and accounts receivable as assets, while their labor costs and accounts payable are considered liabilities. Since that economic context is what encapsulates all our exchanges, society by extension has been trained to classify every living person as either an asset or a liability, depending on which stage of life they're in. Children, the handicapped and the elderly are social liabilities; laborers in the prime of their lives are considered social assets. One group "drains" us of scarce monetary resources; the other group can be tapped to pay those bills. That explains in large part why we pay teachers less to educate our children than we pay engineers to design new construction equipment. Caring for children costs money, yet we get nothing from them in terms of any immediate economic gratification. Meanwhile, engineers design equipment we can produce and sell in the open market for an immediate profit. In the short run, then, because our children don't contribute a nickel to society, we tend to be stingy about how much we're willing to collectively invest in them. Liabilities versus assets; think about it.

As a society we grudgingly invest in public schools because we realize our children will *someday* be important financial assets, but the bulk of our money, time and attention goes toward funding our profit sources in the here and now. We approve of the job our schools are doing only to the extent that they teach each child the same information at approximately the same pace, so they'll all turn out about the same upon graduation.

In actuality, "No child left behind" simply means no child is encouraged to be uniquely him/herself any longer. We're sucking much of the creativity and spontaneity out of our children by requiring them to pass standardized tests year after year; then we wonder why they're all on Ritalin and diagnosed with ADHD. We're shocked by the Columbine shootings and the persistent rise in adolescent suicides, even as we continue to mold our children into cookie-cutter "future assets." By the time they reach high school, many of our children—who began life asking a million questions about everything—profess an *aversion* to learning! How we've managed to take something like learning, which comes as naturally to children as breathing, and turn it into something they abhor is a question we surely need to explore when we examine the educational system and its purpose.

Additionally, with so many parents working outside the home these days, most children aren't even considered assets by their own *parents*, the way they once were when we grew crops and our kids helped out in the fields. Nowadays, many kids aren't even expected to contribute to family operations by doing household chores, so they're not encouraged to develop core competencies. We also fail to value them for what they uniquely can contribute, but instead measure them against each other based on grades, athletics, social skills and personal talents.

When children act up out of frustration or exhibit antisocial tendencies as young adults, we lock them away in juvenile facilities or in prisons rather than invest in rehabilitating them or training them to become the best they can be. Investment in *people* contains many unknown risks; it's much more cost-effective to invest in mechanical equipment with a known performance output and predictable lifespan. We can predict and manage the costs of keeping a person in prison for the rest of his life, but we can't be sure we'll ever recover the cost of educating someone for as long as it may take to empower him to be successful at fulfilling his life's purpose. Because we're focused almost exclusively on money and how to earn more of it, we've chosen to contain our costs—sometimes viciously and ruthlessly, as when we eliminate firemen or close down national parks—rather than pay for something we can't guarantee will provide us with a return on our investment.

To restructure our society around our infinite creativity rather than around the scarce twin commodities of time and money would be to at last unleash the most valuable commodity of humanity—our ability to imagine and freely create. The exchange of time for money can never match our abundant ability to give birth to new ideas out of love for this world, and for each other. Think of it this way: what if, upon our birth, the universe demanded immediate cash payments from each of us in exchange for all the creativity and energy it has poured into us during the eons-long process of evolving us to reach the stage of human development we're at today? Very likely none of us could afford to be born! Thank heaven the universal blueprint *doesn't* call for an immediate cash payment in receipt for all the time and energy it has expended on our creation. Graciously, it's gifted this life to us for however long it lasts, so we can create all the wonders we can imagine and bring them forward for the benefit of every living thing with which we share space. It's still patiently waiting for us to wake up and fulfill our part of that beautiful bargain. How long it will wait is impossible to guess; but since we know we can't count on time to get us to where we want to go, I'd suggest we start now.

BREAKING THE CAPITALISTIC BOND BETWEEN TIME AND MONEY

One of the major challenges in transforming capitalism is embedded in its very nature. The thing is, we've designed a system where none of us are willing (or able) to work unless we're *paid* to do the job. That means the people who hold the power to define and assign humanity's work are those who have enough money to pay for it—the wealthy one percent of Americans who run our economy. *They* decide what work needs to be done and, in a profit-making paradigm, their decisions rest primarily on what generates additional profits for themselves and their own businesses, not on what's good for humanity, the planet or the ongoing sustainability of our species.

The general population is almost totally disempowered through our conscripted participation in a system that concentrates its decision-making power in the hands of a wealthy few. We then empower those few even *more* by providing them with higher profits, which gives them more power to control our labor and creative energies. Because most of us have been conscripted from birth into a long-standing economic system that denies us the things we need to survive unless we have enough money to buy them, our power to choose our own destiny will be continually subverted by the energy, will and domination of the moneyed few—at least so long as we continue to fear (and therefore support) our current capitalistic system.

While democracy may, in its earliest inception, once have had the potential to help rebalance this embedded financial injustice, the problem we face today is that our politicians also need money to succeed. They have also fallen under the domination of the capitalistic system. Without donors to fuel their campaign funds, they have no power to effect social change. And if they try to change things too much by shifting more benefits and power to the people, their donors will vanish. It's a messy problem, one that will likely require a complete restructuring of the way we elect our public officials and fund their political campaigns.

Lessening the grip money has on us, and by extension on our time, won't be easy. We're all held captive to a system that demands we invest time in it in exchange for the money we need to pay our bills. We must begin, then, to take back our time by refusing to live for work that doesn't serve humanity, and by honoring the work we're doing to improve the quality of *all* life on this planet—paid or not. We can learn to respect our free time more than we presently do by not wasting it in mind-numbing or emotionally destructive pursuits, such as endless hours of television viewing or the excessive consumption of alcohol and drugs. The fact is, we've become so accustomed to living inside our minds instead of occupying our whole bodies that learning to engage life by simply showing up for all of it takes a bit of getting used to.

Taking up new hobbies, spending more time with our children, getting ourselves back outside and running and playing again—these are all ways through which we can begin to reconnect with what it means to be fully alive. Stand with your face to the wind and your arms outstretched. Lie down in the grass and let ants crawl over your fingers. Get up before dawn and watch the sun paint the sky crimson. Listen to the birds. Turn off the television and use the extra time to observe the subtle daily shifts in the plants and trees. All these connect us to the wonder of our own physicality, and reconnect us with the life flowing all around us.

I never realized until just this past winter that honeybees hibernate. I found out by watching some honeybees that have been nesting in our house eaves for over five years now gradually slow their movements and then disappear. What a joy it was to watch them awaken and return to the flowers this spring! What pleasure

I've taken from watching my fruit trees bloom when the bees arrive. Each variety of fruit tree has a slightly different growing season and rate, as well as a different time for flowering and fruiting, and I'm coming to appreciate them all like precious children. Paying attention to their differences connects me with them in a way I never dreamed possible; now, when I eat a tangerine or a fig from one of my trees, its as if I'm accepting a gift of love from a friend.

Even in the workplace it's possible to make more time and space to appreciate the living. Connecting with people, not as cogs in the business machine but as living human beings, makes the job better for everyone concerned. Acknowledging and honoring the life force that flows in others is a wonderful way to feel it move inside yourself as well.

When we notice what's buzzing and bursting with creative energy within and all around us, the entire universe suddenly springs to life. That's time well spent as compared to focusing mainly on our role in a mechanical system that labels us either an asset or a liability. See everything as alive and suddenly we recognize the sheer absurdity of our ongoing classification, mechanization, subordination and destruction of life for the sake of short-term monetary profits.

CONCLUSION: VISUALIZING A NEW ECONOMY

If we were to build a new economy based on the underlying creative design of the cosmos, what would it look like? What values would be at its foundation, and what level of consciousness would be required to ensure we didn't repeat the mistakes of our past in a different form?

For starters a new economic model would need to be win/win, far different from the win/lose paradigm under which we've been operating. It would demand that we release our attachment to manufactured lack and embrace the notion that what benefits one advances us all, while what impoverishes one diminishes us all. Our society would need to mirror life, in that what we become must be greater than a simple sum of our parts. It would be founded on the premise that Earth is humanity's home, and that anything we do going forward must be done with reverence for *all* life forms, for our shared natural resources and for the environment that supports and sustains us. Nothing we wish to accomplish must *ever* be considered more important than stewarding and nurturing our home, for no amount of monetary compensation will benefit us if we destroy our own ability to survive.

We'd also need to begin to perceive humanity as a living organism, and to honor each other as cells in that living body. Like cells, we grow under vastly different environmental influences with different likes, dislikes, capacities and passions, but we're all working toward a singular goal: the ability of the human race to thrive. Keeping that goal ever in mind would be helpful as we learn more, grow and do more as a species.

To be more aligned with how nature operates, humanity would be well served to follow the fine example nature has already set. Nature doesn't require any of her participants to pay for their needs before they produce in abundance. She nourishes them without complaint until they've matured and are ready to produce their bounty for the benefit of all. Nor does nature withhold her vast resources due to inability to pay; she freely makes everything she produces available to whichever creatures find themselves in need.

While she teaches us to be mindful of the need to prepare for the winter, she also shows us that hoarding leads to waste, since all things decay. Additionally, she teaches us that to take more for ourselves than is necessary creates shortages and causes suffering for others, which eventually comes back around to us.

Nature encourages competition of the highest sort—not to destroy, but to inspire individuals to be the best they can become. She rewards collaboration both within a species and between species by making it easier for those who cooperate to thrive.

She teaches us that growth must be curtailed when a life form reaches maturity, at which point the bounty and beauty that each life produces—not what it consumes—becomes its purpose. She reminds us that every living thing is exquisitely unique, and is worthy of the opportunity to grow and bring forth all it has to offer.

Nature is patient, in that she's granted us time to discover who we are and why we're here. She's compassionate, in that when our creative time ends she graciously enfolds us into herself. Nature challenges us to grow in core competency by presenting us with obstacles and inviting us to find new ways around them. In short, nature exemplifies all the qualities we humans attribute to unconditional love. Perhaps, then, nature *is* love. Perhaps we humans are as yet the most advanced physical manifestation of nature's infinitely loving consciousness, youngsters in her marvelous garden who are just now learning to emulate her love. Our species, *homo sapiens sapiens* (which in Latin means the one who knows he knows), is a mere forty thousand years old. We're still quite young in relationship to the long and arduous evolutionary journey that life has been taking for eons. On a mother planet that's been evolving toward an ever-higher expression of love for over four billion years, it's not surprising that we've not yet had time to fully grasp how unconditionally loving we humans can be. I suspect we'll realize it once we release our insecurities and false feelings of separation and instead revere the web of life in which we are all embedded.

An economy based on the above principles and realizations, designed by a society that honors life in all its forms and recognizes that whatever diminishes one of us diminishes us all would not include money, bills or debts of any kind, since those instruments give a few of us the power to control and enslave the rest. A new system based on a new level of consciousness would instead be a true gift economy, empowering all to access not only what they need to survive, but also what they feel is necessary to pursue their passions and bring forth their creativity. No one would dictate the activities of others or judge whether the "worthiness" of another's productivity merited them receiving what they felt they needed. We'd learn to trust that each individual understood the value of making a contribution in whatever way he or she felt called to self-express. We'd each take our responsibility to contribute as seriously as we take our current rights and freedoms. Children would be taught at an early age that personal freedom and social responsibility go hand in hand, and that true freedom can only exist when individuals cooperate, practice self-restraint and feel empathy and compassion for all living things.

I envision humanity moving through a transition period as we shift toward a free economy, one that rewards a more responsible, loving level of human consciousness. How bumpy or graceful that transition will be most likely depends upon us. To inspire us to practice self-governance during our transition period, it might help if we wiped out all debts and eliminated money, paychecks and bills, then set up a resource-based asset distribution system. It might look like what happens when we go around "Go" in the game of Monopoly®. Simply by virtue of being alive, all would receive annual credits for adequate food, water, shelter, clothing, medical care, non-durable and durable goods, education and vacations. In exchange for that we'd be expected to work so the system could provide what we need while we rethink and retool the global economy.

Because one size doesn't fit all, everyone would have the option of trading their resource credits to customize their needs to their own situation. A full-time student might swap his durable goods credits for more education credits, while an athlete could trade his vacation credits for extra food calories. The more we exercised self-restraint and the greater responsibility we took for ensuring that what we produced was durable, the more would be available to be shared the following year. The Internet would be instrumental in enabling us to track what was needed globally and to discern where current surpluses and shortages were.

For adults, going to work would be the same as going to school is for today's children. Nobody would be getting paid, but we'd understand and accept its long-term importance. Since we'd no longer be getting paychecks, people would be less inclined to compare the value of their jobs and *all* work would be revered for the contribution it made to the whole. Satisfaction for a job well done would ultimately be its own reward.

No goods or services would be priced; items would be inventoried instead. Imagine that every year we each received ten credits for durable goods products (items designed to last longer than a year). Our choices for that year might include an electric car, a new washing machine, a bed and some solar panels. Given their limited number of credits, people would become predisposed to choose only the highest quality merchandise and ask only for what they genuinely needed, because we wouldn't want to waste our credits on something that might not last, or was only a whim. Industry would need to upscale manufacturing quality to meet consumer demands, so planned obsolescence and waste would disappear. Profits would no longer be business's motivating factor; meeting popular demand would determine which companies survived and which dissolved.

With businesses no longer able to spend money to undermine the science of climate change or discount the effects of pollution to protect their profits, our desire to protect our environment would impact all product choices. Businesses would need to demonstrate a truly wise use of natural resources. No one would gain by cheating or lying about a problematic product, since no one would have a vested interest in a business's survival. Companies that no longer served the public interest (or that did more harm than good) would either disappear or be retooled to make things people really needed.

Everyone who was currently unemployed or underemployed would be able to find work, because money would no longer be the deciding factor for whether or not enough work existed for all. Wherever work needed to be done, a new job would be created. Jobs could be posted locally through the Internet and people could respond based on their talents, passions and skills. Jobs requiring a high skill set could be posted globally and the people who filled those jobs could freely relocate. No one would be required to perform a job that didn't fulfill him or her. Once we reached full global employment the number of hours each person put in could be lowered, enhancing the quality of life for everyone. Many people would work from home or work locally to reduce traffic congestion and energy consumption. Mothers *or* fathers could once again choose to stay home and care for their children. They could work from home during school hours and be available to nurture their children each day when they returned home. Our able, experienced elders and currently unemployed teachers could pour back into our classrooms, enabling us to drastically lower the student/teacher ratios. That would enable children to explore their passions individually and at their own pace, creating a new generation of inspired and creative adults.

We could build new homes for all those who didn't yet have adequate housing, using green technologies and new ideas. We could repair our crumbling infrastructure, clean up our polluted land and water, grow our crops organically, experiment with new technologies and find humane and fulfilling ways to do difficult jobs. We'd manufacture fewer goods to feed our egos, and instead would focus on enhancing the beauty, sustainability, and quality of the things we truly need.

Local gifting warehouses might open, through which we could pass along things we no longer needed. That would enable others to reserve their asset credits for things they couldn't find elsewhere. Recycling would become a natural part of how we functioned, because avoiding waste would be a priority. As for the dirtiest, toughest and least desirable jobs, we could each contribute a couple of hours a month to getting them done so that no one would have a nasty full-time job. Those jobs could be posted as local Internet listings and ranked in order of social urgency, with descriptions of the consequences for us all if they didn't get done. Monthly public service awards could be granted to honor those who contributed extra time toward doing those difficult jobs. Meanwhile our technicians and engineers could use their free time to conjure up ways to automate those jobs.

As for the rich, no one would be forced to surrender their present home or give up any current assets beyond money, stocks, bonds and other financial instruments. The rich would receive the same allocation of resources as everybody else, so they wouldn't be disadvantaged by this social system shift. If their existing boats, planes and vacation homes used too many energy credits they could swap durable goods credits or education credits for energy. Or they could donate items back to the system for redistribution and better social use. Time would eventually take care of any remaining inequities in material assets, since the rich would someday die and the younger generation would gradually forget what life was like when a few had more privileges than others. Since the rich constitute such a small part of the population, what's crucial is how the majority of us would feel about this newly established system. To be rid of the stress related to bills, debts and fears about money would likely unleash so much joy and creative energy we'd be astounded by how much we could collectively accomplish in relatively little time.

We'd make it clear to all that this was a grand social experiment, designed to maximize our personal freedom to express our full potential within the context of our responsibility to the social body. If a large percentage of the population failed to live up to their civic responsibility by contributing work to the system, or if too many of us attempted to "game" the system from greed, the experiment would fail and we'd either return to the old monetary system and pyramidical power structure, or we'd try some other way of being in relationship with one another based on what we learned.

Is this a perfect transitional approach? Of course not. But as Voltaire once said, "The perfect is the enemy of the good." It may in fact be *impossible* for humanity to ever get to perfect, which doesn't mean we shouldn't aim for good and continually try to do better. Many who fear or distrust change will find ways to poke holes in these ideas, from claiming they're naïve and undermine freedom (shades of socialism, Nazism or communism, depending on one's biases), to fearing they will lead to the collapse of human civilization. Of course, since it appears our economic and monetary system is already on the brink of total collapse, what harm can there be in experimenting with radical new ideas? As we've already seen from examining our longstanding beliefs around capitalism, tweaking the old won't accomplish enough to fix what ails our economy at its core.

The most passionate challenge I've encountered whenever I talk about shifting our system from a debt to a resource economy springs from the fear that the dreaded "others" will take advantage of our "good" efforts. We've become so conditioned to believe the worst about each other that we find it nearly impossible to imagine a world in which we're not constantly on the lookout for those who might screw us over for a nickel. Perhaps the reason people take advantage of others is because that's the only way they can see to get ahead in a monetary system, which is stacked against the general population. We'll be able to stop worrying about other people getting ahead at our expense the moment we implement a system that instead eliminates debt and rewards us for lending a helping hand to our brothers and sisters.

The open question we'll need to find an answer for is this: Can humanity, when the weight of the fear of survival is finally lifted off our shoulders, become more loving, generous and supportive of each other? Can we live to thrive, instead of merely survive?

I *know* it can be done, at least on a small scale, because it's already happening all over the world. In September of 2009 I was blessed to attend a spiritual retreat at Hummingbird Ranch in New Mexico. The Hummingbird community itself is a lesson in conscious evolution; its residents are committed to living and working together in ways that honor and protect the land they steward. Their intention is to foster honesty and intimacy, personal growth, regenerative life practices, voluntary simplicity and a shared wisdom culture as they grow and evolve in community together. Additionally, the living school they've built on the land brings together people from all walks of life to share and learn new ways of being within a community.

During that retreat I witnessed two amazing events I'd like to share. First, my friend Barbara Marx Hubbard introduced to our group of about thirty-five people her longstanding dream of creating a global peace room as sophisticated as our present war rooms that would map, connect, coordinate and communicate the best of what's working for us around the world. As we sat in a group circle, Katharine Roske (one of the resident founders of Hummingbird) led us in a meditation on what that peace room might look like to each of us. With our eyes closed we were then invited to offer into the circle our dreams around what that system might become. Eight pages of notes later, what emerged from our collective input was a creative vision of a combination of physical locations and an Internet social synergy system far more magnificent and inspiring than what any of us could have imagined on our own.

Afterward we took inventory of what the group had to offer to assist with the peace room's construction, and discovered that in our little gathering of thirty-five people we possessed nearly all the energy and talent necessary to make that dream a reality. No one seemed overly concerned with whether or not they'd be getting paid to do the work; the mere idea of being part of making that dream a reality was all the payment anybody needed. It was one of the most moving and powerful acts of co-creation that I've been privileged to see.

Later that evening we were treated to a visit from a group that calls themselves the "Superheroes." The Superheroes are bike riders who leave their homes, jobs and families for a month at a time to bicycle around a given state to gift their time and energy to whomever needs their services—for free. No job is too dirty, no task too demeaning for the Superheroes to agree to undertake. At Hummingbird Ranch they chopped and hauled wood so the residents could keep warm in the coming winter. They make a game of it, with each rider taking a name and donning a crazy costume for the duration of the experience. When they arrive in a new town there's an aura of playfulness that accompanies them. Infinity Kid, The Crimson Seeker—I loved hearing their individual names and stories and getting to know each person. Representing both sexes, they ranged from students in their early twenties to professional fifty-somethings.

The Superheroes carry their own tents and supplies and live very minimally during the duration of their ride. If money is pressed on them they'll give it away to a local person in need before they leave town. They will gratefully accept food, as well as space in which to pitch their tents for the night; warm showers and clean bathrooms are also appreciated. Beyond that they have no expectations of any material reward. They do what they do because they *can*—and because they *enjoy* giving to others and spending time in the embrace of a loving community of like-minded individuals.

If people like the Superheroes can do what they do while still embedded in a pay-before-you-go paradigm, how much more might we collectively accomplish if we shifted our system to a take-what-you-need-and-give-all-you-can way of life? The Superheroes demonstrate that greed and fear needn't dominate our thinking any longer, that love, generosity and joy can lift us if we choose to embrace those aspects within ourselves. We already know that we carry within us the basest of our natural instincts all the way up to unconditional love. So far as we know we're the first life forms to become fully aware of what we presently are *and* to imagine what we have the power to become. Having also been gifted free will, it therefore seems incumbent on each of us to decide what we want to become, and then to *be* it.

As Gandhi once said, "You must *be* the change you wish to see in the world." The important point is that we can't wait around for everyone else to become more loving, giving and socially responsible before we take our own leap of faith and do what we know to be right for ourselves and the world. As a species that has long prided itself on its powerful religious faith, this may be the one place and time in history where a *genuine* leap of faith is truly called for. Whatever our individual cultural history or religious background may be, life itself has placed enough trust in us to have evolved us to this stage and encouraged us onward. The question is: Do we humans have enough trust in our *own* collective capacities to aim for this higher vision of humanity that life is revealing to us, right here and now?

I do not know the answer; but I *believe.*

AUTHOR'S NOTE

ONE QUESTION I'M FREQUENTLY ASKED IS WHY, WHEN I'M SO clearly of the belief that the capitalistic for-profit structure no longer serves humanity's highest interests, would I choose to sell this book instead of offer it for free?

That's a fair question, and one I'm happy to answer. First, let me say I didn't write this book to make money. I made a great deal of money in the past and it didn't make me happy. When I write, I do so mainly to enlighten *myself* about what I'm trying to understand. My hope is that the energy I've invested in exploring these ideas will bring healing to others in the way that it has brought healing to my own spirit.

When it came time to release *Sacred Economics*, I seriously considered alternative models of publication and distribution but soon realized I didn't have enough marketing expertise to ensure the book would be noticed by those who might benefit most from its message. I also wanted to emphasize the e-book format; I wanted this book to be environmentally friendly and easy for people to acquire. To ensure the book received the widest possible exposure I also knew it needed to be downloadable from major distributors like Amazon.com and the iBookstore, and I wasn't digitally savvy enough to make that happen on my own. My choice then, was to sign with a publishing company. Ironic as it may seem, I realized that the best way for me to put forth this critique of the existing for-profit system was to *use* that very system as part of the process.

Ten percent of this book's profits will be donated to the Hummingbird Living School, the non-profit arm of the intentional community in New Mexico that I've come to love and revere as a living laboratory for the advancement of human consciousness. An additional ten percent will be donated to the Foundation for Conscious Evolution, a non-profit institute whose mission it is to spread the evolutionary story of humanity, and to help set a vision for where we might want to go. My goal is to use the remaining eighty percent of any profits to establish a non-profit foundation to be called "The Habitat For Human Creativity." The foundation's aim will be to purchase land in a wilderness setting, build structures and gardens that are off grid and self-sustaining, and invite people who wish to explore this new way of being to live there without the pressures and stress of a capitalistic environment. No one within the habitat would be required to spend or earn money; all needs would be met and all services provided by the foundation. All that would be asked of the residents would be that they contribute some of their energy to the smooth daily operation of the community. Beyond that, they would be invited to use their freedom to consciously explore their passions and talents, and to gratefully bring forth the fruits of their labors in service to all of life. I fervently believe that an indirect gifting system is the way our world was intended to unfold, and that the best way for us to connect with that truth is to practice the art of indirect gifting and see where the experiment takes us.

BIBLIOGRAPHY
AND RECOMMENDED FURTHER READING

Ardagh, Arjuna, *The Translucent Revolution,* New World Library, 2005

Aurobindo, Sri, *The Life Divine, Sri Aurobindo,* Ashram Press, 1939-1940

Beinhocker, Eric, *The Origin of Wealth,* Harvard Business School Press, 2006

Bloom, Howard, *Global Brain, The Evolution of Mass Mind From the Big Bang to the 21st Century,* John Wiley & Sons, 2000

Bohm, David, *Wholeness and the Implicate Order,* Routledge (reissue) 1995

Bourne, Edmund J., PhD, *Global Shift: How a New World View is Transforming Humanity, Noetic Books, Institute of Noetic Sciences,* New Harbinger Publications, 2008

Bryson, Bill, *A Short History of Nearly Everything,* Broadway Publishing, 2006

Carey, Ken, *The Third Millennium: Living in the Post-historic World,* Harper San Fransicso, 1995

Chua, Amy, *Battle Hymn of A Tiger Mother,* Penguin Press 2011

Church, Dawson, *The Genie in Your Genes,* Elite Books, 2007

Cusac, Dr. Anne-Marie, *Cruel and Unusual: The Culture of Punishment in America,* Yale University Press, 2009

DeChardin, Teilhard, *The Future of Man,* Doubleday Random House, 1959

Eisler, Riane, *The Real Wealth of Nations,* Berrett-Koehler Publishers, 2007

Elgin, Duane, *Promise Ahead: A Vision of Hope and Action for Humanity's Future,* Harper Collins, 2000

Englehart, Matthew & Terces, *Sacred Commerce: Business as a Path of Spiritual Awakening,* North Atlantic Books, 2008

Fischer, Steven Roger, *A History of Writing,* Reakton Books, Ltd. 2001

Fuller, R. Buckminster, *Critical Path,* St. Martins Press, 1981

Glassner, Barry, *The Culture of Fear,* Perseus Books, 1999

Harford, Tim, *The Undercover Economist,* Oxford University Press, 2006

Hawkin, Paul, *Blessed Unrest,* Penguin 2007

Henderson, Hazel, *Building a Win-Win World: Life Beyond Global Economics,* Barrett-Koehler Publishers, 1996

Hubbard, Barbara Marx, *Conscious Evolution,* New World Library, 1998

Hubbard, Barbara Marx, *Emergence: The Shift from Ego to Essence,* Hampton Roads, 2001

Jacoby, Susan, *The Age of American Unreason,* First Vintage Books, 2008

Kaku, Michio, *Einstein's Cosmos,* W.W. Norton and Co., 2004

Korten, David, *Agenda for a New Economy,* Berrett-Koehler Publishers, 2010

Korten, David, *The Great Turning: From Empire to Earth Community,* Berrett-Koehler Publishers, 2006

Kotlikoff, Laurence J. and Burns, Scott, *The Coming Generational Storm: What you Need to Know about America's Economic Future,* Massachusetts Institute of Technology, 2004

Krishnamurti, J. & Bohm, Dr. David, *The Ending of Time,* HarperCollins, 1985

Leeb, Stephen, & Leeb, Donna, *The Oil Factor,* Time Warner Books, 2003

Lipton, Bruce and Bhaerman, Steve, *Spontaneous Evolution: Our Positive Future, and a Way to Get There From Here,* Hay House, 2009

Marinoff, Lou, PhD, *The Middle Way: Finding Happiness in a World of Extremes,* Sterling Publishing, 2007

Peterson, Peter, *Running On Empty,* Farrar, Straus and Giroux, 2004

Ray, Paul, *Cultural Creatives,* Harmony Books, 2000

Rifkin, Jeremy, *The Empathic Civilization: The Race to Global Consciousness in a World in Crisis,* Penguin, 2009

Satz, Debra, *Why Some Things Should Not Be for Sale: The Moral Limits of Markets,* Oxford Univeristy Press, 2010

Shlain, Leonard, *The Alphabet Versus the Goddess: The Conflict Between Word and Image,* Penguin Group, 1998

Smith, Adam, *The Wealth of Nations, ed.* Simon & Brown, 2010

Smolin, Lee, *The Life of the Cosmos,* Oxford University Press, 1997

Speth, James Gustav, *The Bridge at the End of the World: Capitalism, the Environment, and Crossing from Crisis to Sustainability,* Yale University Press, 2008

Swanson, David, *Daybreak Undoing the Imperial Presidency and Forming a More Perfect Union,* Seven Stories Press, 2009

Swimme, Brian, & Berry, Thomas, *The Universe Story,* Harper Collins, 1994

Taibbi, Matt, *Griftopia, Bubble Machines, Vampire Squids and the Long Con That's Breaking America,* Spiegel and Grau, 2010

Tolle, Eckhart, *The Power of Now,* New World Library, 2004

Tolle, Eckhart, *A New Earth: Awakening to Your Life's Purpose,* Dutton 2005

Twist, Lynne, *The Soul of Money: Reclaiming the Wealth of Our Inner Resources,* W.W. Norton and Co. 2003

Quigley, Carroll, *The Evolution of Civilizations,* Liberty Fund, 1979

Made in the USA
San Bernardino, CA
16 April 2013